Managing the Global Enterprise

Pearson Education

We work with leading authors to develop the
strongest educational materials in international business
and management, bringing cutting-edge thinking and best
learning practice to a global market.

Under a range of well-known imprints, including
Financial Times Prentice Hall, we craft high quality print and
electronic publications which help readers to understand
and apply their content, whether studying or at work.

To find out more about the complete range of our
publishing, please visit us on the World Wide Web at:
www.pearsoneduc.com

Managing the Global Enterprise

Competing in the Information Age

JAMES C. LEONTIADES

Director of the Cyprus International Institute of Management

FINANCIAL TIMES
Prentice Hall

An imprint of **Pearson Education**

Harlow, England · London · New York · Reading, Massachusetts · San Francisco
Toronto · Don Mills, Ontario · Sydney · Tokyo · Singapore · Hong Kong · Seoul
Taipei · Cape Town · Madrid · Mexico City · Amsterdam · Munich · Paris · Milan

PEARSON EDUCATION LIMITED
Edinburgh Gate
Harlow
Essex CM20 2JE

and Associated Companies throughout the world

Visit us on the World Wide Web at:
www.pearsoneduc.com

First published 2001

ISBN 0273-64691-5

British Library Cataloguing-in-Publication Data
A catalogue record for this book is available from the British Library

Library of Congress Cataloging-in-Publication Data
Leontiades, James C.
    Managing the global enterprise / James C. Leontiades.
        p. cm.
    Includes bibliographical references and index.
    ISBN 0–273–64691–5 (limp)
    1. International business enterprises—Management.   2. International business
enterprises—Communication systems.   I. Title.

    HD62.4.L458 2001
    658′.049—dc21   00–046620

10 9 8 7 6 5 4 3 2 1
05 04 03 02 01

Typeset in 9/12 Stone Serif by 35
Produced by Pearson Education Asia Pte Ltd.
Printed in Singapore

Contents

List of figures

List of boxes

Publisher's acknowledgements

We are grateful to the following for permission to reproduce copyright material:

Figure 2.1 adapted with the permission of The Free Press, a Division of Simon & Schuster, Inc., from *COMPETITIVE STRATEGY: Techniques for Analyzing Industries and Competitors* by Michael E. Porter. Copyright © 1980, 1988 by The Free Press; Figures 8.1, 10.2, 11.1, 11.2, 11.3, 11.4, 11.7, 12.2 and 13.1 and exerts from Chapter 13 from J. C. Leontiades, 1985, *Multinational Corporate Strategy*, Lexington Books; Figure 8.4 reprinted by permission of *Harvard Business Review* from 'Impact of Strategic Planning on Profitability', Schoeffler, Buzzell and Heany, March–April 1974, copyright © 1974 by the President and fellows of Harvard College, all rights reserved; Figure 11.6 from *Financial Times*, 23/24 April 1994, p. 11; Figure 13.2 reprinted from *Long Range Planning* 11, S. J. Q. Robinson and D. P. Wade, 'The Directional Policy Matrix – Tool for Strategic Planning', copyright (June 1978), with permission from Elsevier Science.

Whilst every effort has been made to trace the owners of copyright material, in a few cases this has proved impossible and we take this opportunity to offer our apologies to any copyright holders whose rights we may have unwittingly infringed.

Introduction

Nearly all companies are engaged in a competitive contest, a sort of game. The game itself changes as new players enter and some leave, as rules, strategies and even scoring systems alter. The really big winners are those companies that are at the cutting edge of innovation, moving ahead of the competition to take advantage of new methods and strategies that will one day be adopted by others.

Globalisation is just such a change. It has altered the nature of the competitive contest, not slowly and incrementally – but quickly and fundamentally. It has introduced new definitions of what constitutes 'winning' and quite different forms of competitive behaviour.

Globalisation is but the latest extension of a trend which has a considerable history. Man's horizons have been expanding continually, perhaps since he or she learned to walk on two legs. Certainly, institutions which operate internationally have been with us for a considerable time, particularly if one considers the early multinational companies and, much before them, organisations like the Catholic Church or the Dutch East India Company. We are now witnessing a transformation in the way some international institutions operate. This is so recent and far reaching that its significance has not been fully assessed.

Driven by several developments, but particularly the recent innovations in information technology, we see the emergence of organisations that operate in a manner which is quite different from their international predecessors. Corporations that qualify as 'global' rather than 'international' represent a new form of enterprise. Their ability to see and act globally opens up new possibilities that an increasing number of firms are pursuing to their advantage.

This change has not gone unnoticed. The declared aim of many chief executives today is to make their companies 'global'. But like many new concepts which have emerged suddenly, there is a lack of agreement as to what this means.

The terms 'global' and 'globalisation' are sometimes used to refer to mere geographic spread, the fact that a company or institution is represented in many parts of the world. At other times they may be used to refer to a growing similarity between institutions and consumer preferences in different parts of the world, as in the globalisation of markets. These terms have also been used more generally to describe a growing international interdependence between various interest groups, institutions and nations.

More relevant from the standpoint of this book is globalisation as it relates to companies and the management of companies which are 'going global'. What is a global enterprise and how is it different? What new opportunities does it offer for competitive advantage? These and associated issues are the subject of the following chapters.

The book begins with an analysis of the forces driving company globalisation, particularly the development of a 'global reach' on the part of management. It considers the unique characteristics of global players and the new competitive behaviour they introduce. The aim is not simply to describe but also to offer methods and techniques that will help managers deal with subject areas which include the following:

- **Competitive strategy**: The emergence of a new competitive environment, characterised by global rivalry, alters the positioning of all companies in the industries affected. The major options for positioning the firm globally are presented, their strengths and weaknesses evaluated.
- **Decision making**: The new competitive behaviour characteristic of global companies affects decision making, introducing a strong element of gamesmanship into the way managers perceive and evaluate new opportunities, including foreign investments.
- **Sources of competence**: The global enterprise has access to new sources of competence and competitive advantage. Practical examples are given on how these have been developed and implemented. The costs as well as the benefits of such efforts are presented.
- **Marketing**: The globalisation of markets, while sometimes exaggerated, offers new opportunities for companies able to carry out the necessary research and analysis. We examine the procedures for introducing globally standardised products, their opportunities and limitations.
- **The role of headquarters**: Alternative modes of the relationship between the coordinating centre and locally based operations are discussed.
- **Organisation**: Structure tends to follow strategy. Going global will require changes in the way the firm organises its activities. Some of these may involve altering the firm's formal organisation structure but there are also other mechanisms that can bring about the necessary coordination.
- **Scorekeeping**: A new global perspective also requires a global interpretation of tracking the firm's performance and the development of a global scorecard.
- **Environmental analysis**: Interpreting the global competitive environment is essential – but existing guidelines for interpreting the firm's environment have major weaknesses when applied globally. A framework is provided designed for interpreting the global competitive environment.

These and associated issues are the main subjects treated. Their presentation is directed at practitioners and those who hope to become practitioners.

I should like to acknowledge the contribution of Ranjay Gulati of the Kellogg Graduate School and Peter Clark of University College Dublin for their advice and recommendations on certain portions of the manuscript. My special thanks to Chrystalla Demetriou who provided invaluable assistance with the drawing of the various charts and the task of putting together the completed manuscript.

1 Global reach

Towards the latter part of the nineteenth century a revolutionary development fundamentally changed the structure of American and European industry. It also changed the way managers thought about their business.

This was the era that saw the emergence and the rise of nationwide companies. Prior to this, companies had operated as local businesses. The introduction of the railways and the telegraph, together with improved means of high volume production both encouraged and made possible the geographic expansion of coordinated company operations beyond the local environment. The time and money required to manage across great distances were sharply reduced. It became economic and practicable for management to direct the firm's business on a truly national scale.

The wider scope of company operations extended the boundaries of the group of firms comprising 'the industry' to national proportions. Companies found themselves facing new competitors in a new competitive environment, whether or not they had taken an active part in this transformation. The wider geographic scope and size of some of the new national firms fundamentally altered the competitive relationship of all firms in the industry. Local firms that might once have been considered relatively large and relatively impregnable found themselves fighting for their corporate lives against new, more powerful competitors.

Some of these new national companies made use of the greater scope of their operations and their nationwide access to resources and customers to develop new sources of competitive advantage. Managers had to rethink their strategies. Those firms that were not able to find a place in this quite different national competitive environment were either acquired or disappeared. The new competitive situation was characterised by numerous mergers and acquisitions. Waves of such amalgamations welded together many smaller local firms into national corporations. United States car producers were reduced from several hundred competitors into fewer than half a dozen in the space of a few decades. Similar restructuring took place in oil, steel, food processing and most of the major industries.

All this has a familiar ring. Today, many companies are once again experiencing a fundamental change in their own scope of operations as well as that of their competitors. Familiar national and regional boundaries are increasingly irrelevant. An ever greater number of firms find themselves in a competitive contest of new, global dimensions. One which differs radically from the more traditional view of international business.

Once again traditional notions as to what constitutes 'our industry' and 'our competition' are being challenged. There is a struggle for industry leadership, this time on a world scale. At the centre of these changes is a general trend, referred to as 'globalisation', affecting many firms and industries. Many companies are 'going global'. But what does this mean? In particular, how will this globalisation affect the conduct of business and the way companies are managed?

EARLY THINKING ON INTERNATIONAL MANAGEMENT

For much of the era following World War II, the teaching of international management turned on the importance of national differences. Much was made of the cultural, institutional and other distinctions differentiating one country from another. Generations of students were exposed to examples of national differences and peculiarities. At best, such exercises underlined the importance of understanding national cultural differences. On occasion this degenerated into a preoccupation with national oddities. The fact that white is the colour of death in China, that some nationalities have different eating habits, dress strangely, place different values on time, etc., preoccupied and entertained generations of students. The underlying message was nevertheless serious – success in international business depended on the ability to adjust the firm's products and practices, adapting them to the differing tastes and business conditions found in various countries. Adjustment to local differences was at the heart of such instruction.

However, in the mid-1970s research into the actual practice of leading companies marketing their products internationally revealed that, contrary to the accepted wisdom, there was a high degree of standardisation in the methods and products used by many firms in different countries. Two academics based at Harvard University in Boston, USA published the results of their research showing that many of the most successful companies doing business internationally employed less adaptation and more standardisation than predicted in the prevailing views on the subject.[1] In surveying companies marketing their products across a range of European countries, the researchers found there was a high degree of similarity in their marketing programmes. The products were often much the same, as were some of the other elements of their marketing programmes.

The challenge presented by these findings to the prevailing orthodoxy stressing national differences was unmistakable. Subsequent investigation provided further evidence supporting this early research. A certain commonality of treatment across a wide spectrum of countries appeared to be not only acceptable to consumers of different nationalities but also a way of reducing duplication and costs. Products which worked in one country were often effective in another – why reinvent the wheel? A powerful body of opinion emerged to the effect that along with diversity, there were also many similarities between countries. Furthermore and perhaps more significantly, these similarities were growing stronger. This view, almost heretical by previous standards, carries far reaching implications for how firms manage internationally.

THE MYTH OF GLOBAL MARKETS

With increasing frequency managers have been urged to think in terms of the growing similarity between world markets. In fact, the movement towards globalisation has often been associated with a growing homogeneity between national markets. Consumer tastes around the world, it is said, are becoming more similar.[2] Some authorities speak of a world market transcending national barriers and characterised by small and diminishing national differences. Companies and designers, it is suggested, should think about designing globally standardised products for a consumer rapidly becoming similar from country to country. Global product standardisation provides the basis for economies of scale in production and design, giving such firms an advantage over their more traditional market tailoring of products to suit various national market requirements.

How valid is such advice? Nothing is more obvious than that some standardised products may be successfully marketed internationally. Levi's jeans and Coca-Cola, the classic global products, have been marketed in much the same form in most countries of the world. That does not mean that the various locations around the world where these products are sold are all part of a single global market.

Products are only one element of a market. Inspection of most standardised products which are marketed globally, be they jeans, watches, computers, television sets, etc., will reveal major national differences in other features, such as distribution, storage, pricing, advertising, financing, packaging and labelling. These in turn reflect unique national characteristics in legislation, taxation, consumer preferences and all of the many factors that act to bring together the supply and demand for a particular product or service. Taken together, all these various agencies and activities which facilitate the exchange of goods between potential buyers and sellers for a particular product are integral parts of 'the market'. Once we cease to interpret markets in the very narrow and misleading sense of simply the product, their inherent individuality becomes strikingly evident. Firms engaged in international marketing must also be familiar and able to adjust to all of the features which together form a market, not just those associated with the product itself.

Even so-called standardised products and services incorporate subtle differences which are purposely introduced to adjust to local requirements. McDonald's fast food restaurants do not offer precisely the same products and product lines in the many countries in which they operate, neither is Coca-Cola the same in all countries. Close observation reveals that small but important changes have been made to adjust to local tastes, legal requirements, supply availability, technical specifications and so on. Though these small product adjustments are not always very obvious, this is not to say that they are unimportant. Even slight changes may be crucial to success. A small variation in the taste of coffee can make a great deal of difference to certain coffee customers.

Companies marketing such products around the world have been successful precisely because they recognise the individuality of markets even as they introduce such globally 'standardised' products. The key to their success has been to identify the differences which invariably exist in different parts of the world, then to take steps to tailor their overall marketing programmes to these differences. The message here is that even behind standardised products there is considerable adjustment to local conditions. Successful product standardisation requires an ability to make extensive cross-national comparisons, evaluations and decisions.

Having said that, there are no doubt numerous examples of growing similarities between different national markets. For example, the rising income levels of the past few decades have made it possible for consumers in many countries to acquire durable consumer goods that at one time were limited to only a few. Worldwide media, promotion and communication have spread product ideas and an appetite for goods and services that are highly similar. Trends that span national boundaries have emerged for certain items. This applies not only to jeans but also to music, software, banking services, hamburgers, fashion accessories, books and many other goods and services.

But it is also easy to find examples that go in the opposite direction, towards decreasing similarity and away from standardisation. Increased competition is forcing some companies to differentiate their products from one country to another in order to adjust to local taste differences. More flexible production methods also make it possible to economically produce numerous product variations to suit national differences. One major coffee company now supplies its world markets with 35 different types of coffee to cater to the divergence in tastes between one locality and another.

The same applies to services. The Sky TV channel initially relied on standard programmes and a standard language (English) to reach viewers across an area stretching from the Middle East through most of South East Asia. Along with some of its competitors it has now moved in the opposite direction; Mandarin and other local languages are widely replacing the former English standardisation and there is keen competition to buy Asian film libraries. Japanese firms are establishing design studios in Europe and the United States to tailor their products more closely to the needs of local markets.

Persistence of national differences

If there is truth to the statement that national markets overall are becoming homogeneous, forming a single market to replace previously multiple national markets, then we would expect to find this process most advanced within the European Union. For several decades this group of European countries has been engaged in a systematic and far reaching effort of unprecedented proportions to build a single regional market. Starting from a common Western cultural base, literally hundreds of pieces of major legislation have been enacted into law with the specific purpose of removing the barriers separating the national markets of member countries. Despite much progress, the European Union's own studies indicate that this goal has not been achieved. After several decades of legislation and action specifically aimed at developing something that could qualify as a single European market – no such market has yet emerged.

Any close inspection of national markets makes one thing abundantly clear. There are enduring differences between national markets which are not likely to disappear in the foreseeable future and which it would be folly for managers to overlook.

This does not imply a return to the era of national differentiation, the view that all markets and countries must be treated individually. Globalisation involves something quite different. Individual adjustments still have to be made to adjust to local conditions. There are no 'single world market' prescriptions. But in certain instances, international standardisation based on a consideration of conditions in many markets, may provide the best approach. Local adjustment and international standardisation may coexist, depending on the situation. The 'situation' here refers to both the local situation as well as the needs and opportunities presented by the broader, global context. Thanks to recent improvements, it is now possible to combine both, but this requires the ability to acquire and interpret the necessary information.

GLOBAL REACH

Interpreting globalisation in terms of the emergence of homogeneous markets or globally standardised products misses the point. The really seminal change that is behind many of the changes ascribed to globalisation is not that associated with marketing or markets but rather with management's new information capability which enables managers to 'see' and direct operations at great distances and the impact this has had on methods of management, competition and competitive behaviour.

Advances in information technology, including both information transfer and the ability to manage information, have given management a 'global' reach, i.e. the distance over which management can directly monitor and manage the firm's operations is now global. Of course, companies have managed business operations in distant parts of the world for many years. Information from these international operations has always been recorded and transmitted to the corporate central offices. But until fairly recently, such information was very limited. In the earlier years transmission was by cable or even letter. The later introduction of the telephone was a considerable improvement – but expense and other considerations limited this method during the early years. There was a distinct gap between the information available to the 'man on the spot' and the manager in a distant country. The former had a large amount of local information which was obtainable rather quickly, the latter did not. This greatly limited the ability of the managers to manage anything beyond 'local'.

This gap between the information available locally and that available several thousand miles away has been greatly reduced. Just as it is possible today for a surgeon located in one country to view and direct an operation on a patient located in another country, so too has management's ability to monitor and direct business operations at a distance radically improved. Making use of technical advances in electronic forms of information transmission, companies are able to move vast amounts of information over great distances. Managers now have ready access to current and detailed information on markets, competitors and government actions in distant parts of the world on a scale never before possible. The General Electric Company uses the internet to check factory equipment thousands of miles away. Banking staff in one part of the world are able to monitor and service customers doing business with a branch in another part. Even more important is the fact that computer systems are able to link inventory, financial, marketing and competitor information into a global reporting network which provides the firm's top managers in a distant country with much of the same information available to the man on the spot and at virtually the same time. With the introduction of the internet, both companies and individuals are linked in a communications network that is revolutionising not only the way firms manage internally but also how they relate to customers around the world.

As far as the transfer of information is concerned, distance has become irrelevant. Speed of transfer is not the major consideration. This has not changed since the day of the telegraph. More importantly, there has been a major decrease in cost and an increase in the amount of data which it is practicable to transfer. Increased convenience is also a major factor not to be underestimated. Only a few decades ago, making a telephone call across some 50 miles of the English Channel required the better part of a morning to secure the necessary connection. Improvements in communications, including digital dialling, mobile phones, facsimile machines and the internet, continue to improve the ease with which managers obtain information at great distances. There has also been an enormous increase in 'comprehensiveness', i.e. the scope and depth of data transferred and processed ready for use. It has now become practicable for banks to have instant access to individual profiles of millions of their customers. Computers and the internet have, furthermore, increased the availability of 'real time' information – data available the instant it is generated, in whatever part of the world it is needed. All this has had a major impact on management and the way companies are managed. The roots of this change can be traced back to earlier epochs and different types of organisation.

BOX 1.1

The transfer of information

Throughout history, the transfer of information over distance has been at a cost. Moreover, there was usually a rough correlation between this cost and the distance travelled. The greater the distance, the greater the cost.

Recent changes in information technology have changed all this. The cost of communicating information over distance, which has historically declined over the years, has now been almost eliminated. With a relatively small initial investment in computer equipment information can be transferred over the internet at no additional cost irrespective of distance. Other forms of information transfer, mainly various types of telecommunication, are rapidly heading in the same direction. Distance is rapidly becoming irrelevant with respect to such cost.

Figure 1.1 shows the historic cost/distance relationship steadily declining. The present and future situation will be one of almost costless information transfer, with zero marginal cost. ■

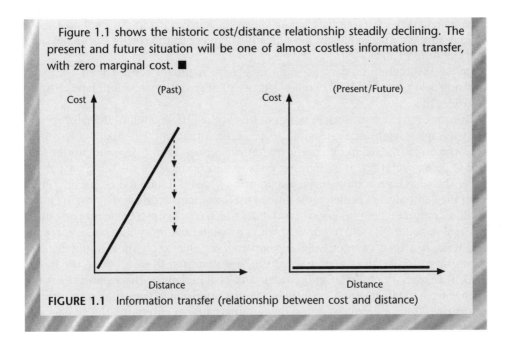

FIGURE 1.1   Information transfer (relationship between cost and distance)

It was approximately two hundred years ago that Wellington found himself hard pressed to actively direct his army at Waterloo across a front of only two miles. By dint of hard riding, he was able to see and 'manage' the conduct of his troops over this distance, roughly the same managerial 'reach' Alexander the Great had enjoyed some 2000 years earlier. Strategy, tactics, the organisation and management of the battle – all were shaped by the limitations imposed by the communications of the time.

In the days of sail, the captain of the ship was absolute master, making all the major decisions. Given the communications of that era, there was little alternative. Today, shore based shipping companies routinely direct the destinations and operations of their ships, sending detailed instructions and advice to their captains in mid-ocean. Captains no longer make the same decisions as before. They still have primary responsibility for the ship but a captain now receives advice and instructions in mid-ocean over even relatively minor issues relating to cargo and destination. He also receives decision support from home base, including information on other ships, port conditions, weather patterns and so on. These are two quite distinct methods of international communication and management.

Not so long ago negotiations between countries were carried out through distant ambassadors who were empowered to make key policy decisions on the spot. The lengthy time interval required to communicate with their government made such arrangements a necessity. On occasion, they even had the power to declare war. Today, equipped with the latest local and international information by satellite, the head of state is in effect able to direct international negotiations in distant parts of the world – in a way not possible only a few decades ago. This extended 'global reach' provides major advantages in the conduct of foreign policy. One such advantage is better global coordination between a country's various embassies. Much better information on a global scale is another. These changes have greatly altered both the role of the ambassador and the head of state.

Unlike Wellington, modern generals are able to maintain contact with events on the battlefield across hundreds of miles. Military strategy and organisations have changed to reflect this.

The same forces are at work in business. Just as the introduction of the railways and the telegraph extended the geographic scope of the corporation nationally, changing its character, so too the recent improvements in management's ability to communicate with and to direct operations at ever greater distances are doing the same thing on a global scale. There has been another major leap in management's information capability. Freed from the constraints of earlier, more limited means of transferring and managing information, companies have developed capabilities which enable them to identify new international opportunities and to pursue them in a manner not previously possible. For the first time, managers of international companies are able to obtain a comprehensive view of the global business environment in 'real time' and to react within the framework of an overall global plan and coordinated global initiatives. This represents a major change from the fragmented, country by country approach of the earlier international companies. It has introduced a new type of international enterprise, the global company, every bit as significant as the earlier emergence of the national corporation.

To better understand the unique characteristics of this new corporate player, let's first look at its more familiar predecessors.

EARLY MODELS OF INTERNATIONAL ENTERPRISE

The study of international business has focused on two types, or models, of international enterprise. For the sake of simplicity, we shall consider these in terms of the following stereotypes: the export company and the multinational enterprise.

The export company

The simplest way into international markets is the export company. The export company penetrates foreign markets and conducts international business by turning over the management of its foreign activities to a system of middlemen. The traditional exporter relies on intermediaries such as shipping agents, brokers, financial institutions and a variety of import agents to take their goods to customers. These take over the actual management of the firm's products in foreign markets. The primary task of the exporter is to select and organise such agencies into a sort of extended distribution system.

Such intermediaries are usually national in character, legally incorporated and limited in their sphere of operation to a particular country. A manufacturing company exporting goods to France will have importing agents and other middlemen there who take over and guide the marketing of the producing firm's products in that particular country. Another set of middlemen will take over in Germany and yet another in Italy.

Having in effect contracted out the management of marketing its products abroad to various agencies, the exporting firm relies on these agencies for information. But, since these agencies are generally independent companies with their own goals and objectives, the information they provide has frequently been inadequate and available to the exporter only after considerable delay and typically limited to the particular national location comprising their sales territory.

The management of the early exporting enterprise developed when communications provided, at best, a fragmented view of world markets and competitors. Management's view of the various markets and competing companies had to be pieced together from summing up, on a country-by-country basis, information from its various foreign agencies relating to their respective national sales territories. Its power to act on these reports was constrained both by the limited nature of communications facilities as well as the independent nature of the agencies themselves.

The export enterprise was nevertheless well suited to operate within such limitations. The independent character of its foreign based agents, many of them incorporated as separate companies, meant that they did not require rapid and frequent contact with the exporter. It is readily observable even today that, valuing their independence, many of them wish to avoid too close a contact with the exporting company.

In spite of its drawbacks, this form of enterprise offered companies a ready access to foreign markets with minimal investment of resources and management time on the part of the exporter.

The multinational enterprise

The other familiar model is the multinational company. The multinational enterprise is one of man's most ambitious and successful organisations. Such companies establish their own facilities abroad, enabling them to overcome many of the limitations of the export model. Foreign affiliates, staffed by the parent company's own managers eliminate or drastically reduce reliance on international middlemen. Firms such as Shell, Unilever and Philips have been able to use their foreign based companies to gain direct, on the spot, knowledge of competitors and markets as well as the control necessary to engage in effective rivalry against local competitors. In their ability to operate vast, internationally dispersed organisations, multinational companies have been considered by some to be the most effective international company structure.

But if one talks to managers in such multinationals it is often difficult to locate anyone who is actually directing or planning operations which cross national boundaries. Most can and do say quite truthfully that they are entirely occupied with duties that are purely domestic and carried out within a single national environment. Even today, in many such firms planning and acting across such boundaries is relatively rare.

This inward oriented management was the rule during the early days of the multinationals. Companies such as Singer, Ford and Unilever originated and developed their earliest organisations in an era when the major mode of international communication was the telegraph and international travel was by steam or even sail. They developed long before computers and electronic information transfer or even direct telephone dialling had become common practice. The archives of some of the early pioneers yield photographs of managers departing for foreign shores on the decks of steamships,

---

BOX 1.2

Establishing foreign bases

The procedure used by the early multinational companies to establish and operate huge foreign networks of plants and facilities around the world is conceptually very simple and, in fact, not so different from that used by the Roman Empire and Catholic Church.

Basic procedure

- The parent company provides initial resources to set up a new company in a foreign country.
- The 'business idea' and operating systems are transferred from the parent to its foreign based company.
- The new company eventually develops its own capabilities and becomes largely self-sufficient, requiring minimal support and guidance from the parent.
- The new company makes periodic reports to the parent, which retains ultimate control. ■

---

surrounded by the machinery that would be used to start the new foreign venture. It was not expected that they would be heard from for many weeks or even months. Communication by undersea cable was very limited and sometimes unavailable. Hence it is not surprising that such firms adopted enterprise forms which minimised the need for rapid and frequent international communication.

The great achievement of the multinational enterprise was to overcome the difficulties of managing at a distance without the benefit of modern communication and transport. This it did through geographic decentralisation, i.e. by treating each country as a separate and independent business environment. A company subsidiary in a foreign country was treated as a stand alone local business, little different from any other national domestic company except for its foreign ownership. A simple device but highly effective in minimising the need for international communication.

Ownership of such overseas affiliates was international but management was essentially national in function and outlook. The multinational's locally based managers viewed markets and rivals on a national basis, concentrating on their own domestic market, much like any other domestic company. The early multinational company was basically a cluster of such national units, with minimal coordination between them. Hence the reference also to this type of multinational as 'multi-domestic' or 'multi-local' companies.

Insofar as a global perspective and any form of global management could be applied to such firms in their early days, it was confined largely to financial reporting. The various subsidiaries of such multi-domestic companies were required periodically to report their financial performance to the parent company. Data from the various international subsidiaries was summed up to arrive at the parent company's view of total worldwide performance.

THE INTERNATIONAL FIRM AS A COLLECTION OF LOCAL BUSINESSES

During these early years, the organisation, strategies and management methods of both enterprise models, exporters as well as multinationals, evolved in a way that did not require rapid communication over long distances. Management of foreign operations was typically delegated to units, located close to the scene of the action. In the case of the multinational company, this was to a subsidiary, i.e. 'our man in country X'. In the case of the exporter, the delegation was to import/export agencies. Any picture of events in multiple foreign markets had to be distilled, after considerable delay, from many individual local pictures, themselves often based on non-comparable data.

Each enterprise was in effect a collection of local businesses linked loosely to a corporate centre. More than any other device, this locally focused approach, delegating the firm's operations to local management in each country, underpinned the organisation, thinking and management of international business prior to the development of modern communications and the accompanying trend towards globalisation. The geographic scope of such companies was global but their thinking and methods of operation were local.

Having disaggregated the world into a series of domestic businesses, the management of such firms were not well equipped to take a world view or to coordinate operations across more than one country. Indeed, the decentralised business units frequently encouraged a sort of tunnel vision – concentrating on managing the local business to the exclusion of all else. For firms operating a number of such local businesses in different parts of the world, this often meant that the left hand did not know what the right hand was doing. Managers concentrating on the local business in their own location would be unaware of events in another country. This could mean, for example, that new investment to expand plant capacity in one country might be made even if the parent company had excess plant capacity in another. The same multinational of this type might have excess managerial and technical skills in one of its local businesses while suffering a shortage of the same skills and talents in another. With little communication and no incentive to look beyond local borders such situations could continue indefinitely.

Reinventing the wheel in such situations was not uncommon. Ideas developed at considerable cost in one part of the world were cast aside or redeveloped within the same company's operations in another part of the world. Perhaps the most important lack was the inability to mobilise the international firm's resources globally in a coordinated manner. Subsidiaries located in different countries but belonging to the same parent company have even been known to engage in price competition and other forms of rivalry against each other.

The above descriptions of the multinationals and export forms of enterprise represent stereotypes, generalised descriptions which apply particularly to the earliest forms of these companies.

A NEW APPROACH

Change did not come all at once, but incrementally. With the new ability to communicate over long distances quickly and cheaply it became patently clear to some companies that there were opportunities for global linkages and cross-border operations that offered potential advantages to companies able to identify and take advantage of them. More and more firms recognised and began to use the potential of improved communications and transport to overcome the limitations of the early multinationals, to manage their foreign operations differently.

Some of the first signs of the new approach were evident in the trading companies of Asia and Japan. Earlier than most, these companies, trading in imports as well as exports, developed global intelligence and information that provided management with an up-to-date world view of their business operations, as opposed to a compilation of outdated and fragmented individual national and regional perspectives. Western export companies also made major strides in this respect, developing the information gathering ability of their international distribution channels as well as their own ability to integrate and interpret such information on a world scale.

The new approach to international management has had a major impact on the multinational enterprise. The early versions of this type of firm, the multi-domestic companies, have gradually been giving way to new interpretations. More modern versions of the multinational firm have moved away from the fragmentation of the early models, coordinating across borders towards a more global approach. Observers have variously described these latter multinationals as 'geocentric companies', or as 'transnationals'. Whatever the name, the change has been to move away from the multinational enterprise as a loose collection of local businesses. The change has been towards the multinational seen and managed as an international network of companies with considerable global coordination and a world view.

Improvements in information technology and the greater internal capability of many companies to collect, process and interpret information from many countries has contributed to this. This has enabled such firms to pursue objectives and strategies quite different from those of the more traditional international competitors. There has been a major shift, a change in competitive behaviour which transcends the traditional distinction between enterprise forms. The key difference between the new and the old approach to international business today is not one of organisation structure or catering to a global market. It is much broader and more basic than that. Improved information capability has changed management's view of the world and the position of their business within it. It has changed their view of international competition and the global threats and opportunities. In other words, it has changed management's perception of the way the game is played.

Companies making use of modern methods of communication and mobility are able to 'see' their markets and competitors and to shift resources globally in a way not possible by earlier companies engaged in international business. With a different vision of their environment, such firms are able to mobilise their resources on a global scale behind strategies which introduce new possibilities for competitive advantage.

As in the earlier era, which saw the rise of the national firm, there has again been a radical improvement in the ability of management to mobilise and direct operations at greater distances than before. This recent extension of management's reach, this time on a global scale, has introduced major changes in both the firm and its relationship to its business environment. Once again as in the earlier era, the improvement in management's ability to manage over great distances has been accompanied by widespread mergers, acquisitions and alliances. Industries are being restructured, this time globally rather than nationally. All companies, including those that wish to remain purely local, are having to adjust to a new global competitive environment. As in the rise of the national corporation, this will introduce a new competitive situation, with new winners and losers.

There are also other differences today in comparison with the era which saw the rise of the national company. Unlike the early national corporations, global companies operate across countries and regions that still retain major essential distinctions conditioned by history and traditional boundaries. Local differences in government, culture, institutions, currencies and legislation continue to require individual treatment. Even companies attempting to develop globally standardised methods and products, must recognise and adjust to local situations that differ both in magnitude and character from those encountered by national companies operating under a single national jurisdiction.

Management in global companies must operate at two levels. Their managers will continue to require the knowledge and judgement, the feel for the local market of 'our man in country X'. They must be able to recognise and make adjustments to local conditions. But now there is an additional dimension. Knowledge of the local situation will increasingly have to take account of and be integrated into a broader worldwide perspective of the firm and its business. Management in such companies must also be able to see, think and act globally. The ability to operate at both levels, rather than simply as a collection of locally focused companies, opens up new opportunities. Such firms are able to coordinate their worldwide resources behind global strategies. They compete differently in a different competitive contest.

The remainder of this book will examine the new global game of business. Who are the new global players? What are their characteristics? How does the game differ? What must management do to make the company a global player and develop new sources of global competitive advantage?

SUMMARY

- Just as the introduction of the railways and the telegraph promoted the rise of the national corporation, so the introduction of the new information technology is fostering the emergence of global companies. As in the earlier era, these new players are challenging traditional notions of what constitutes 'our industry' and 'the competition'.
- Early thinking on international management stressed the importance of national differences. But research has shown that many successful companies employ a high degree of standardisation in their international marketing. More recently managers

have been advised that foreign markets are becoming homogenous. Reference is made to 'the globalisation of markets'. This goes too far. Truly global markets are a myth. Though there are a growing number of similarities between national markets, many essential differences remain.

- The really essential change behind globalisation is management's new information capability. Advances in information technology have given management a global reach. Managers now have the capability to see and direct operations over vast distances. They are able to view their global markets and competitors in real time. This has changed the way firms are managed.

- Early international companies were managed as a series of local businesses. The new information capability means management can now take a holistic view of the company, managing its worldwide operations as part of an integrated global network.

- These changes are altering the competitive environment, affecting all companies. Local firms will also have to adjust.

- Managers in global companies must operate at two levels. Local knowledge is still important. But knowledge of local situations will have to take account and be integrated into a wider global perspective. The change is a fundamental one, introducing a new competitive contest which will have new winners and losers.

NOTES AND REFERENCES

1. Sorenson, R. Z. and Weichmann, U. E. (1975), How multinationals view marketing standardization, *Harvard Business Review*, May–June, pp. 39–42.
2. Levitt, T. (1983), The globalization of markets, *Harvard Business Review*, May–June, pp. 92–102.

Chapter

2 A new competitive league

Whether in sports or business, competition is most intense against those players considered to be in the same competitive league, the direct competitors. Successful competitive strategy begins with a close knowledge of such rivals: who they are, their objectives, particular strengths and weaknesses as well as other characteristics.

As more and more firms capitalise on management's global reach to extend their operations beyond national boundaries, they encounter new rivals. In fact, these same companies may have been established in their respective countries for many years. Management may have been aware of their existence. They may even have been included in company reports as 'other foreign companies'. But that is not to say they were perceived as rivals. Globalisation is changing the players that comprise the firm's direct competitors, those firms that are perceived as rivals. Even more significant is the change this is bringing about in the way such companies compete.

APPEARANCE OF A NEW COMPETITIVE LEAGUE

In recent years an increasing number of international firms have come to realise that they have been competing against many of the same firms in different parts of the world. Firms such as Nestlé, Toyota, IBM and Sony could see that whether the location was Bangkok, Bonn or New York, they could count on finding many of the same familiar competitors.

Improvements in communication have made it practicable for these and other companies to track and monitor their foreign markets and competitors globally. This, together with their numerous international operations, has enabled them to assemble an information base giving them a world picture of markets and competitors. Such companies were among the first to glimpse evidence of another competitive contest, quite different from that taking place at the local level.

Assessing competitors, their sales, resources, profitability, overall capabilities and strategies globally gives a quite different view of rivals from that which is seen when viewing them on a national, country-by-country basis.

A company which is a leader in certain parts of the world might well be losing globally. A large share of certain national markets might be inconsequential in global terms. International patterns of geographic expansion which are easily revealed when viewing markets globally can also be overlooked when viewing the same markets separately. Where information is global and resources (including human resources) are readily transferable around the world, country-by-country analysis of competitors is of limited use and very likely misleading.

Competitors such as these have to be interpreted globally. This wider perspective is required not only to assess the current situation and performance of global players, but also their strategies and objectives. Better information technology and mobility make this possible, indeed, inevitable. It is not only a matter of interpretation. When rivals are viewed globally, when they can observe and monitor each other across national boundaries, the nature of rivalry also changes. Companies find themselves competing in a new global competitive league. This brings about major changes in their behaviour. Competitive behaviour between global players is radically different from that which characterised the more traditional forms of international business. To appreciate the nature of this change, let us first consider the distinction between international competition and global rivalry.

International competition vs. global rivalry

International competition in its broader sense has been with us for centuries. The rise of international commerce brought early producers of commodities, agricultural products, pottery, wine, crafts and many other types of produce into international competition with each other. The development of efficient international markets in many products and commodities has enabled companies to market their products abroad with little or no detailed knowledge of their competitors. Such firms are engaged in competition, but not the form of competition known as rivalry.

A simple example is the small cotton farmer in Georgia, USA. Even though he may be competing directly against similar cotton farmers in Egypt, Australia and the Sudan, he will have little knowledge of the activities of such competitors.

His cotton travels to various destinations, local and foreign, through the intermediation of the international cotton market. The cotton farmer will probably sell his cotton to a local agent, a cotton broker who is the first step in a chain of agencies which purchase and sell the cotton. A series of such market agencies, including cotton brokers, storers, export agents, import agents, producers, wholesalers and retailers take ownership and control of the cotton. The decisions of these agencies will determine the final destination of our cotton farmer's cotton, the price paid at various stages as it progresses through the market, the form of the final product and many other features. Few if any of these decisions will be influenced by, or even known to our cotton farmer.

Of course, cotton farmers from other countries are also seeking to sell their produce to many of the same agencies and customers. Our Georgia cotton farmer is clearly competing against them with his goods and hence engaged in international competition. But not having personal knowledge of these foreign cotton producers, their costs, prices, product quality or availability, in countries such as India, Egypt or Australia, he is in no position to take competitive action against them. He may have a general idea that such producers exist, but he will have little or no knowledge of their individual characteristics, production schedules and future plans. Nor, within this system, is such knowledge required.

The local producer will be interested in the price he will receive from the local purchaser, sometimes only a few miles away. Once he has sold his cotton he has no international influence over his goods. Adam Smith's unseen hand in the form of the international cotton market takes over. Our cotton farmer is in no position to see or plan and manoeuvre against particular cotton farmers in Africa, Australia, Egypt or other parts of the globe to improve his competitive position. In other words, he is not engaged in international rivalry, even though his goods are part of the international competition among world cotton producers.

Global rivalry

Firms such as Sony, Nestlé, Procter & Gamble and other global companies are in a quite different position. They have the internal resources to both monitor their markets and competitors globally and to act upon such information in a purposeful and coordinated manner. They are engaged in rivalry on a global scale. Rivalry is a particular type of competitive behaviour quite different from that described above with reference to our small cotton farmer.

This distinction becomes clearer if we consider certain global industries. Computer firms such as IBM, NEC, Bull, Siemens and Toshiba can hardly fail with today's communications to see that although they are competing against each other in various national markets, they are all part of a wider global competitive contest. Unlike the cotton farmer, they 'see' each other globally and take action accordingly. They plan and manoeuvre on a world scale for competitive advantage. In other words, they have become global rivals consciously competing directly against each other in different parts of the world. They are aware that the success or failure of one is highly relevant and affects the positions of the others. If Toshiba becomes the market leader in laptops, this is carefully studied and analysed by Olivetti, Compaq, NEC and the other firms producing closely similar products.

If IBM is losing market share in the USA, the effects of this for its future strategy are not limited to the USA. The implications are studied by its rivals in other parts of the world. Each global rival observes the movements of the others irrespective of national boundaries. A gain or loss by one, from whatever source, is important information for the others. They see and appreciate that their actions and fortunes are interdependent in whatever part of the world they may be located. A government subsidy to Air France has definite implications for American Airlines. A new drug developed by Merck is of interest to Glaxo. Compared with the cotton farmer, they see their competitors differently, rivals in a sort of game which knows no boundaries.

This type of competition, known as oligopolistic rivalry, is a particular form of competitive behaviour which was at one time largely confined within national borders. Firms engaged in oligopolistic rivalry know their competitors. They are able to track and monitor their behaviour. They see them as part of a competitive contest in which all such rivals are engaged, the actions of one affecting the others. It is a quite different sort of competition from that associated with our cotton farmer and many other international business enterprises. This is the critical change which globalisation has introduced, the extension of this type of competitive behaviour on a world scale.

Many of the more traditional exporters are still in much the same position as our cotton farmer – relying on the international market to take their goods to global customers. The multi-domestic type of multinational, through its international subsidiaries, is aware of foreign rivals – but in the past this awareness has been only on a country-by-country basis. Rivalry in such companies has typically been conducted in foreign countries through various subsidiaries based there, each of these focusing on its own local competitive environment. Limitations of information and the ability quickly to assemble and communicate data on a world scale necessitated a local or multi-local interpretation of the competitive environment and its rivals.

Driven by the continuing advances in information technology, many exporters as well as multinational companies are now extending their vision beyond national boundaries. The ability quickly and cheaply to acquire and transmit information on competitors in different parts of the world is becoming available to more and more firms – in some cases even to small farmers. As global information on markets and competitors comes increasingly within their reach, such companies are changing their competitive stance, moving from local to global rivalry.

But information by itself is not enough. Managers must also be in a position to use the vast amount of data now available from distant corners of the earth. If they are to make sense of the enormous new possibilities which technology has opened up, they must be able to interpret this expanding amount of international information. What tools and concepts are there which can assist them in this task?

CONCEPTS OF INTERNATIONAL BUSINESS

For almost 200 years the most influential theory relating to international business activity has been the theory of international trade. In its classic form this explained trade in terms of a nation's characteristics, particularly its endowment of natural and human resources. Countries rich in agricultural resources were considered to have a competitive advantage in products that derived from such resources. Most famously, it was explained that this (an abundance of appropriate climate and land resources) was the reason Australia exported sheep and Portugal wine.

While this theory and its more modern variations continue to provide insight at the national level, helping to explain why certain countries are successful in exporting particular product categories – its value for managers has been limited. The fact that a country is well placed to export a particular product does not mean that all firms in this business will be successful. Some will succeed, others will fail. The theory of international trade provides little direction to managers that will help them to place their firm among the winners. It provides little guidance regarding their strategy, marketing and other decisions that face them.

Perhaps for this reason, there has been a recent emphasis on international business theories, those more concerned with explaining the behaviour of companies rather than nations. A major strand of such theories deals with multinational companies and foreign direct investment – providing explanations of why companies invest and produce abroad.

But neither the foreign investment theories nor the earlier international trade theory address the recent changes in the firm's competitive environment to global proportions or the implications of this for strategy and other key decision areas. However, there are some notable exceptions that come close. One of these is Raymond Vernon's international product cycle theory. Developed during a period characterised by a slower pace of change, some of the key assumptions on which this theory is based are now obsolete (see Chapter 9 for a fuller discussion of this theory). Another exception is the type of industry analysis discussed below.

Industry analysis

A much more fruitful approach for purposes of strategic analysis and decision making for a new competitive environment is that body of theory which takes an industry based approach. The field of industrial organisation has provided evidence that industries have relatively stable characteristics which influence the competitive behaviour and performance of their member firms. Understanding these characteristics, which vary from one industry to another, is important in understanding the competitive environment of firms in that industry. Moreover, if globalisation is associated with a fundamental change in rivalry and competitive behaviour, then surely this field of study is potentially useful in understanding the types of changes that it has introduced.

Michael Porter is probably the best known of the recent line of authors on this subject. He has drawn on previous theory and research together with his own contributions to develop his widely accepted 'five forces' model for interpreting the competitive environment.[1]

However, the structural analysis of industry, as reflected in Porter's model and elsewhere, has typically been based on research carried out in national industries. At one time this was realistic. The member firms of many industries consisted mainly of national companies competing against each other within the same national territory. It was natural to speak of a British shipping industry and American, Norwegian and Japanese shipping industries. Also, a German machine tool industry and a French machine tool industry. In short, the definition of industry for many years was simply understood to be national. Official statistics on industry even excluded from their definition of 'the industry', all foreign companies which did not have a production base in that country.[2] Today, this is clearly nonsense. Speaking of a British, American, French, Brazilian, etc. aircraft industry is not only not very helpful, it is positively misleading. This raises a question mark over the validity of the Porter type model in industries whose scope is global rather than national.

BOX 2.1

Michael Porter's five forces model

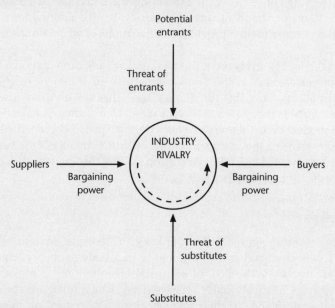

FIGURE 2.1   Five forces analysis of industry competition
Source: Adapted from Porter, M. E. (1980), *Competitive Strategy*, The Free Press, p. 4.

Porter's model (Figure 2.1) identifies five major industry characteristics, or 'forces' influencing the industry competitive environment and its attractiveness. These are:

- **Threat of entry**: The threat of new entry into the industry is a major factor influencing the industry environment. The extent of this threat depends on entry barriers to the industry. Industries that require large up-front investments in finance and/or technology to become competitive, such as steel and automobile manufacture, qualify as having high entry barriers. Also a monopoly guaranteed by the government may be said to provide a high entry barrier. Such an industry enjoys a degree of security quite different from that in industries (such as retail groceries, bakeries, household repairs) that have few entry restrictions.

- **Intensity of rivalry**: The intensity of rivalry among member firms is another of the five forces driving competition within an industry. This may vary. For example, industries with a high concentration of large firms will exhibit a quite different intensity and type of rivalry compared with industries made up of many small rivals. Competition is likely to be more intense and even cut-throat in the latter situation. The rate of industry growth will also influence rivalry. Slow growing, stagnant industries leave member firms with little choice but to take sales away from competitors.

- **Bargaining power of suppliers**: The bargaining power of industry suppliers is another force. Firms in industries dominated by a few large suppliers are likely to be squeezed by the prices suppliers are able to charge for their products. The labour force is also a supplier. Its bargaining power can vary enormously from one industry to another depending on factors such as unionisation, labour scarcity, difficulty of training for required skills and so on.
- **Bargaining power of buyers**: The bargaining power of buyers also influences the competitive environment. In industries such as soap, toothpaste or other toiletries, where there are many small buyers, their bargaining power is limited. They are unlikely, for example, to have sufficient bargaining power to be able to force companies selling these items to reduce their prices. The opposite is the case in those industries with only a few large buyers, such as government hospitals purchasing medical supplies.
- **Pressure from substitute products**: Substitutes are a form of competition. Companies in industries with many substitute products are more vulnerable to competitive pressures. For example, the introduction of synthetic textiles exerted severe competitive pressure on producers of wool and cotton goods. ■

Defining industry globally

A possible solution is to redefine industry globally. If the industry is global, we simply apply the five forces model to industries defined globally rather than nationally. However, once we broaden the definition of industry in this fashion, to global proportions, we find that some of the accepted methods of industry analysis, including Porter's five forces model, lose much of their effectiveness. Global industries are fundamentally different. They are not simply national industries on a larger scale. New variables influencing the behaviour and performance of the global players are introduced which are not included in models designed for national industries.

GOVERNMENT AND GLOBAL INDUSTRY

The major new variable is government. As Porter points out, government is potentially able to influence 'all aspects of industry structure'.[3] However, the structural analysis of industry (not only in the case of Porter's model but more generally) proceeds on the assumption that we are dealing with a single country and a single national government.

This was acceptable as long as industry analysis was nationally limited. Once we move to the consideration of global industries, this clearly is no longer the case. Global competition takes place across many countries each with its own government. This introduces multiple national legal systems, legislation, regulations and institutions affecting industry structure. In other words, we can no longer speak of 'the five forces' as if this referred to a single set of five forces. Since government itself varies, the five forces also vary from one country to another. Global industry is characterised by many variations of the five forces, as many variations as there are countries.

Industry entry barriers, for example, may vary dramatically from one country to another. Global banks and other financial institutions contemplating entry into new national markets must normally obtain a licence. This can represent a formidable entry barrier and one which is by no means similar from country to country. In other words, organisations applying for a banking licence will face different levels of entry barrier, depending on the country at issue. Of course, there are numerous other government related barriers for banks, such as required liquidity reserves and capital requirements, which also vary by country and multiply once we view industry globally.

Companies interested in owning or operating broadcasting networks or airlines also face a wide variety of entry barriers in the form of nationally diverse government restrictions limiting foreign participation in such industries. In some countries, governments altogether forbid foreign entry into these industries. Others do not.

Pharmaceutical companies must comply with stringent health regulations, a major entry barrier which again differs by country. Of course there are also the traditional barriers of national tariffs and quotas as well as work and residence permits.

Similarly, the power of suppliers depends on which part of the world, which country, we are talking about. The power of Hong Kong suppliers, for example, is vastly different from suppliers located in, say, North America, or Western Europe. Institutional differences, such as unions, are part of the explanation for these discrepancies. So too are differences in labour availability, industry safety regulations, legal and other factors.

Buyers in different parts of the world will also have different degrees of bargaining power, since they are governed by quite different consumer protection and legislative requirements. They may also be organised differently. In some countries and in certain industries buyers will have formed buyer groups to increase the scale of their purchases and to influence their bargaining power. In other parts of the world, this is not the case.

Even the threat of substitutes differs. Petroleum companies doing business in Brazil have to consider the competitive threat of substitute fuel derived from sugar cane and other vegetable sources. Pharmaceutical companies marketing their products in China and South East Asia have to compete against a number of local herbal substitute remedies not prevalent in the West.

The nature and intensity of rivalry among industry firms will also differ internationally. In some countries monopoly legislation is highly restrictive. Certain mergers and acquisitions which are perfectly legal in one part of the world are prohibited in others. Price rivalry will be limited in certain countries with resale price maintenance legislation. Rivalry by way of advertising encounters a variety of regulations which vary by country.

Once we take a global view of industry, it is no longer possible to speak generally about suppliers, buyers, substitutes and the other forces. Global industries are much less homogenous than national industries. Global players compete against each other across highly diverse industry environments. Indeed, understanding this diversity is a key skill required of global managers.

This same diversity severely restricts the usefulness of the structural analysis method. Within global industries, there are not five forces but many multiples of this number. Countries retain unique government, institutional and other features that shape the five forces as they apply nationally. In effect, each country has its own five forces, introducing a level of complexity that undermines the usefulness of this approach as applied to global industries.

GLOBAL INDUSTRY AS THE BASIC UNIT OF ANALYSIS

Despite the limitations noted above, the industry based approach remains a useful concept for the global enterprise. Perhaps Porter's most valuable (and underestimated) contribution was introducing the concept of industry as the relevant competitive environment for the firm. He established that the essence of the firm's environment was the industry (or industries) it was in. The task of management was to adjust the firm to the external threats and opportunities there.

This focus on industry has greatly facilitated and sharpened analysis of the firm's competitive environment. Firstly, using industry as the basic unit of analysis helps to simplify what we mean by the firm's competitive environment, eliminating many extraneous factors. Since competition between baby food producers has little to do with the producers of jet engines, it makes sense to view these two sets of competitors separately.

Secondly, the definition of competitive environment by industry is justified by the interdependence of its member firms. Since the actions of any one competitor actually or potentially affect all the others, they represent an interdependent system which should be viewed as a whole, i.e. an industry. Interpreting business activity between rivals without an analytical framework that encompasses all of the competitors, places managers in the same position as the general who sees only one part of the battlefield.

Both of the above reasons apply to global as well as national industries. If firms engage in rivalry on a global scale, which is clearly the case, then industry defined globally provides a basis for defining the players and the playing field of relevance for the global enterprise. Moreover, this industry based concept of the global firm's competitive environment is superior (for both of the above reasons) to the country-by-country analysis so often used in the past for this purpose.

Early foundations of global industry analysis

The focus on global rivalry and industry is not new. It has already been the subject of considerable research. Stephen Hymer and a number of other distinguished academics have gathered substantial evidence supporting the importance of rivalry on a global scale as a major influence on international business decisions. In a radical departure from conventional doctrine, Hymer explained foreign investment in terms of oligopolistic rivalry on a world scale. Protection of market share from foreign rivals and the defence of the firm's home market were by themselves sufficient reasons for companies to invest abroad.[4] Today this seems more and more like common sense. The remainder of this text will follow in the footsteps of these pioneers. We will focus on industry, defined globally, as the relevant competitive environment of the global firm.

Shifting from local to global

Our particular interest in the following chapters will be the changes that take place when companies move from a national to a global perception of their competitive environment. It is this shift, a change in management's mindset of what constitutes the firm's competitive environment that is at the root of many of the changes associated with globalisation. Driven primarily by advances in information technology, management's view of the playing field is changing, moving rapidly towards a global perspective.

Figure 2.2 shows three different views of the firm's competitive environment. Some firms have no perception of their international rivals and rivalry. Even organisations whose products find their way abroad, like our cotton exporter, may be in this position if they do not have the information required to engage in oligopolistic rivalry.

Multi-domestic companies with subsidiaries based abroad (and most exporters) view international competition on a country-by-country basis. They see several individual playing fields. Such firms relate to industry rivals nationally, developing competitive strategies for each country individually (position 2 in Figure 2.2).

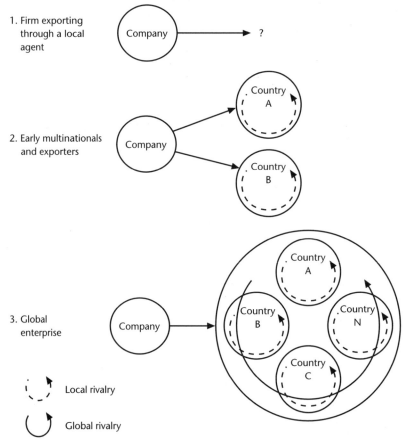

FIGURE 2.2 Three views of international rivalry

Global firms (position 3 in Figure 2.2) see the world as an integrated competitive arena. Such firms are able to engage in oligopolistic rivalry at both the local and global levels. Local rivalry, however, is seen as a sub-category of a wider, global industry rivalry. The primary strategic aim of management is to relate the firm's strategy and operations to this global perception of their competitive environment.

The shift many firms are now making from a country-by-country view to a global perception of rivalry, introduces a quite different view of what constitutes the firm's environment. Competitors and markets come to be viewed in an entirely new light. Change of a fundamental sort is introduced in the way management deals with strategy, marketing, scorekeeping, organisation structure and associated decision areas.

Before proceeding to a consideration of these, let us spell out more precisely what is meant by a global enterprise.

THE GLOBAL ENTERPRISE

The chief external sign of the global firm is the conduct of rivalry on a global scale. Global firms are global rivals. They see the whole world as the playing field. In order to do this such firms must have a corporate intelligence capability which enables them to 'see' and interpret their business, its threats and opportunities, on a global scale. This requires a decision making structure which permits them to coordinate their world-wide resources behind global competitive strategies. In the final analysis, it is a state of mind; management must 'think global'. National and regional competitive environments are viewed as part of a larger, global pattern of markets, suppliers, resources and rivals. This global perception of rivals and rivalry will often give such companies an edge over more locally focused competitors.

The North American television producers, when there were a good number of these, were certainly aware of foreign competitors, such as Sony and Hitachi. The crucial fact remains that these foreign companies were not treated as rivals which had to be matched and attacked globally.

While the US television producers kept their eyes firmly on their domestic market, defining that as their competitive arena, their foreign competitors began to target rival companies outside their home market. At first, they concentrated on smaller markets, building up their capability there. During the early years of this globalisation, Japanese producers sent only 1% of their production to the USA. Their global presence increased, but US producers did not see the connection. Ten years later they were shipping over 60% of their production to the American market. Their more global approach enabled them to spread their costs over a larger volume of production, to reduce unit costs and to acquire resources which ultimately gave them the market power to under-price and to acquire the American producers. Both sets of competitors were engaged in competition, but only the Japanese were engaged in global rivalry.

Firms like our cotton producer or those exporters who rely on the mechanisms of the international market to guide their goods to various world destinations are not global companies. Such firms have no systematic knowledge of their competitors, they do not have the capability to engage in worldwide rivalry. Multinationals that deleg-ate most management decisions to local subsidiaries engaged in local rivalry are also disqualified as global companies, no matter how large or internationally dispersed the parent company may be. Unlike traditional 'international' companies, global firms coordinate their worldwide operations closely. This makes it difficult to identify their performance with a particular country or region.

Citibank has recently made sizeable gains in a number of European countries, but focusing on its performance in any particular country, such as Germany, tells us little either about its own overall performance or how it performs relative to other banks. With the use of electronic funds transfer, a dollar earned in Hong Kong is readily available to Citibank operations in Berlin, New York, Rio or Athens. It is not 'located' in any one place. It is part of the firm's global assets, to be employed to meet its needs or opportunities wherever they may be.

A dollar lost is similarly lost to all parts of the global system. Of course, the same applies also to Barclays, HSBC, Sumitomo and other world banks.

Who qualifies as 'global'?

Are there any companies that fully qualify under the above criteria? Probably only a few, though many now come quite close. The majority of companies in this category will be made up of exporting and multinational companies that have moved away from the more traditional models described in the previous chapter, developing capabilities that enable them to assemble intelligence and coordinate their actions on the necessary world scale.

Both exporters and multinational firms may qualify as global companies. The familiar distinction, based on equity ownership of foreign based facilities, as the key difference between these two enterprise forms, is irrelevant. Global companies are identified by their actions, the way they behave, engaging in global rivalry, rather than characteristics such as the ownership and location of their assets.

Some exporters clearly qualify as global companies, as do many multinationals. For example, the Toyota automobile company was classified by most observers as a global player even when its international activities were confined to exporting. Toyota operated and competed on a world scale long before it began establishing its own foreign based facilities. Unlike most traditional exporters, Toyota developed the capability to monitor its rivals globally. Similarly it actively coordinated many of its international activities in pursuit of competitive advantage in world markets.

Japanese trading companies, although predominantly concerned with exports and imports, were among the first companies to develop the necessary information base and coordinating capability to qualify as global. These commercial giants had long ago acquired the information resources required for global rivalry. Unlike their Western export counterparts, they did not rely on market intermediaries (e.g. import agents) for their information, establishing their own offices and data collection centres in many parts of the world.

By the same reasoning, certain of the larger Western exporting companies, such as Boeing, Rolls-Royce, Pratt and Whitney, also qualify as global companies.

It follows that the term 'global enterprise' may also include franchisers who have the necessary information and ability to coordinate globally. McDonald's probably qualifies as global, as do certain companies franchising international hotels, and businesses such as consulting, accounting and advertising. Companies engaged in licensing technological know-how may also be included in this category.

Smaller players

The term 'global' conjures up an image of industrial giants, an erroneous impression. In the past, the main obstacle to the globalisation of all firms, but particularly the smaller enterprises, has been the costs of global information. That is, the costs of a global intelligence capability. These costs fall into three categories. First there is the cost of accumulating information regarding the firm's external environment, mainly its global markets and rivals. There is also the cost of communicating information about the company to its global customers. Finally there is the cost of processing and transmitting global information within the firm itself.

Such costs are now changing dramatically. New advances in information technology have reduced costs in all three categories and are set to lower them much more. The information 'entry barrier' to becoming a global company has been drastically reduced. It is now within the reach of even the smaller firms to acquire the necessary global information about foreign markets.

Amazon.com is no longer unique. Starting as a relatively small firm it has used the internet to become a global player, perhaps the first in an industry consisting of small national firms. The internet has made it possible for Amazon.com to access millions of potential international buyers around the world, something that was considered prohibitively expensive for a bookstore a short time ago. Other retailers are following this example. Insurance brokers and dealers in equities have been quick to use the low cost internet to market their products nationally. Once the organisation is in place the cost of going from national to global in terms of the necessary information is now far different from that which existed only a few years ago.

The entry of smaller firms into the global category will increase the number of global competitors, sometimes above the numbers usually associated with oligopolistic rivalry. However, advances in information processing capability work strongly in the opposite direction, making it possible for management to track and individually monitor a far larger number of competitors as rivals.

GLOBAL INDUSTRIES

Global industries are those in which a significant number of the member firms are global companies. They are characterised by oligopolistic rivalry on a global scale. It is not possible to place any precise number on how many or what proportion of the member firms should qualify as global. 'Significant' will vary with the size and character of such global rivals in relation to other competitors in the industry.

In forwarding the above definition, we recognise that industry boundaries are constantly changing, particularly today, making precise demarcation of one industry from another difficult. Rather than get immersed in academic distinctions regarding industry boundaries, we shall proceed to use the term 'industry' in the generally accepted sense of a group of firms competing against each other with similar products or services. Whatever the difficulty of formal definition, it is a fact that companies engaged in oligopolistic rivalry (whether local or global) are in practice able to identify their rivals. They are able to calculate with a useful degree of precision their (market) share of industry sales. In practice, identifying the firm's industry in such cases is something firms find they can do.

It is also evident that some companies and their associated industries are global in scope while others are populated primarily by local competitors. Globalisation has not affected all industry sectors equally. It has not had the same impact on bakeries, for example, as on financial institutions. The industries that are far advanced towards globalisation tend to be those where the number of competitors is large enough to afford the high costs (historically) of a global information capability. The pharmaceutical industry, consumer electronics and investment banking are some examples of industry sectors that are among the most global. Other sectors, including certain foods, furniture producers, crafts, bakeries and local newspapers are among the least global. Most firms will find themselves in sectors which are neither at one extreme nor another. But the overall trend is clearly towards an ever increasing proportion of global competitors. It is not difficult to find examples of food producers, furniture companies, crafts, bakeries, newspapers and other organisations usually thought of as local players moving rapidly towards globalisation.

Secondary drivers of globalisation

In addition to advances in information technology, there are a number of secondary factors driving globalisation. Since their impact varies from one industry to another, they help to explain the industry differences noted above. They include the following factors.

Increasing knowledge intensity of products

The rapid increase in the knowledge intensity and particularly the technological inputs required to produce many of today's products and services has provided a major impetus towards globalisation. It is no accident that the most global companies also tend to be those with high R&D expenditures. As investment in technology increases, so too does the pressure to spread the cost of such investment globally rather than locally.

Fixed costs, which are at the root of economies of scale, at one time took the form of investment in buildings and machinery. Today, these are diminishing in relative importance. Much more important today are the fixed costs in the form of soaring investment in R&D expenditures.

Whatever accounting convention may dictate, the really important fixed costs of many products is in their intellectual content. As the cost of developing new designs, drugs and other innovations continues to escalate, so too the pressure to widen the scope of a firm's operations, to coordinate its activities in a way which will defray such costs over a wider (global) customer group, increases.

Mobile customers

With increased mobility, it is not surprising that there are many potential customers interested in doing business with firms that can provide a global service.

An American chemical company which prided itself on the recent reorganisation of its European operations from a series of quasi-autonomous national units into a new European-wide organisation, was surprised to find that some potential new customers were dissatisfied. They were not complaining about the larger size of the new organisation. Just the opposite. They found it too small and narrow in its policies and practices.

These potential customers were from South East Asia where they had long been purchasing their chemical supplies from this same company's regional offices. On embarking on an expansion into Europe these customers were demanding that the American chemical company offer them chemicals and prices comparable to those that they were accustomed to in South East Asia. They felt they should be able to deal with a single global decision point within the firm. They were not happy at the prospect of negotiating with the separate Asian and European businesses of their supplier, each with its own agenda.

The chemical firm's European offices had no knowledge of either the prices that its counterparts charged in South East Asia or the specifications of the materials and chemicals it supplied there. Since the chemical firm's operations in the two regions were operating with a high degree of autonomy, they had developed their own prices and products independently of each other. An apparently reasonable request from an important customer went unanswered. Shortly thereafter management launched a new drive to transform the firm from a regional organisation into a global company.

Deregulation

In industry after industry, whether it be airlines, banking, telecommunication or other, governments have moved to deregulate, lifting restrictions which heretofore presented formidable entry barriers, particularly to foreign companies.

In the United States the government has lifted the restrictions that limit the stake of foreign ownership in telecommunications and airlines. A similar lifting of restrictions against foreigners is affecting many previously regulated industries. This has enabled firms in such industries to move beyond their local national markets more easily. Companies previously confined by regulations to a particular national industry are thus expanding internationally to become global players.

Closely associated with such deregulation, in effect if not in principle, is the international movement to adopt more uniform industry standards. The fact that there are ever more globally applied industry standards governing the configuration of CDs, computer software, video tapes and many other products and services reduces geographic entry barriers and facilitates the global mobility of rivals and their products.

Reduction of tariffs and quota barriers

Progress in lowering trade barriers through multi-governmental agencies such as the World Trade Organization, the European Union and other trade organisations has had a major impact on the ability of firms to operate and compete cross-nationally and globally. Prior to such reductions, these barriers restricted the geographic scope of rivalry by discouraging firms from pursuing opportunities requiring cross-national mobility of goods and other resources. In doing so, they were also responsible for the small, uneconomic size of many companies, particularly in Europe. Constrained by national barriers that prevented the transfer of goods and finished products to other countries, many firms developed production facilities producing below the optimal size. They were nevertheless able to operate profitably due to the protection such barriers provided against foreign competition. The removal of the barriers exposed the uneconomic nature of such nationally limited and protected facilities. By the same token it opened up new opportunities for more globally oriented companies.

Multi-business companies

Within a multi-business company producing a variety of products and/or services, some businesses may fall within industry sectors affected by globalisation while others may not. Some businesses within the same company may be global while others remain local. In the interest of simplicity we will continue to discuss globalisation in terms of single business companies competing in a single industry sector. The principles developed here and in subsequent chapters also apply to multi-business companies, each business considered individually.

Local companies

Even local domestic companies, if they find themselves competing within industries that include global players, will have to develop a global view of their business. If some of their competitors are global, the strategies, commitments, resources and vulnerabilities of such competitors can only be understood from that perspective. Understanding the local actions of a global firm cannot be done successfully looking only at the local level.

All of the above changes are having a major impact, reshaping the nature of the competitive contest. As we shall see in the following chapter, they are also altering perceptions of how to play the game, even the definition of 'winning'.

SUMMARY

- The development of a global reach enables companies with this capability to perceive their international competitors in a new light. In an earlier era, international companies were engaged in international competition but not international rivalry. Such companies now have the ability to view their competitive position globally and to engage in oligopolistic rivalry on a global scale. That is, they are aware of the actions of individual competitors in other parts of the world and are able to adjust their behaviour accordingly. Industries containing such players are outgrowing national boundaries, becoming global rather than national.
- A fruitful approach towards interpreting this new global industry competitive environment has already been developed based on the theory of industrial organisation. But this theory and recent conceptual models based on it are not fully applicable on a global scale, i.e. to interpret global industries. Such models have typically been based on national industries. Global industries are different. New variables, notably those related to the fact of multiple governments, are introduced which greatly limit the application of models such as Porter's five forces model.

- Despite its limitations, an industry based approach remains a useful concept for interpreting the environment and behaviour of the global enterprise. The focus on global industry and global rivalry has in fact already been the subject of considerable research. Much of the content of this book builds on this work.
- Global players are firms which engage in global rivalry. It follows that the term 'global' may apply to exporters, multinationals, franchisers and licensors. Global industries are those which have a significant number of such global players. Globalisation has not affected all industry sectors equally.
- In addition to the new information technology, there are a number of secondary factors driving globalisation. These include the increasing knowledge intensity of products, mobile customers, deregulation and reduction of tariffs and quotas.

NOTES AND REFERENCES

1. Porter, M. E. (1980), *Competitive Strategy*, The Free Press.
2. For example, Richard Caves points out that ratios of industry concentration are calculated 'on the basis of sales by domestic producers only'. Caves, R. (1967), *American Industry: Structure, Conduct, Performance*, 2nd edn, Prentice Hall Inc., p. 8.
3. Porter, M. E. (1980), p. 28.
4. Hymer, S. H. (1979), in R. B. Cohen et al. (Eds), *The Multinational Corporation: A Radical Approach*, Cambridge: Cambridge University Press, pp. 61, 62, 82, 143.

Chapter

3 Global gamesmanship

It is fundamental to any game that winning or losing depends on performance against other contestants. There is little comfort for the athlete who has improved his or her own performance if others have improved even more. A high jumper may add centimetres to the height of his jump and still lose if others jump higher. In games of rivalry it is relative performance that counts.

So too in business, performance is ultimately judged in comparison to the firm's rivals. The firm that invents a path breaking new pharmaceutical or integrated circuit is still losing if its rival comes up with a better product. This would seem obvious – but so often it is not. One of America's largest companies frustrated over the low ratings it received from shareholders, invited a leading Wall Street analyst to explain to them why, despite all their improved performance, their shares were still depressed. The analyst conceded that the firm was making progress – the problem, he pointed out, was that 'everyone else is making more progress'.[1] Globalisation by changing both the players and the scope of their rivalry is changing the basis for such comparisons as well as the nature of the competitive contest. When rivalry was largely a local phenomenon, mainly limited to national firms competing against each other, whether the firm was winning or not was judged against the performance of other local players. Competitive strategy was similarly locally limited, addressing a contest between local firms.

This country-by-country view of competition and competitive strategy may have been suited to the situation of the early multinationals and exporters, with their more limited horizons and multi-local approach. But for companies engaged in global rivalry, it makes very little sense.

As indicated in the previous chapters, the broadening of management's 'reach', the ability to manage over a wider geographic scope, is leading many firms to adopt a global view of rivals and rivalry. Competitive strategy becomes global rather than local.

Winning means outperforming rivals globally. Once a company defines winning in these terms, the game as well as the way it is played changes.

THE FOREIGN INVESTMENT DECISION

To illustrate, let's take a look at the foreign investment decision. How do firms go about evaluating foreign direct investment opportunities?

Capital budgeting

The accepted wisdom has been that companies considering foreign investment projects should base their decision on estimates of their future financial profitability. Textbooks on the subject stress that multinational companies use capital budgeting procedures to evaluate proposals for such projects originating within the firm. These assess the future profitability and investment associated with various possible foreign investment projects which the firm might undertake. Investment proposals are submitted from various parts of the firm. The aim is to identify the expected financial return of such projects, adjusted for risk and time scale. The priority is on selecting those with the best risk–return characteristics as the prime candidates for investment.[2]

Theorists explaining the rationale behind foreign direct investment have offered various explanations but here again a central theme is the notion that the incentive for foreign investment reflects the expectation of financial gain. Indeed, it is expected that such foreign investment projects should earn superior returns to those of locally based companies. Otherwise it would be better for the shareholders of potential foreign investors to invest directly in local firms.[3]

Environmental analysis

Closely related to the financial analysis of capital budgeting is investigation of the various environmental factors associated with the investment site. Environmental analysis of local demand conditions, political factors, local competition, etc., underpin the financial calculations.

Any major investment decision also involves considerations of strategy. These may sometimes be kept in the background, the project proposal for a new investment may be submitted directly to environmental and capital budgeting analysis (see Figure 3.1). But, whether implicit or explicit, strategic considerations are part of the investment decision making process. Indeed, there will be instances in the case of so-called 'strategic investments', those judged to be essential to the firm's future overall strategy, when strategic considerations will be the dominant influence on whether or not to invest irrespective of financial estimates of future profitability.[4]

So long as rivalry was conducted nationally, between competitors in the same country, foreign investment motivated by strategic considerations of global rivalry did not enter the picture. Globalisation has changed this. As competition and the need to counter competitors are perceived on a world scale, possibilities for global rivalry related strategic investments assume a new importance. Certain investments whose

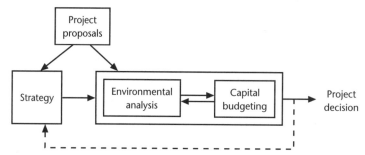

FIGURE 3.1   The foreign investment decision process

primary aim is to contain or limit rivals in other parts of the world may be justified, even if they are not the investments with the highest return.

For the global player the question of what constitutes the best foreign investment now has to consider, not only the financial profitability estimates of capital budgeting, but also the logic and benefits of strategic investments such as those indicated below.

FOREIGN INVESTMENT AS GAMESMANSHIP

Once the firm's vision of rivals and rivalry becomes global, whether and when to invest can best be understood as part of a series of interconnected moves in a game which is now played globally. In games of rivalry, a brilliant defensive manoeuvre can be just as valuable as a goal scored. Not all of the moves need to be profitable in order to win.

In the context of global industry, manoeuvring and jockeying among rivals on a global scale introduces a form of gamesmanship which may by itself provide sufficient justification for new investment. Investment in a particular project may simply be an interim move, yielding on its own, little or no return. Company strategy may determine that the payoff of simply maintaining the firm's present competitive position or placing competitors at a disadvantage is in itself sufficient to make the investment worthwhile.

Blocking moves

Preventing entry into the 'home' market

A competitor is moving into the firm's home territory – what should be its response? Research indicates that companies sometimes invest abroad mainly to block a foreign rival from moving into the blocking firm's own 'home' market.[5]

A preemptive blocking investment into the rival's own territory may also be aimed at distracting a rival, keeping them preoccupied and focused on their present location. Forced to fight harder for their present territory, the rival may find it more difficult to assemble the necessary resources and the managerial time and energy required to pursue expansion in other parts of the world. The blocking firm may consider the investment as money well spent if it allows it to operate with greater freedom and less threat in its own home market. The ultimate objective of course is a higher return to the firm doing the blocking – very possibly in another part of the world – with little apparent connection to the investment that initiated the blocking.

It is no coincidence that the computer industry, one of the few where the Japanese producers have had to battle hard for their own home market, is also one of those in which Western firms invested at an early date to establish their own Japanese based facilities. IBM and Apple were willing to invest to build their own facilities in that country, taking on the (locally) much larger Japanese companies at a time when the vagaries of the Japanese language, software and the Japanese market made anything approaching a good return on such investment a distant, high risk proposition. In terms of short to medium term return for their money, there were certainly better prospects elsewhere.

Analogously, Texas Instruments established semi-conductor production in Japan during the late 1960s contributing to the considerable delay experienced by Japanese manufacturers in developing their own semi-conductor facilities.[6]

Perhaps the main 'return' from Coca-Cola's initial investment in Japan was to eliminate some major potential rivals.

Blocking rivals from a foreign location

A blocking investment may also be aimed at excluding rivals from a particular foreign location (foreign to both the rivals and the blocking investor). When General Motors became the first automobile company to invest in a plant assembling cars in Australia, this move blocked the entry of other interested competitors from Europe and the United States into that country for many years. Such 'early entry' blocking is a particularly effective manoeuvre in developing countries. The limited size of such markets will often only sustain one or two competitors. Early entrants are able to establish a supporting infrastructure, building their distribution system, relations with local suppliers and local government. This makes it very difficult for subsequent follower investors. The latecomers have to overcome the dual handicap of capturing market share in a limited market as well as the usual disadvantages of being an outsider. The strategic value of such moves becomes particularly obvious in those situations where a once small market develops rapidly, as is the case today in many of the emerging markets. Coca-Cola, which had once left the Indian market for cola drinks, decided to re-enter that market when its development accelerated. It found it had to re-enter India as a relative outsider, facing fierce competition from an entrenched Pepsi-Cola as well as other established competitors.

Governments have long been familiar with and sensitive to the effects of such blocking, particularly as it relates to foreign investment within their boundaries which may, even unwittingly, block the development of local firms. Many countries have passed legislation relating to investment by foreign firms specifically to protect home companies against such blocking moves by foreign rivals.

Brazil, Mexico and India are just a few of the many countries which have selected certain 'strategic' industries for special protection from incoming investments by foreign rivals.

Blocking through licensing

Licensing may also be used as a blocking manoeuvre. Awarding a licence, particularly an exclusive licence to a foreign company producing the same types of products or services, is a form of investment. The licensing firm is in effect investing its technology and possibly other assets such as brand name and reputation. Licensing of foreign companies may be used for two types of blocking.

First, the licensing firm is able to provide technology to strengthen allied companies that might act to block potential rivals. If the licensed technology represents a significant innovation, it gives the licensee an added competitive advantage with which to block and/or slow the rise of other, potentially more dangerous competitors to the licensor. By selecting which firm to license the licensor effectively chooses which firm to strengthen. Of course, the strengthening may work to the disadvantage of the licensing company if the new technology is used against it. But careful framing of the licensing conditions and particularly its territorial restrictions, can avoid this. Companies receiving the new technology may also be potential allies and are often chosen with this in mind.

BOX 3.1

Pilkington restraining rivals through licensing

The British glass maker, Pilkington, used the licensing of its numerous innovations in glass making technology to transfer its know-how to selected companies in different countries. Provided by Pilkington with its revolutionary float glass technology, these licensees found they enjoyed a competitive advantage over other glass producers.

This not only enabled Pilkington to choose which companies would enjoy the competitive advantages conferred on them by its technology, giving them an advantage over other rivals, it also helped the British firm to develop close working relationships and alliances, with its foreign licensees.

Furthermore, by incorporating the appropriate restrictions in the contract the licensor in such cases is able to specify and limit the territory over which the licensee may use the technology. This enables the licensor to dictate the geographic scope of the licensee's operations, in effect blocking it from particular countries and regions. Obviously, the terms of such agreements could ensure that such rivals were excluded from invading the territory of the licensor.

The United States Justice Department, in referring to a settlement it had reached with the British glass maker, stated that Pilkington had put 'tough restraints' on its licensees, allegedly placing geographic restrictions on them which limited them to particular national territories. In its statement, the Justice Department referred to a 'licensing stranglehold' that kept American companies from building plants overseas. It was estimated that the changes introduced by this settlement between the Pilkington company and the Justice Department could enable American companies to win contracts for up to half of a projected 50 new glass plants expected to be built over the subsequent six years, most of them in South East Asia and Eastern Europe.[7] ∎

Follow the leader

In choosing a new location, some firms have been known to simply follow their rivals. A classic study of foreign investment provides evidence that rivals not only watch each other but also imitate each other's actions. Such imitation includes the choice of foreign investment locations.[8]

This follow-the-leader mentality is not as naive as it may appear. The foreign investment decision in a new territory is typically made under conditions of incomplete information, the type of situation appropriately described by Igor Ansoff, the well known strategist, as 'partial ignorance'. This is especially true in the early years of such foreign investment. Given this lack of information there is necessarily a high level of uncertainty on the part of the potential investor. If a company contemplating foreign investment sees one of its rivals taking the lead – investing in a particular foreign market – it might understandably consider that this rival may have superior access to information. The rival may know something that the follower does not. Such thoughts become even more pressing if other rivals join in, following the lead of the first investor. All of these leaders may, of course, be mistaken. But suppose they are not? If the investment is a success, it may mean the rival or rivals gain access to important new markets or resources. The leaders thereby acquire new advantages which upset the existing competitive balance.

Let us suppose that the new location proves to be unfavourable. The rival firm being followed will probably also be affected. The relative positions of leader and follower may thus remain unchanged. If the leader has indeed found a favourable new location, the follower may profit from this as well as the leader. Following the leader thus provides a form of insurance against a change in relative competitive position. Not following the leader into a new location that turns out to be 'good for business', risks the possibility of the rival leader gaining an advantage.

On balance, a strong case can be made for a follow-the-leader strategy in situations characterised by inadequate information, uncertainty and a large upside potential.

Many of the recent investments by Western firms in China reflect just such a pattern, firms following each other in close succession to make investments with enormous potential, but entailing a high degree of ignorance and uncertainty.

The same leader–follower pattern is observable in other parts of the world. Within a very short space of time, Peugeot-Citroën, the Ford Motor Company, Volkswagen, Mercedes-Benz and General Motors all announced the establishment of car making operations in India. The financial press reported a 'stampede' of car companies to that country.[9] Can it be a coincidence that all of these rival companies discovered the attractions of this location at about the same time?

Exchange of threats

The Chinese say that the best strategy is the one that secures the objective without the battle. A proposal to invest abroad may be used to signal a foreign rival to stay away or to moderate its rivalry. The intention would be to persuade the foreign rival to stay out by threatening to attack it elsewhere, as in its home market, if it did not. A threatening signal of this sort to a foreign rival may be supplemented by news releases and promotional campaigns to highlight the warning. If the rival has already made an entry, a counter-investment in the rival's territory may be used to persuade the rival to limit its invasion.

When the German software company, SAP, located its new development headquarters in California, very near the headquarters of Oracle, its United States rival, the chief executive of the latter was quoted as saying: they (SAP) are 'giving us hell' here in the United States, we are going to do 'the same to them in Europe'.[10]

This type of exchange between global rival firms may culminate in reciprocal investments in each other's territory. A pioneering study of international investment patterns found that investment by a company into a foreign market, particularly as between one developed country and another, may be expected to elicit a response from local firms in the recipient country.[11] Motivation for such investment, sometimes referred to as an 'exchange of threats', is best explained in terms of oligopolistic rivalry on a global scale.

Avoiding dangerous players

Avoiding dangerous rivals is itself a valid strategy which can influence the foreign investment decision.

An executive with one of the international oil companies investing in Cuba commented: 'What attracted us to Cuba was not having to compete with the big United States oil companies.'[12]

Sometimes this evasion of rivalry may be temporary, allowing the firm time to develop its competitive capabilities. Just as an athlete in the early stages of training will avoid going up against recognised champions, so too will some companies in the early stages of globalisation sometimes avoid direct competition with their most powerful rivals. This may be either a long-standing policy or a temporary strategy. It allows the company time to prepare and develop its capabilities.

With this in mind, some global competitors sometimes seek out investment locations which will temporarily avoid or minimise the threat of rivalry, allowing them to develop their skills gradually – even if it means not investing in the larger and more lucrative markets until they have had a chance to fully build up their capabilities.

During the early stages of their international expansion, a number of Japanese car companies entered several of the small Nordic car markets, specifically to test and further develop their products and capabilities. The severe northern climate was ideal for testing early product designs. The smaller of the Nordic countries, Norway and Finland, also had no indigenous automobile producers. There were no established home based companies to seek special government protection against foreign investors.

The experience gained in these countries enabled the Japanese car companies to further develop their designs and marketing skills in preparation for the main contest in the larger markets of Europe and North America.

Dividing the playing field

Global rivalry inevitably involves major expense, risk and often, duplication of effort. In its extreme form, such competition can appear wasteful and even destructive. One response is to eliminate, or at least moderate it, through some form of collusive agreement dividing markets among the various rivals. It has been argued that this can 'rationalise' production, ensuring that the excesses of rivalry, such as cut-throat pricing, wide swings in production, the closing down of some firms, wasteful expenditure on advertising, etc., are reduced or eliminated. However, the advantages which appear so logical and attractive to the contracting parties are often secured at the expense of the consumer who may have to pay higher prices or lose other benefits of free competition. For this reason many (but not all) such collusive arrangements are considered illegal.

Despite this, certain companies have responded to the globalisation of world markets by agreeing to divide the market. On some occasions this has taken the form of geographic division. This type of defensive manoeuvre, limiting the territory of rivals, also influences their investment decisions. The strategy is one with a lengthy history. The most famous example is the 1930s decision of three rival chemical firms to divide the world market for a wide range of chemical products. The agreement between the three companies allocated world markets for chemical products, requiring each firm to limit its activities to agreed national markets.

There is little doubt that such practices continue even among those (relatively few) countries with stringent anti-monopoly legislation. One report refers to a 'memorandum of understanding' between two of Europe's largest and most prestigious producers of high speed trains 'to divide the world market among themselves'.[13]

Not all such agreements are illegal. Some, particularly those relating to the allocation of export markets, are perfectly legal. In many parts of the world rivals are permitted to agree on which national or regional markets they will share and where they will compete.

Developing competitive capabilities

The outcome of any game depends in large part on the relative capability of the various players, i.e. their ability to develop and sustain particular competitive capabilities and competencies which give them an edge.

Certain locations which are not in themselves attractive as sites for investment may nevertheless warrant company resources if they contribute to the firm's overall global competence. This effect is particularly noticeable in those industry sectors where providing a global service is important. For example, the bank that can offer its customers access to its services around the world has a distinct competitive advantage not available to those doing business on a purely local basis. For an increasing number of companies, providing a global service network is essential. It provides the potential for competitive advantage which may well be worth the cost of investment in individual project locations that do not make a positive financial contribution.

Just as some companies support loss making products because they contribute to the success of the overall product range, so too some firms find that certain loss making locations may be justified when viewed as part of the firm's overall strategy for developing specific capabilities.

A major motive for company globalisation is the greater flexibility and speed with which global services can be offered within a single corporate entity. Recognising the value of such worldwide coverage has led some companies to form cooperative arrangements, for example, an arrangement that permits the customers of a bank in one country to be serviced by the facilities of a different bank in another country. However, arrangements of this sort between independent organisations have their limitations. Once fixed, the introduction of changes to such agreements require renegotiation, with no guarantee that the suggested changes will be accepted. The global company that has invested in and owns its own worldwide facilities has greater control over the management of the operation and greater security regarding any con-fidential information that may be associated with it. However, it is a near certainty that some of this investment will be in projects and countries that, considered individually, would not qualify as the most profitable.

Strategic location

Are there certain key locations in which companies which aspire to be global players must have a strong presence? The expansion of rivalry across national borders, putting some competitors in head-to-head competition for the first time will inevitably lead to a shake-out in this trend. The main battleground is very likely to be the countries and regions that comprise the major markets of the world for these sectors. Con-sidering the importance of economic power and economies of scale in many such industry sectors, there is good reason to believe that firms that aspire to become global players must develop a strong presence in these major world markets if they wish to be among the survivors.

In the telecommunications industry, the American market accounts for over half the worldwide sales of mobile telephones. It is also much the largest world market for computers, pharmaceuticals, aircraft and many other products. No matter how strong the position of a company in the smaller markets of the world, it is unlikely that any firm can become a major global player in these industries without a sizeable com-mitment in this market.

In other words, the investment location decision is closely related to management's aspirations as to the type of company they want to be. Companies which aim to become 'world class' will often be required to invest heavily in the major world markets for their products. These may not be considered the most profitable markets, but investment there may nevertheless be a necessary prerequisite for global player status.

The Japanese writer and consultant, Kenichi Ohmae, identifies a group of three so-called 'triad' markets which he claims are crucial to becoming a world class player.[14] For companies that aspire to this category, a strong presence would appear to be necessary in at least two of the three triad markets (Europe, North America and Japan).

Extending the firm's scope into the triad is responsible for no small percentage of the international mergers and acquisitions that have characterised the movement towards globalisation. In explaining a recent acquisition aimed at making his company a global player, Bill Castle, chief executive officer of Amersham International, stated: 'This will help Amersham to achieve market leading positions in each of the world's three major nuclear medicine markets – Europe, North America and Japan'.[15]

Of course, the triad deployment strategy presupposes that the company wishes to become a global player. Not all companies agree on the desirability of this goal and some of those which may have had this as an objective have subsequently changed their minds. Maytag, the American washing machine company, followed its rival, Whirlpool, into the European market as part of its globalisation strategy. More recently Maytag decided to pull out, even selling some of its European operations at a loss. The chief executive of Maytag concluded that while some products were suitable for globalisation, washing machines were not among them. Rival Whirlpool continues to move in the opposite direction. The company is designing a standard washing machine which it plans to sell (with adaptations to individual market requirements) to markets throughout the world. The chairman of Whirlpool comments to the effect that 'there is no way to conclude from Maytag's experience that this isn't a global business'.[16] The decision is one many companies face. The choice is especially stark for those companies that have originated and started their operations in one of the smaller home markets.

BOX 3.2

The pull of large markets

Companies such as Nokia and Ericsson, from Finland and Sweden respectively, recognised early in their development that they had little choice but to become international. At first, the aim of expansion for such firms is usually one of simply tapping the larger customer base available abroad, growing the business. With the emergence of global competitors a new element has been introduced. Investing in certain key markets has now become a matter of survival. Moving into these markets is a prerequisite to developing the necessary customer base and sheer financial strength required to support the firm's ability to compete against other global players. Quite simply a firm cannot be credible as a global player if it is not represented in the major markets of the world.

In certain industries, reaping the full benefits (lower unit costs) of efficiencies of scale requires production volumes only available by producing for the largest world markets. Production of this magnitude typically entails considerable investment. It is abundantly evident that companies producing passenger aircraft, ships and pharmaceutical products, must sell their products in the major markets of the world in order to attain the necessary production volume required to keep their costs competitive.

At one time companies could remain viable, avoiding competition with larger firms by sheltering within smaller national markets protected by tariffs and other barriers. So long as these markets remained isolated this was a workable strategy. Companies within the protective barriers of these smaller markets could afford to operate without the advantages of global volume, passing the extra cost on to the consumer. This is no longer the case. Such firms will increasingly find themselves challenged.

Today, both Nokia and Ericsson are aware that not only success but also survival in their business (mobile telephones) requires a major presence in the larger markets of the world. The mobile phone company that attempts to produce a new product only for a specific national market is doomed to failure. It will soon be undercut by a competitor able to spread the high development cost of such products over a wider customer base. In such research intensive industries the ability to defray R&D expenditures across the major world markets has become a necessary condition for remaining competitive, hence the stream of investors, even from the developing countries, who feel that a presence in North America, Europe and Japan is essential. ■

The lowering of trade barriers and transportation costs means that there are very few national markets immune today from the attention of global rivals. The choice is often one of either entering the major world markets early, while the global industry is in its formative stages, or retreating behind the ever less effective barriers of protected, smaller markets. Global firms that have moved first, even if initially at a sacrifice in profitability, will have an advantage difficult for follower firms to overcome. Having carved out a place in the larger markets, thereby gaining access to economies of scale and market power, can make them formidable competitors in other parts of the world as well.

But Kenichi's designation of North America, Japan and Europe as the 'triad' markets, regardless of what product or service is produced, is surely misleading. These regions certainly encompass the main markets for many products and services, possibly the majority. Hence it is unlikely that companies in most industries can attain global status without competing in and very likely investing in this triad. However, there are clearly product and service sectors where this generalisation does not hold. In a number of agricultural and animal products, including veterinary medicines, farming tools and livestock products, any list of the major markets of the world should include Australia, Brazil and other countries of Latin America.

In certain other product sectors, market size is closely keyed to population size. Examples include birth control devices, insulin and certain low-cost pharmaceutical and over-the-counter drugs. For these sectors the key world markets may well be India and China. In any case, given the pace of change and market conditions, it would be surprising indeed if the leading market position for a particular product or service remained consistently within the borders of certain specified countries or regions. Today's key markets will not be the same tomorrow. That we can be sure of. But the general notion that certain core markets are crucial and of strategic importance as regards the possibility of becoming and remaining a global player is probably valid. However, it is just as well to keep an open mind about which countries or regions qualify for this category.

The overriding message is clear. For companies that intend to compete globally, investment must take account of the strategic need to maintain a strong presence within certain key markets. For certain specific project proposals, the importance attached to such geographic positioning may well outweigh narrower considerations relating to return on investment.

As the world business environment becomes increasingly globalised the type of gamesmanship outlined above will become more widespread. The ability of global companies to see their rivals and competitive arena on a world scale introduces and heightens the role of investment decisions motivated by considerations of competitive strategy. The very concept of what constitutes 'winning' is altered from that employed in more locally oriented international firms that do not take account of global rivalry and the potential benefits of strategic investments.

To be sure, the firm's global investment objective over the longer term may be profit. However, closer and ever more numerous linkages across national boundaries will increasingly blur cause and effect. Investment in one part of the world will increasingly be only one part of a chain of events whose ultimate return is far removed from the location in which the investment is made.

For a global company, investment, costs, benefits, losses and profits have to be assessed and balanced on a world scale. Local performance is secondary, an interim goal. Global performance is the objective.

SUMMARY

- With the appearance of rivalry on a global scale, competitive strategy itself becomes global as does the definition of whether the firm is winning or losing the competitive contest. Once a company defines 'winning' globally, an element of gamesmanship is involved. An illustration is provided by way of the foreign investment decision.
- So long as rivalry was conducted nationally, between competitors in the same country, foreign investment motivated by strategic considerations of global rivalry did not enter the picture. Traditional explanations of foreign investment stressed the prospect of a contribution to profitability. With the onset of global rivalry, strategic investments, which yield little or even negative financial rewards, become an important part of the global firm's competitive strategy.
- In such cases, an investment abroad may be motivated by the intention to block a foreign competitor. The blocking move may be directed at blocking the competitor from the (blocking) firm's own home market or another foreign market.
- Blocking moves may also be implemented through licensing, the licensor using its agreements with licensees to prevent them from entering certain markets.
- Foreign investment may also be based on a follow-the-leader strategy. Particularly where there is very little information on a foreign market, the usual investigation to assess profitability may be bypassed in favour of following a rival. This at least ensures that parity is maintained, i.e. the move may not result in profits but at least the rival does not gain a competitive advantage.
- Analogously, foreign investment may be motivated by a desire to avoid the firm's most powerful competitors, pursuing a policy of dividing world markets and developing the firm's competitive capabilities.
- Firms that aspire to become global players may find it necessary to invest in certain key world markets, even if they are not the most promising in terms of profitability. This decision is particularly relevant for successful firms that have developed their base in the smaller markets of the world.
- Even though profit may be the global firm's long term goal, any particular investment by such companies will increasingly be only one part of a worldwide chain of events in which not all the links are profitable.

NOTES AND REFERENCES

1. *The Wall Street Journal Europe*, 12–13 June 1998, p. 1.
2. Eiteman, D. K., Stonehill, A. I., Moffett, M. H. (1998), *Multinational Business Finance*, 8th edn, Addison-Wesley, pp. 583–9.
3. For a comprehensive review of such theories see, Calvet, A. L. (1981), A synthesis of foreign direct investment theories and theories of the multinational firm, *Journal of International Business Studies*, Spring/Summer, pp. 43–59.

4. Dunning, J. H. (1993), *Multinational Enterprises and the Global Economy*, Addison-Wesley, p. 56; Hout, T., Porter, M. and Rudden, E. (1982), How global companies win out, *Harvard Business Review*, September–October, pp. 98–108. Also Hymer, S. H. (1979), in R. B. Cohen et al. (Eds), *The Multinational Corporation: A Radical Approach*, Cambridge: Cambridge University Press, pp. 61, 62, 82, 143. Strategic investment motivated by objectives related to competitive strategy on a global scale is a prominent theme in the writings of a number of the authors featured in this chapter, including Knickerbocker, F. T. and Graham, E. M.

5. Aharoni, Y. (1966), *The Foreign Investment Decision Process*, Boston: Division of Research, Harvard Business School, pp. 68, 69.

6. Kim, W. C. and Mauborgne, R. A. (1988), Becoming an effective global competitor, *Journal of Business Strategy*, Jan/Feb, pp. 323–37.

7. *Financial Times*, 27 May 1994, p. 18.

8. Knickerbocker, F. T. (1973), *Oligopolistic Reaction and Multinational Enterprise*, Boston Division of Research, Harvard Business School.

9. *The Wall Street Journal Europe*, 19 October 1994, p. 10.

10. *Business Week*, 8 August 1994, p. 48.

11. Graham, E. M. (1974), *Oligopolistic Imitation and European Direct Investment in the United States*, unpublished doctoral dissertation, Harvard Business School. See also, Aharoni, Y. (1966), pp. 68, 69.

12. *Financial Times*, 16 April 1998, p. 7.

13. *Financial Times*, 26 July 1995, p. 9.

14. Ohmae, Kenichi (1985), *Triad Power: The Coming Shape of Global Competition*, New York: The Free Press.

15. *Financial Times*, 12 October 1994, p. 24.

16. *The Wall Street Journal Europe*, 24 June 1998, p. 9.

4 Global competencies as a source of competitive advantage

Teams engaged in competitive sports carefully analyse their own performance as well as that of their competitors. Hours are spent watching replays of previous matches. Why did we win/lose? Knowing just what the team is good at, its competitive advantage, can help it to become better.

If the team is able to develop new areas of superior performance not previously known to its rivals, this not only gives them a competitive edge, it changes the very nature of the competition.

For many years, economists have preached that the source of international competitive advantage was to be found in the national attributes of particular countries. Nations engaged in trade would do best, it was proclaimed, in those products which drew on the particular resources that they had in relative abundance.

From this perspective, competitive advantage springs from the location, the country itself. The emphasis is on national attributes rather than the individual enterprise. Management is assigned a passive role. If a country has an abundance of certain resources, it is assumed that companies will spring up to capitalise on this and employ these resources to gain competitive advantage.

Today there is a new stress on the role of management and the firm. It is companies that compete for markets, and it is the company that not only acts as the agent or carrier of competitive advantage but creates it through its actions.

With the increased mobility of companies and resources locational considerations, i.e. which country the firm is located in and its particular attributes are increasingly irrelevant. Many of the new product areas such as software, integrated circuits, and so on require very few resources other than human skills or technology both of which are highly mobile. Software companies can and do draw on the talent they require from many parts of the world. There are specialised search companies which do nothing but recruit software technicians and scientists from wherever they may be located to wherever they are needed. The resources that count today are predominantly human skills and expertise which are mobile rather than those fixed in any particular national location.

Furthermore most companies today are themselves mobile. They can locate their operations wherever the necessary requirements for success, be they markets or resources, are to be found. In short, the initial requirements, the 'raw' materials required to succeed are not specific to particular countries or locations. Apart from patents and other proprietary rights, they are available to most companies. But anything that is available to all cannot be a source of competitive advantage.

The potential for uniqueness and hence a possible source of competitive advantage is within the companies themselves, the way they organise, combine, direct and manage themselves and their resources to develop certain things (competencies) which they can do better than competitors elsewhere in the world producing similar goods and services.

Achieving competitive advantage requires that the sources of the firm's competencies, whatever they may be, are identified, nurtured and developed. Like so many other simple formulas, translating such advice into action may not be so straightforward. Where do we look for this competence? What are its sources?

CORPORATE COMPETENCE

Many firms have only the very vaguest notion of the competence or competencies which are behind their ability to compete. Perhaps they have been in business over a number of years and the special skills, technology or assets which underlie their competitiveness have become so familiar that they are taken for granted, a part of the scenery. Also, changes in technology, competition and market trends can eliminate winning skills and capabilities or even turn them into liabilities.

The company that sells a single unit, even if it has sold much less than its competitors, has outperformed them in terms of that single sale. For that one product or service, it has excelled. Does this reflect a source of competence? It may. However, if it is based on chance or superior performance of an extremely short duration, then it is not a competence. The search for competence seeks to identify and develop those capabilities that will enable the firm to excel consistently. Sustainable competitive advantage requires that such competencies are of a type not readily duplicated by others. The aim is to develop capabilities which provide competencies of an enduring nature.

The source of the firm's competence may take various forms. Competence may derive from its technology, managerial skills, product design, equipment, or other resources underlying the capabilities in which it excels. Frequently it is also based on the way various skills and resources are organised and put together; the way a particular set of capabilities is combined may be the basis of superior performance.

Sources of global competence

Recently there has been a shift in the types of competence associated with firms operating on an international scale. In the normal course of its development, the typical company will begin as a local player with local competencies. Initially such firms typically undertook foreign expansion in order to exploit whatever competence they had developed within their domestic market. Companies that had developed a particular product or process that was successful in their 'own' country not infrequently found that this could also be successful abroad. The success of such firms in foreign markets was based on their ability to successfully transfer their domestic competence into another environment.

Microsoft's initial expansion abroad was based on skills and competencies with software which it first developed in its United States domestic market. These have sometimes been modified to suit local conditions. For example, certain adaptations to its software were developed especially for China. But the core competencies behind Microsoft's international expansion were clearly those that the company had developed initially in its domestic market and then transferred abroad.

Within multinational companies, this transfer of competence makes use of foreign based subsidiaries as the main transfer vehicle. During the early stages of their establishment in a new environment, these subsidiaries draw on the parent company's strengths and its domestic competencies, applying these in the new situation. Subsequently, they may move beyond this stage, developing additional sources of competence in the new environment.

The advent of globalisation and global companies introduced a new type of competence. The subsidiaries of the early multinationals did not work together in any systematic fashion. They operated with a high degree of independence, making it difficult if not impossible for them to combine and coordinate their efforts towards the development of new, joint competencies. Acting independently they were not able to develop the sorts of competencies that required the international coordination of their activities.

The appearance of global players changed all this. Taking advantage of their new 'global reach', such firms operate their worldwide facilities as part of a globally coordinated network. This enables them to tap new possibilities for acquiring additional capabilities: sources of competence over and above those available to either local companies or the more traditional forms of international enterprise.

Today, developing new sources of competence is perhaps the most important motivation of all behind the decision of companies to 'go global'. These new competencies are not simply a means for securing foreign markets. For such companies, the distinction between foreign and domestic is meaningless. Competencies acquired through global operations may be used to attack rivals in whatever market, foreign or domestic, they may be located. In a world of increasing global rivalry, new competencies are not only a potential source of new business and competitive advantage, they are often essential for the firm's very survival against other global competitors.

Any company contemplating the costs and benefits of globalisation would do well to examine carefully the new global sources of competence and the contribution these can make to increased competitiveness. The following are some examples.

Competence based on a global service

The early development of a capability for servicing its customers around the world gave American Express a competence based on the ability to provide global financial services for travellers. Wherever the American Express customer may decide to travel, the company is able to provide facilities ready to honour its financial instruments. These facilities are part of a global network offering a recognisable, standardised service which the traveller will find available and familiar from one country to another.

Besides providing American Express with a competitive advantage over companies with a more limited network of facilities, it also serves as an entry barrier. Competitors have to develop their own global service capability before they can even begin to compete effectively against American Express.

Merrill Lynch, the brokerage company, enjoys a similar advantage through its worldwide network of operations which provide a global service to its retail brokerage customers. In the words of its chief executive, Merrill Lynch aspires to 'provide access and support to capital anywhere in the world'.[1]

One of the firm's competitors confirmed the sense of this, explaining their own lagging performance by attributing it to the fact that they did 'not have an integrated global distribution system' such as Merrill Lynch's. This statement coincided with the announcement by the competitor of its plans to restructure itself into a global organisation.[2]

In an age of travel, the ability of health insurance companies, such as the British based BUPA, to offer medical insurance services to clients in whatever part of the world they may be provides a similar edge over locally limited competitors.

The worldwide services offered by these companies capitalise on the global firm's ability to operate and coordinate a global network of facilities and personnel able to deliver a consistent and coordinated level of service globally, almost irrespective of distance and location. This provides a powerful advantage over local firms rooted to a particular national territory. It also gives them an advantage over the old style multinationals: the latter operating as a collection of local businesses have the necessary geographic scope but not the necessary coordination or global intelligence to operate such networks. In the future, the greater mobility of both individuals and companies will make this type of competence increasingly valuable.

Competence based on universal usage

Another closely related but quite distinct competitive advantage accrues to firms whose products or services are so widely known and used that they have become 'universal' global products, i.e. products known to have achieved worldwide acceptance and usage. This global acceptance is itself a major source of competence.

A product that enjoys such universal usage is said to enjoy a 'positive externality'. This simply means that its very universality is considered an additional benefit that contributes to the attractiveness of the product; the more widespread it becomes the more attractive it appears. For example, many people choose to hold dollars simply because they are known and used globally. The more widely the dollar is used the greater its attractiveness from this source. The Japanese yen or the German Deutschmark may have certain other advantages but many people will still choose dollars because of their greater universality. Acquiring the benefits of such universality has become a major strategic issue.

BOX 4.1

Advantage through universality

The QWERTY keyboard is not the most efficient layout for a typist, but it is the most widely used by keyboard producers because it is already so well known and widely accepted. Similarly, Microsoft built its empire on the widespread adoption of DOS, its personal computer operating system which became the world standard for most personal computers. This not only gave Microsoft an early advantage over competitors, it also spurred other software producers around the world to develop new software products for Microsoft rather than competitive, less widely used systems. These new software products further increased the scope of Microsoft systems' usage, contributing to a self-reinforcing effect and increasing that firm's competitive advantage. ■

Achieving universality, better still becoming accepted as a world standard, has obvious attractions as a source of competitive advantage. Certain products, such as blue jeans, may achieve global universality as a matter of fashion, almost without conscious effort, but this is rare.

Achieving worldwide universality requires a degree of market knowledge and worldwide coordination that requires the capabilities and vision associated with global companies. Most such products must be designed from the outset to take into account the diverse requirements of different national markets. Software for example must be designed so that it is widely compatible with many types of computers in different parts of the world. Secondly, the firm seeking such global usage must develop a strategy for gaining and maintaining worldwide acceptance. This requires constant monitoring of world markets and competitors. In many cases it will also require close coordination of international logistics and distribution systems designed to keep abreast of emerging trends and to maintain compatibility with newly emerging product requirements.

The efforts of companies to acquire the benefits of global usage for their products and services reverses the traditional wisdom of keeping innovations close to the chest. The classic example is that of Apple Computer Inc. Apple followed the familiar path of keeping new innovations as proprietary information and refusing to license competitors. The new logic indicates just the opposite. With the benefit of hindsight, it has become evident that proprietary standards not widely shared and copied create 'technological islands' limiting the firm to doing business only with those equipped with similar technology. Apple subsequently moved, perhaps too late, to a much more open attitude towards licensing its technology.

It may even pay to give technology and products away free. Firms trying to attain this virtuous circle, wider usage of their product stimulating more demand, go out of their way to introduce their products to the largest possible number of consumers, sometimes even giving away proprietary rights or other assets in an effort to persuade individuals and companies to adopt their own software, service or product. The stakes are great. One thing is clear, where global coverage, uniformity and compatibility are assets in this contest, global players start with a decided advantage.

The struggle to be on the right side of emerging new product standards is behind many global alliances. Failure to reach agreement on a common standard can disrupt and even prevent the successful launch of a new product. Such agreements often require compromise with rival firms even if it means the sacrifice of a new technology developed at considerable cost. Numerous examples are to be found in the battles now underway between electronics companies struggling to have their products adopted as 'world standards'. Sony was willing to sacrifice its technological leadership in the emerging new digital video disc (DVD) products. Rather than see a splintering of standards and a possible market failure, Sony joined with its rival Toshiba, agreeing to a standard based largely on Toshiba technology.[3]

Competence based on global market power

Experienced managers know that market power can be more important than efficiency. Having access to larger markets global players are able to reach a size well beyond that of most local companies. This together with the ability to mobilise and coordinate their sales and other resources globally enables them to focus their power in a way old style multinationals cannot match. For example, they are able to structure their prices and marketing policies, including cross-subsidisation from one part of the world to another, to sustain a price cut or an expensive promotional campaign in selected countries. In short, they are able to structure and draw on their worldwide market power, targeting selected companies, areas and countries.

Competence based on global sourcing

The advantages available through international sourcing of supplies and purchasing are familiar, usually associated with the idea of trade theory. Individuals as well as companies have historically benefited from the lower costs of materials and labour associated with imports from low wage countries. Using traditional imports to lower supply costs is still an important source of competitive advantage. Modern communications make such supplies even more accessible. But global companies are often able to extend this sort of competitive advantage further, beyond that available through international trade alone. By coordinating imports (and exports) internally through the company's own facilities and contacts rather than relying on exports and imports through international markets open to all, global companies can secure additional sourcing advantage. Moreover, this latter type of international sourcing cannot be as readily duplicated.

BOX 4.2
Global sourcing

Amstrad, the British producer of consumer electronics, used its global reach with foreign supply sources to acquire an advantage over its local British competitors. These mainly produced their own supplies of electronic components for their products or purchased them locally. To a greater extent than its competitors, Amstrad developed a capability for tapping the cost savings available through importing. To do this Amstrad developed special facilities and close direct contacts, negotiating agreements with factories in Singapore and other suppliers around the world. By such direct agreements with suppliers, contracting their facilities to supply parts specifically designed for its products, Amstrad was able to outperform competitors relying only on international markets.

Its capability for dealing with suppliers around the world gave Amstrad a competence and competitive advantage many competitors could not match. Without such direct supplier contacts, competitors had to rely on whatever imports were available on the open market. Such open market purchases can be effective for standardised items, as in certain steels, textiles, jeans, wool, agricultural products and other commodities or near commodities. They do not work well in those cases (increasingly numerous) where purchasers require supplies tailored to particular needs and specifications.

By forming contracts and agreements in advance with foreign based suppliers, Amstrad was able to provide them with its own design requirements and measurements, enabling them to supply the company with parts and electronic components especially suited to the timing and technical needs of its new product introductions. It was thus able to capitalise on the lower labour costs and other advantages arising from locational differences, obtaining reduced costs on parts and supplies to a greater extent than competitor firms. ∎

Global purchasing power

Historically, a major source of competitive advantage of the larger firms has been the ability to convert larger sales volume into greater bargaining power which they could use to obtain lower purchasing costs. The ability of the global firm to link global sales with centralised purchasing can greatly increase the potential gains from this source. Such firms are in a better position to leverage their global sales volume into increased bargaining power and its associated cost savings.

Putting this into practice requires not only globally coordinated purchasing procedures, but also company standards designed to achieve extensive uniformity of parts and processes.

Scania, the Swedish truck producer, claims that it gets lower prices by purchasing supplies and components for its new world truck at global volumes. However, as

Scania management points out, achieving such volume economies relies on world-wide coordination by way of the standardisation of components and the adoption of standardised specifications and procedures by its manufacturing plants in the many different countries where they are located.[4]

Competence based on global volume

The most familiar source of competence open to global companies is that stemming from the efficiencies of global size and volume, potentially leading to lower unit costs of production.

It is sometimes assumed that all large firms operating internationally can enjoy the benefits of large volume production. This view is mistaken. The larger volumes associated with producing for global markets do not automatically lead to greater economies of scale. Far from it. Efficiencies of large scale attach to the size of the production unit, and not necessarily to the size of the firm. The two are often quite different.

In a company with production facilities in several countries, the size of the production unit in each country may be quite small, with little or no relation to the size of the total enterprise. What appears on paper as a large company may comprise numerous small production units, none of which is large enough to reap significant economies of scale.

For a company with multiple production facilities, global efficiencies of scale are only achieved if the various individual plants, whatever their geographic location, are closely coordinated and organised into a single production unit. However, such a company may also simply build (as is most often the case) separate facilities in a number of countries, all operating independently. Such facilities will be producing at national volumes, no better than other local producers. Production output may be global in the sense that total output is both produced and distributed over markets in many parts of the world, but there will be no efficiencies of global volume production. What appears to be 'large volume' in terms of the total enterprise is no larger than that of its individual production units.

Global volume efficiencies derive from production volumes aimed at meeting global demand, usually for a standard product. Multinationals seeking the advantage of global volume find that this often requires specialisation and coordination which goes counter to their practice of treating each national subsidiary as an independent unit. A single production unit in country A may produce the company's total global requirements for a particular part, another production unit in country B produces its total global requirements for another part, and so on. The supplies of these various component parts are programmed to come together at the times and in the quantities required to produce the final product. This is then distributed to the firm's markets around the world (see also the following chapter).

Efficiencies of large scale of this sort have usually derived from a more efficient use of 'fixed costs', as represented in investment in the buildings and equipment required to produce a given product. Much more significant today are the fixed costs associated with investment in 'knowledge'. That is the costs of investment in the ideas and other know-how required to produce products and run the company. These have increased dramatically. The growing emphasis and importance of knowledge assets, such as successful product designs, copyrighted material, patents and formula associated with new innovations make globalisation particularly attractive. These fixed costs, unlike those in buildings and equipment, are infinitely 'spreadable'. If a pharmaceutical company spends 500 million dollars to develop or purchase the formula for a new drug, it does so with the knowledge that its cost can be spread over the totality of its sales. The more customers buy the product, the lower the unit cost each has to bear to write off the original investment. Unlike investment in plant and equipment costs, there is no fixed capacity beyond which new buildings and equipment are required. The same formula that produced the first unit of a new drug can be used to supply the needs of the entire United States and Europe and still be used to supply China and the rest of Asia, each time lowering the unit cost of the knowledge investment required to produce the new drug.

Though wider access to world markets makes possible magnitudes of production which are greater than those available to firms limited to individual local markets, reaping these benefits requires much more than just high volume. Mechanisms have to be in place to disseminate and implement globally consistent methods of instruction on the use of the new drug; internationally consistent safety standards and methods of testing are required as well as uniform regulations and procedures for storage and distribution. All this requires coordination on a global scale. In other words a company very different from the early multinationals, a global enterprise.

In the final analysis, the new formula or design may still prove a failure. Global products inevitably represent a compromise, a trade-off between the advantage of the lower costs associated with producing similar products at high volumes and the advantage of greater marketing appeal through producing many different products, each especially designed for particular markets and customers. It is not difficult to get this balance wrong.

It is only recently, through modern methods of research and communications, that it has been possible for companies to set out purposefully to design products acceptable to consumers in many different countries. Prior to that, it was something of a lottery. To be sure, a few products were able to duplicate the success of Coca-Cola, appealing to customers in multiple national markets even though they were developed locally for a particular national market. Many more failed. Even with modern methods, designing new global products that appeal to customers in multiple national markets involves considerable risk. A number of marketing specialists maintain that even with present methods, it is at least as much an art as a science.

Global leader image

Reputation as an industry 'leader' has always counted. Subsequent to the rise of the national firms, companies vied with one another for the title of national leader. The same effect is now evident in the advertising campaigns and promotional efforts of a number of companies, such as ICI, British Airways or Hewlett-Packard, to achieve recognition as 'world class'. Status as a global player can in itself provide a certain advantage over more local players.

The desire of consumers to feel that the wisdom of their purchase is confirmed by others, that is, other consumers around the world, is part of the attraction. In the case of the global player there is also the psychological impact at the political level to consider. Governments negotiating agreements with foreign companies may react more favourably to a company name with worldwide recognition.

Political negotiating power

Governments negotiating with global firms will be aware of the ability of these companies for worldwide coordination and the negotiating advantages this confers. For example, governments wishing to increase exports will quickly realise that such companies are in a position to use their global network operations to plan and control their exports to the advantage or disadvantage of particular countries and regions. One of the phenomena associated with globalisation is the rapid growth of intra-company trade, trade between different parts of the same company. The global firm is often able to guarantee interested governments of an assured level of exports (perhaps to other parts of the same company, e.g. exporting parts from their production in country A to be used in products they produce in country B). By the same token, the ability of global players to use their facilities to coordinate global logistics flows can also apply to imports.

The global oil producing companies with supply sources in various parts of the world have more than once demonstrated their ability to coordinate oil movements so that supplies to traditional customers are maintained, even during revolutions and other events beyond the control of any single government. Similarly, their worldwide marketing outlets and their ability to use these to export oil have been one of the major bargaining strengths that have enabled them to exert leverage on the governments of oil producing countries.

Competence based on global vision and strategy

Whether any of the potential competencies outlined above are actually transformed into competitive advantage depends on the ability of the global player to pull them together.

Firms able to develop a global vision of their industry sector, its markets and competitors, have access to opportunities and strategic possibilities not available to the firm viewing the world on a country-by-country basis. The former is able to search the world for opportunities.

The wider scope of vision of the global firm confers an ability to prioritise and select from among global rather than locally limited strategic options. This is perhaps the most important source of competence available to global players. It is the necessary prerequisite for developing a global strategy: the ability to see the playing field globally. It enables the global player firstly to identify the strategies of other global players. The company is then able to coordinate and focus resources according to a vision that positions the firm within its global market and competitive environment.

The local player has a quite different vision. Viewing the world on a local (or an international, country-by-country) basis, the latter does not see its opportunities in the global context nor does it have the ability to focus resources from different parts of the world in pursuit of global objectives.

Because of this narrower vision local firms may be sub-optimising: resources in one national compartment being devoted only to opportunities within that compartment – even though better opportunities may exist (outside management's field of vision) in an adjoining country. Threats from global companies are viewed piecemeal, on a country-by-country basis – even though the plans of such companies only make sense and can be fully understood if viewed globally.

This places the local firm at a considerable disadvantage against global companies. These two types of enterprise are seeing and playing different games. The odds are against the local player, just as someone who can see only part of the playing field is at a disadvantage relative to a player who enjoys a view of the whole.

A NEW TYPE OF MULTINATIONAL

The usual method of expansion employed by multinational companies has been to transplant themselves abroad through investment in subsidiaries that were able to transfer their competence to new markets. In the early multinational companies, close coordination of their internationally dispersed facilities was not technically practicable. The competencies of such multinationals were necessarily local in scope.

The new global multinationals now emerging are in effect global coordinators. They may retain some or all of the original local competencies. However, they have also shown themselves to be capable of developing new global competencies based on their ability to see and coordinate their operations around the world. They bring together diverse skills, innovations, supplies and resources from different parts of the world in a way that cannot be duplicated by other types of companies or through international trade.

Of course, not all of the new sources of competence noted above will be available to every global firm. Quite the contrary, successfully accessing such sources of competence will vary from one company and industry to another. More to the point, converting the competencies potentially available to the global player into reality requires considerable vision, effort, imagination and planning.

Today, most companies assuming this role are among the largest in the industrial world. This is already changing in favour of smaller companies. The main distinguishing function of the global enterprise, global coordination, does not necessarily require either vast resources or foreign subsidiaries. It requires an information gathering and processing capability which until recently has been beyond the powers of most small companies. Modern communications developments and particularly the internet are changing this. In the future we will see global companies consisting of little more than a central coordinating office and an intelligence function. The investment of such a company would be largely limited to observation posts dedicated to information gathering in the major world markets. The main assets would comprise a clear notion of the firm's particular global business, its markets and strategy, together with the ability to negotiate agreements with suppliers (which may include research and design firms) and distribution networks. The principal role of this central office would be to provide the vision and coordination binding the various contractors together into loose confederations and linking them to global customers. The core of the company would be exclusively focused about its major competence, the ability to coordinate resources and markets around the world.

A number of firms approximating this model have already emerged. Some of the internet companies, such as Amazon.com, approximate this type of global company. The communications capability opened up by the internet is moving other companies in this direction (see also Chapter 11). For the time being at least, the majority of global players will be represented by companies, many of them multinationals, following a more evolutionary path. The following chapter provides some insight into how one company has pursued the road to globalisation.

SUMMARY

- Competitive advantage in international business was at one time explained largely in terms of national location. Companies, it was thought, reflected the advantages springing from the endowments (especially the natural resources) of the particular national location in which they were sited. Today, it is more nearly the other way around. Natural resources are increasingly irrelevant. Nations draw whatever trade advantage they may have from companies within their borders that have developed particular competencies. Companies and the particular competencies they are able to develop are the main source of competitive advantage.
- A firm's competence is something which it does better than the competition. It may derive from its skills, technology, design equipment or other attributes. Frequently it is based on the particular way these are combined, organised and managed.
- Global companies have access to competencies not available to more locally oriented competitors. Developing such global sources of competence is perhaps the main motivation behind the decision to go global.
- Providing a global service is one such competence. Global firms are able to capitalise on their global scope and coordination to offer a uniform service to customers almost irrespective of their location.
- Universal usage may in itself be a source of competence. Global firms are in a better position to promote and develop products that become widely used throughout the world. The fact that Microsoft's Windows software for personal computers has become so widely used throughout the world provides it with a powerful competitive advantage.
- Market power on a global scale is another competence which such firms can bring to bear. Global players are able to focus their resources on particular local situations. For example, reducing their prices against local competitors (cross-subsidisation).
- More than other companies, global firms are able to use their global network to take advantage of international differences in wages and material costs to lower the costs of their supplies. They are also able to centralise their purchasing, using global purchasing power to secure cost reductions from suppliers.
- The most familiar competence and source of competitive advantage for such companies is their ability to tap the efficiencies of large scale associated with global production. However, this requires the production of globally standardised products and/or components. Also, the close coordination of production facilities which may be located in different countries.
- Such companies may also use their global position to project an image as a leader of their industry. They may also gain certain advantages from governments based on their ability to coordinate exports, imports and other resources on a global scale.
- Probably the most important competence of such companies derives from their global perspective and the advantage this gives them in developing global strategies.

Because of their generally narrower focus, local firms are often at a disadvantage in this respect, missing the sort of strategic opportunities that require a view of the whole playing field and not just a part of it.

- All of the above competencies require global coordination and vision. These are the unique internal characteristics of the global firm and the general source of its competitive advantage. In the future, we may well see the emergence of companies which are 'global coordinators', specialising in coordinating resources globally, though they may have few assets of their own.

NOTES AND REFERENCES

1. *The Economist*, 15 April 1995, p. 15.
2. *Financial Times*, 4 August 1997, p. 14.
3. *The Wall Street Journal Europe*, 15 May 1997, p. 1.
4. *Financial Times*, 6 January 1997, p. 10.

5 Competitive advantage: laying the foundations

Ask a winning team the secret of their competitive edge and they will most often refer to things like training, team spirit, a successful recruitment policy, an inspiring coach and so on rather than any specific competence. Competencies are crucial to competitive advantage but perhaps even more important are the supporting systems that develop and make them possible.

Global companies have access to quite different competencies and competitive advantage than do local companies, but getting there, attaining global competitive advantage, requires changes in what we shall refer to in the following sections as the firm's 'infrastructure', i.e. the organisation, skills, resources and support systems which underlie and make possible those things the company does exceptionally well.

What sorts of changes in this infrastructure are required for the company which is going global? How are they brought about? Behind any particular company competence, whatever it may be, will usually be found an extensive history of developing the necessary support systems and skills that make the competence a reality. These changes will obviously vary with the company and the situations. However, we may use the following example of one company's efforts in this direction to gain some insight both as to the process and as well to some of the actual changes required.

BUILDING THE FOUNDATIONS

The Ford Motor Company offers an interesting case study of changes in competencies and associated competitive advantage.[1] Over a period of years, a series of incremental changes led the company away from the old style multinational model centred about individual country markets towards a different type of enterprise based on a quite different approach to competitive advantage.

Initial expansion into foreign markets was based on capabilities and techniques that Ford had developed for its domestic American market. Its earliest efforts at such expansion took the form of exports, distributing its domestic products to other countries where they quickly found ready acceptance. Exports were soon overshadowed by the establishment of locally based Ford facilities in Europe which were able to assemble and produce locally. Here again, Ford's success lay in the transfer of its domestically developed competencies. The firm's car designs, production methods and management systems were effectively transferred to Europe. Even minor details relating to procedures were governed by a procedures manual referred to within the company as the 'Ford Bible'.[2] Initially, these transplanted competencies were sufficient to meet the requirements of European consumers and to acquire for the firm a considerable competitive edge over its fragmented European competitors.

Inevitably, the straightforward transfer of domestic products, technology and procedures eventually encountered difficulties. The market for cars expanded rapidly, new competition developed, consumers became more demanding and less willing to accept products designed for a quite different market. In Britain, for example, the fact that the steering wheel of Ford cars was on the 'wrong' side eventually became a major handicap.

Ford's overseas operations responded by becoming less dependent on American transfers, rapidly developing their own design and production capabilities geared to local needs. In Europe, these facilities were organised around two production centres, one in Britain, the other in Germany. Each operated with a high degree of independence, designing and manufacturing cars for local European markets. Competence at this time was based on locally developed capabilities, much like any other European car producer. These facilities were in effect local companies.

In adopting 'localisation', Ford was not alone. In a report describing the policy of General Motors, the chairman of GM described the firm's policy towards international operation as follows. 'The policy which the Corporation is following in the development of its overseas business . . . consists of making General Motors a local institution in each country in which it is operating.'[3]

REGIONALISATION

The growing movement towards a European common market, eventually eliminating the trade barriers still separating some of Europe's largest countries gave impetus to plans for closer integration among Ford's European facilities. This thinking was reinforced and closely associated with the growing intensity of cross-border rivalry among European producers, leading to pressure on profit margins. The costs of operating production facilities producing two entirely different lines of Ford cars were also rising. Against this background, Ford restructured its European operations.

Early in its move towards regionalisation (and well before there was any conscious effort on the part of its management to go global) Ford found that the fragmented ownership which characterised the financial relations between the firm and many of its European affiliates made close coordination among its various plants and offices difficult. For example, the parent company owned 59% of Ford of Britain, which in turn owned 60% of Ford of Denmark, which owned 60% of Ford of Sweden, which owned 60% of Ford of Finland.[4] In preparing for a more regional approach Ford altered its ownership structure, buying a 100% equity interest in its major installations.

In 1967 Ford established a European headquarters in Great Britain. The new headquarters was responsible for coordinating all of Ford's European operations, eventually producing a single line of Ford European cars. This eliminated the duplication of design teams producing separate car lines in Germany and Great Britain. Production of Ford automotive components was concentrated in larger, specialised plants producing higher volumes at lower unit cost. These parts were then transhipped to assembly plants which produced the final automobile.

With the establishment of its European headquarters, Ford's operations in Europe changed fundamentally. From a collection of loosely coordinated subsidiaries each focused about national market requirements, these facilities were integrated into what eventually became a single European enterprise.

Management's perception of what constituted the market and the customer also changed. Previous arrangements for data gathering and market research viewed information on a national basis, interpreting the national markets and customers. The new organisation included specialists and information systems which collected and interpreted markets on a regional basis. National differences were carefully observed, but national markets were no longer treated as isolated from each other. They were seen as part of an integral European region whose various parts were characterised by both similarities and differences. A fleet of Ford aeroplanes situated near the new headquarters enabled Ford managers to schedule weekly and even daily trips to the company's widely dispersed European facilities. Europe was no longer a collection of national compartments but treated as a single playing field.

The transformation changed Ford's competencies and the basis of its competitive advantage. Prior to the integration of its European operations Ford's size and nation-centred structure gave the company less access to efficiencies of scale than some of its competitors. The refocusing of Ford's production around a single European line of cars altered this, giving Ford access to production volumes (and potential economies of scale) greater than those of its European rivals.

Additional savings were obtained through centralised purchasing of materials and components on a European scale. Savings also appeared in marketing, as in the case of common advertising campaigns in many (but not all) of Ford's markets. Inventory costs were reduced and the capability of Ford's European wide service network improved.

The new regional approach was put to the test in producing the Ford Fiesta, Ford's first successful regionally designed and produced passenger car. Its success was followed by a series of Ford all-Europe cars.

Regionalisation also gave Ford greater leverage with governments. During negotiations over a proposed new car plant in Spain, Ford was able to bargain effectively with the Spanish government by using the ability of its new regional structure to absorb a high level of exports from the proposed new Spanish plant.[5] Confirming the benefits of Ford's regionalisation a few years later, General Motors moved in a similar direction. Abandoning its traditional emphasis on the autonomy of its foreign subsidiaries,

GM altered its national focus shifting towards a more regionally integrated structure in Europe.

GLOBALISATION: THE NEXT STEP

In 1994 Ford announced it was adopting a new global organisation structure. Under the title of 'Ford 2000', the company introduced a sweeping reorganisation. Essentially, its aim was to expand on many of the same benefits achieved during Ford's Europeanisation drive, this time on a global scale. Once again there would be a drive to reduce the duplication inherent in producing multiple car lines.

As in its drive towards regionalisation, Ford's global restructuring was pioneered by the development of a new world car. In this case, the Mondeo.

Ford of Europe carried primary responsibility for the basic engineering and integration of the various components of the new car. Its engine and transmission were engineered in the United States. Four of Ford's design centres in Europe and the United States were involved in its design.

The first phase of the new organisation structure turning Ford into a global car producer entailed bringing together Ford's previously independent North American and European regional automotive operations into a single operating unit, Ford Automotive Operations. The new Ford organisation was divided along product lines into five vehicle programme centres (VPCs), four based in the USA and one in Europe. Each VPC had worldwide responsibility for the design, development and engineering of a particular product group. The new global approach would eventually extend to manufacturing, each vehicle programme centre assuming responsibility for all Ford manufacturing plants associated with its product group.

This would mean that certain Ford plants in North America (those producing small to medium-sized cars) would fall within the European based VPC and be managed from Europe. European plants producing cars falling within the jurisdiction of the North American VPCs would be managed from there. Subsequent changes were planned aimed at integrating Ford's Asia–Pacific, South American and African regional organisations into the new global structure.

A major objective of the change was cost reduction through the development of global products but this did not necessarily mean identical cars would be marketed around the world. The cars produced by the new organisation would be highly similar in terms of many of their components. As Alex Trotman, the Ford chairman at the time pointed out, 'We can't allow human and financial resources to be wasted duplicating vehicle platforms, powertrains . . . and other basic components'. At the same time, the Ford chairman maintained that the 'design and feel' of vehicles could still be varied substantially to suit local tastes.[6]

Globalisation is the latest in a series of changes which have altered Ford's competencies over time. Figure 5.1 illustrates some of these changes.

To transform itself into a global company, Ford quite literally had to reconstruct itself, laying the foundations for an entirely new type of enterprise with different competencies. Developing such a global enterprise required changes in Ford's organisation, skills, systems and procedures, as we shall describe.

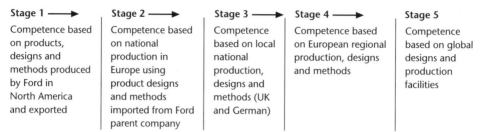

FIGURE 5.1   Changes in Ford's competence in Europe

A new organisation structure

The new Ford organisation created by the new plan was in the form of a product/functional matrix, with senior managers reporting to two bosses. For example, certain managers within one of Ford's local operating units would have a reporting relationship to one of the five global vehicle product centres. The same manager could report as well to the head of one of Ford's various functional headquarters, such as production, purchasing, marketing and sales. (See also Chapter 11.)

A major effort was made to avoid the dangers of confused accountability often associated with matrix structures. The new global organisation reduced the number of reporting levels from 14 to seven. Its objective was 'to push authority and accountability down within the organization as far as it will go'.[7]

Global information systems

The type of information required for a global company cannot be obtained by simply putting together market and competitor intelligence relating to individual national markets and rivals. Firstly, this leaves out information on those markets the company is not in. Secondly, pulling together information compiled on different national markets viewed in isolation fails to provide insight into the shifting positions of global rivals or the dynamics of global market trends which transcend national boundaries. A rival's global product positioning and market share will be quite different from that occupied by the same firm in individual countries; both are important. New procedures are typically required to gather new information and integrate new and old information into a worldwide information system.

In implementing its new, global information systems, Ford discovered that many of its computers were not compatible. The less coordinated mode of operations which preceded globalisation meant that the various Ford affiliates had purchased different computer systems, unable to communicate with each other. Under Ford's old nationally centred organisation there had been no need. The new approach required major changes to ensure communication between the various national and regional information systems.

Today, a Ford designer in one part of the world may be working on a drawing in collaboration with another Ford designer thousands of miles away. They are not only able to see each other but to work on each other's drawings. A designer in Germany is able to take part in redesigning a drawing of a new model as it is displayed on a computer terminal in Detroit.

Supply relationships

Developing the advantages of global sourcing and purchasing power required major changes in Ford's supply networks which had previously been organised along national and regional lines. The company's relationships with its suppliers were reformulated under the jurisdiction of a centralised purchasing staff which negotiated contracts with suppliers on the basis of the new (much larger) global volume of production, seeking correspondingly greater reductions in price. Suppliers were selected on the basis of global price and quality comparisons. Many were dropped altogether while others received contracts for much larger orders. Some 250 of Ford's largest suppliers world-wide were asked to collaborate in a united effort to reduce costs.

Changes were also introduced in the form of company-wide purchasing procedures aimed at taking full advantage of the greater leverage of global purchasing power. Ford management estimated that savings to the order of one hundred million dollars were obtained from this source alone.[8]

Functional skills

The cross-national character of Ford's move towards globalisation required new skills. For example, Ford found significant variation in customer car preferences among the various countries of the world comprising the market for its 'world cars'. Identifying these diverse consumer requirements and then designing new world cars calculated to appeal to world customers, required skills in marketing research quite different from those used in satisfying national customer requirements. Similarly, developing inter-national advertising programmes required changes in the relationship between Ford management and its advertising agencies.

Despite the remarkable decline in some tariffs and other national barriers, numerous restrictions remained which hampered the cross-border movement of Ford products. These included constraints and differences between countries in taxes, currencies, industry regulations, transportation costs and other factors. Experts knowledgeable in managing the movement of Ford resources across such barriers were required.

Planning systems

Globalisation also called for changes in Ford planning systems. For example, its 1994 reorganisation required the new vehicle programme centres to develop new global product plans. These would indicate where each product would be made and include estimates of planned operating capacity at the different production sites and associated information. For the first time such plans would cover Ford's worldwide operations. The global scope of the new product plans enabled Ford to optimise the match between its production in one part of the world and market requirements in another – a product needed for Ford in Brazil might best be met by a Ford product already available in Europe. Global product planning enabled the company to reduce drastically the number of car models produced worldwide without reducing the number available in any particular location, producing savings in Ford's overall design and development costs.

Manufacturing systems

To achieve the higher production volumes that would achieve efficiencies of scale and reduce Ford's unit costs required a reordering of Ford's production facilities. Production lines and equipment had to be reorganised. Major shifts of production from one country to another involved numerous discussions and new agreements with governments on questions relating to quotas, duties, investment incentives and similar matters.

Decisions had to be made on which plants should produce which products. In some cases, the higher volumes required retooling. For example, the large stamping machines used to form exterior body panels in the United States and Europe were different. Ford eventually made a major investment decision to standardise on the European presses. Using identical production tools in the United States and Belgian plants producing Ford's new global car, the Mondeo, saved the company approximately 25% on expensive jigs and dies.[9]

A closely associated change towards globalisation was the move towards the worldwide standardisation of Ford parts and components. As part of the general effort towards achieving higher production volumes, there was a major reduction in the variety of Ford products and components worldwide, permitting Ford factories to produce higher volumes of a much smaller number of items. There was a reduction in the number of engine and transmission options Ford offered worldwide by 30%. The number of car horns was to be reduced from 30 to three, batteries from 40 to 14, steering wheels from 50 to 11, carpeting in the boot of its cars to be in a single material and colour throughout the world.[10]

Common standards

To bring this about, engineering standards at Ford's various plants had to be attuned to a uniform global standard. Hundreds of technical staff were flown across the Atlantic to help the firm develop common global engineering standards. To assist in the worldwide implementation of new quality control procedures, the company put together a special team of troubleshooters which it airlifted to whatever locations had quality control problems. Major improvements were made in anticipating and fixing problems prior to actual production.

Workforce and work practices

Substantial restructuring was also required in workforce and work practices. Ford took its quite separate American and European design teams and merged them into a single unit with worldwide product responsibility.

Prior to this, there was an evaluation of which part of the Ford organisation, Europe or America, had the most efficient practices. The American system for coordinating the parts of prototype products was considered superior and selected for worldwide use, while the European practice of tracking engineering costs arising from warranty claims at the plant was chosen as the preferred procedure.[11]

Not all such change came about without friction. Merging design engineers of different nationalities from different Ford facilities was not without its problems, echoing some of the difficulties encountered earlier.

During the early stages of Ford's Europeanisation there were signs of considerable friction between Ford's English and German workforces. The newspapers of the day carried reports of falling worker output and morale, particularly when strikes in certain of Ford's British plants disrupted the new integrated production system. But with increasing personal contact and cross-border experience between Ford personnel of various nationalities, these difficulties proved to be merely temporary.

Personnel management

Ford's cross-national integration entailed changes in the career structure and promotion patterns and plans of managers. Career and promotion structures that were previously locally oriented were changed to accommodate the new thinking. Change in direction had started much earlier with Ford's Europeanisation. Career paths that were at that time nationally oriented, for example, promotion and evaluation nationally limited, became European in scope. Globalisation extended this one step further. The career ladder itself assumed a more global orientation, opening up new job opportunities as well as making available a greater inventory of managerial talent for specific job vacancies. It became much more likely for a Ford manager in Europe to move to Ford operations in North America and vice versa.

Rotation between widely different parts of the system was no longer reserved for a small cadre of headquarters personnel. Teams of specialists moved about freely across Ford's various worldwide operations. Factory managers in one country could find themselves managing plants in countries they had not previously considered as part of their career pattern. Short term movements of personnel became commonplace. Ford managers travelled weekly and sometimes daily between Ford's European plants as well as between Europe and North America.

External alliances

Globalisation brought about changes in Ford's external links with other companies. The new global structure which placed responsibility for small cars in Ford's European headquarters had repercussions on Ford's strategic alliance with Mazda, the Japanese firm partially owned by Ford.

The earlier Ford relationship with Mazda had largely limited cooperation between the two companies to North America and Asia. The new global organisation, which gave Ford's European headquarters responsibility for the size of car produced by Mazda, brought the Japanese firm into a much closer relationship with Ford's European operations.

Plans were made for a new arrangement whereby Ford-produced cars in Europe were sold there under the Mazda name (Ford was doing the reverse in Australia – selling Mazda-produced cars under the Ford name.) This would make it possible for Mazda to replace cars it had previously imported into Europe with cars produced by Ford in Europe but carrying the Mazda name, thereby saving substantial amounts in import

Ford changes	Action
• Introduction of global car	Design and production of Mondeo
• New organisation structure	Introduction of new global matrix organisation
• Establishment of global information systems	Move to implement worldwide computer compatibility
• Change in supply relationships	Supply network restructured. Worldwide purchasing centre established
• Development of new functional skills	International market research, advertising
• New planning system	Development of global cycle plan
• Manufacturing reorganised	Global reorganisation of production
• Common standards	Adoption of common engineering standards
• Global best practice	Identification and adoption of Ford global best practice
• Workforce	International merging of work teams
• Personnel	Change towards global career structures for managers

FIGURE 5.2 Steps to secure global production efficiencies at Ford

duties and transport costs.[12] The new relationship would enable the Japanese firm to enter the European market with locally produced cars, without investment in new plant. Additionally it meant that Ford's European factories would operate at higher, more efficient levels of capacity utilisation.

Ford's experience as a regional company, particularly in Europe, undoubtedly helped it on its way towards globalisation. But many changes were required. Figure 5.2 summarises some of the steps Ford took to develop a global competence in production.

THE STRATEGIC DIMENSION

What really drives globalisation? At first glance the steps outlined above give the impression that globalisation such as that at Ford is motivated primarily by cost saving and the pursuit of economies of scale. Undoubtedly, these are important. But is it that simple? Such economies lend themselves to documentation, and hence are frequently cited as evidence of results. However, this neglects strategic considerations which are more difficult to pin down but very probably more important.

Ford saw earlier than most the advantages to be gained from moving beyond the fragmented, nation-centred model of the international enterprise. Its move towards regionalisation enabled its managers to see all of Europe as the playing field, to interpret markets, trends and consumer needs on a Europe-wide basis – translating that into products produced and marketed across Europe by a single organisation. This enabled the company to focus its resources differently. Without the concentration of its Europe-wide resources behind the Fiesta car made possible by regionalisation, it is doubtful whether the initiative to produce the new car would have been undertaken. The new Fiesta repositioned Ford in Europe, enabling it to compete for the first time in the small car sector. This helped Ford to overcome its former weakness in small cars, thereby enabling the company to counter the threat of Italian and Spanish small car producers.

Strategic considerations can also be discerned in Ford's subsequent decision to globalise. Japanese car producers had made major inroads into Ford's home market, reducing its market share. They were threatening to do the same in Europe. Producing only a single standard line of cars which they marketed globally, the Japanese were better able to afford the rapidly rising product development costs which have characterised the industry. Ford's globalisation strategy was clearly aimed at matching some of the advantages of its Japanese rivals. A specific target for the new global Mondeo was the Honda Accord.

Ford's European restructuring had overcome some of the problems associated with fragmentation in the European market, but it had little impact on its position relative to the Japanese car producers. The many Ford internationally dispersed production facilities, focusing on local markets and producing multiple car lines, represented a logistics network which had clear disadvantages (as well as certain advantages) compared with the more concentrated Japanese network of facilities. The situation was not one that could be addressed by incremental improvements and a superior car design here and there. It required a strategic change of direction aimed at overcoming the disadvantages of Ford's fragmented international network of subsidiaries, while capitalising on its advantages. As in the case of Ford's regionalisation programme, the contribution of the new approach to management's ability to interpret the world as a single playing field, focusing the firm's global resources behind global objectives was crucial.

PATHS TOWARDS GLOBALISATION

There is no single right road to globalisation and global competencies. In the automotive industry, the different players have developed along diverse paths, influenced by their different starting points, histories, objectives and contexts. Those that pioneer reap the rewards of being the first mover – but they also assume the risks of the innovator. Getting the timing right, the best balance between being too early or too late, too little and too much, is a challenge all firms embarked on globalisation face.

Globalisation at General Motors

General Motors embarked on globalisation somewhat later than its major rival. Like Ford it began from a European base of two quite distinct lines of cars, each produced by a separate national subsidiary company, Vauxhall in Britain and Opel in Germany. Here again, a major objective was cost reduction through integration.

Instead of following the Ford formula of establishing a new regional headquarters, GM chose to make one of its national subsidiaries, Opel in Germany, the focal point of its Europeanisation drive. The Opel subsidiary assumed the prime responsibility for designing and developing a single European line of cars. Essentially the same line of cars was produced by Vauxhall, GM's British subsidiary.

Whereas Ford had merged its two major design and production centres into a single completely new organisation, GM chose a more gradual approach. GM's British subsidiary, Vauxhall, produced the Opel designed product, but 'badged' them with its own name. In subsequent years, GM marketed essentially the same line of cars under both the Opel and Vauxhall names. Gradually the Vauxhall brand has become less prominent and there have been reports that it might be dropped altogether.

GM's move from regionalisation to globalisation also differs. Instead of forming a new worldwide organisation to produce a range of global cars, GM embarked on globalisation by extending its European line of Opel cars to countries beyond Europe to include markets around the world and production bases in Taiwan, Turkey, Brazil and Mexico as well as many European countries.

Opel has become the main instrument for coordinating GM's diverse international products outside North America. The German subsidiary has become the focal point and world coordinating centre of a line of cars no longer confined to Europe. But unlike Ford, GM has continued, until recently, to develop and produce a separate line of cars for North America. There are clear indications (such as plans for an Opel-produced Cadillac) that closer integration is now planned between the firm's North American and European operations. GM's chief executive has gone on record as favouring further rationalisation of the firm's product line, stating that in his view it makes little sense to build near-duplicate products for different regions of the world.[13]

Until now, there has been less evidence of a global vision or strategy at GM. However, in the mid-1990s GM created a global strategy board. This brought together the heads of GM's North American and international units to meet quarterly to allocate responsibility for future projects on a global basis.

Seeking a local/global balance

Tracked over time, it appears that both Ford and GM have been searching for the right balance – between global and local operations – adjusting their infrastructure accordingly. It is also clear that this 'right balance' has constituted a moving target. What was considered right at one point in time, has changed with changes in external conditions such as new technology and lower tariff barriers. Both firms have pursued the competencies associated with globalisation, but have interpreted the changes required to attain these somewhat differently. GM, moving less quickly than Ford, may claim that its path to globalisation has involved less costly reorganisation and disruption. Ford may say that its approach seized the benefits of globalisation more quickly. However that may be, it is clear that the general direction of change in both companies as regards globalisation has been broadly in the same direction, a steady, long term reorganisation of their structure and systems in pursuit of the gains and competencies associated with globalisation.

Was it worth it?

Both Ford and GM have 'gone global', radically altering themselves in a race to develop new competencies. Have they been successful? Unfortunately there is no quick verdict regarding the outcome of such efforts. It is worth noting that Ford's Europeanisation programme encountered numerous difficulties during its early years. A considerable amount of time elapsed before the effort could be judged successful. Similarly, globalisation at Ford has also encountered its own set of early problems. Although the development of global cars was aimed at reducing new product development costs, the development of the Mondeo itself, at 6 billion dollars, exceeded original estimates and was considered by many as too expensive. Also, the new worldwide product development centres caused some confusion; some thought they resulted in duplication of work.[14] There was also the usual disorientation among staff that follows any major reorganisation. Initial sales under the global organisation structure did not meet expectations. Both sales and profits declined during the early years but rose strongly a few years later.

General Motors also encountered set-backs, and 'unprecedented' press criticism on events associated with the globalisation of its German Opel subsidiary. European engineers felt that American engineers had acquired too much influence over the design of Opel products. Management denied that such problems had anything to do with GM's globalisation drive.[15] In 1999, the new manager of Opel indicated his scepticism about the prospects for 'world cars' interpreted as identical products in all markets. But he went on to conclude that cars that share the same basic design and components in different markets around the world 'can work'.[16] On this point, the two American car companies appear to be in agreement.

Having had several years to evaluate the results of such efforts, other automobile producers seem to be moving in the same direction. The subsequent emergence of a new global player, formed by the joining of Daimler-Benz and Chrysler adds further impetus to the globalisation trend, as do the steps made towards partnership between Renault and Nissan. Scania the truck producer has embarked on the production of a 'global truck', reorganising itself in ways that echo many of the changes at Ford.

The Japanese path

Historically, the competence and supporting infrastructure of Japanese firms differed radically from that of the American ones. By the time the Japanese entered foreign markets after World War II, communication and the economics of long distance transport had changed radically. Exporting no longer carried the same penalties as during the earlier era of American expansion abroad. The cost of ocean crossings had declined to such a degree that the pressures to save on transportation costs were much less than those encountered by Western firms during their earlier international expansion. Hence there was initially less pressure on the Japanese to establish foreign based production facilities.

During the early years, Japanese automobile producers were able to make use of their efficient, low cost workforce as their major competence against Western competitors. Even after Japanese wages approached Western levels, they were able to maintain a cost advantage. The base of their competence shifted to modern production methods combined with new, Japanese developed, production methods.

Using large, specially designed ships, their efficient production centres in Japan were connected to consumers around the world with what amounted to a floating pipeline of cars. With modern communications, new car orders received from different parts of the world were swiftly communicated to Japanese factories in minute detail. These orders were then quickly transformed into new products in closely integrated production facilities which required no concessions to national differences of worker culture, production practices or legislation. Exporting remained the preferred option even after Japanese cars had attained sales volumes far beyond those that caused earlier exporters to switch to local production.

For the Japanese companies globalisation and associated cost savings came early and one might almost say naturally. Starting with a single, domestically based, product range and an export orientation, the Japanese factories were in effect producing global products designed for world markets virtually from the outset. Their production facilities were already closely coordinated, not only with each other but also with a highly developed network of suppliers, all operating initially from within the Japanese home base.

A global view of the playing field was encouraged. The geographic isolation of the Japanese producers plus the impoverished state of the Japanese economy during those early years pushed Japanese producers to look abroad. They thus avoided the temptations of focusing primarily on a large home market while treating overseas sales as marginal extras, a state of mind which characterised many of the Western producers.

Well before the Americans, the Japanese car producers had developed a global intelligence and marketing network. For example, in designing their new cars, the Japanese solicited their international distributors around the world for their advice on performance, comfort, safety and other product features. This was in contrast to their American competitors, whose efforts in market research at that time were local rather than global, conducted by their subsidiaries for the particular geographic regions falling within their assigned jurisdictions. The low cost labour advantage of the Japanese was eventually supplemented by competence in the design of globally standardised cars and high product reliability.

But with time, the very success of the Japanese led to political pressures on them from foreign governments. These took the form of various gentlemen's agreements limiting Japanese imports into Europe and the United States. This in turn encouraged the Japanese producers to build local production facilities, thereby avoiding these restrictions.

The early foreign based facilities of the Japanese producers were initially limited largely to assembly plants, referred to as 'screwdriver' factories, reflecting their heavy reliance on imported parts. During most of their early development, they continued to rely on their home companies for product design and development. It is only recently that a few of the Japanese facilities abroad have developed the capability for independent product development. Without this capability, most of their overseas plants were necessarily dependent on their parent companies. Global coordination on matters relating to product development, design and production methods continued to be carried out largely by the Japanese parent as it had been from the beginning.

They thus circumvented one of the main obstacles to globalisation encountered by their American rivals, large autonomous foreign subsidiaries with a vested interest in local rather than global operations.

The eventual, limited transfer of the Japanese production and design competence to their new foreign facilities proved surprisingly successful, counter to the expectations of many of their rivals. Even without a wage differential and without some of the other advantages of their home based facilities, the Japanese producers abroad managed to transfer much of their capability for low cost production, maintaining a competitive cost advantage over their American and European competitors through superior productivity. Productivity measurements showed that the Japanese foreign plants were more productive than their Western counterparts, even when compared with facilities of rivals located in the same country. With the disappearance of their low wage advantage, this edge in productivity was increasingly traced to superior production methods as well as to products designed and produced on a global scale.

The value of the yen, which was rising during much of this period, occasionally threatened the Japanese productivity advantage. However, this was largely neutralised by a strategy of steady improvements in productivity, plus expansion into Western markets and the eventual dispersal of Japanese component production to low wage cost South East Asian countries.

GLOBALISATION AND INFRASTRUCTURE

Globalisation for both the American and the Japanese automobile producers, required major changes in their infrastructure, the complex of elements required to support corporate competencies. This may even include the firm's ownership structure and alliances among the many diverse elements required if these relate to some form of competence.

Compared with the Japanese, the American car companies, Ford and GM, began their globalisation from a different starting point. They both began equipped with extensive networks of quasi-independent national subsidiaries already in place. Much of their restructuring in pursuit of globalisation turned about their efforts to integrate their foreign based subsidiary operations.

The infrastructure challenge faced by the Japanese during this era was almost the reverse of that of the Americans, how to introduce foreign based subsidiaries into export oriented companies already characterised by a high degree of globalisation.

In recent years there has been a trend towards convergence. Competitors from both countries are developing many of the same global competencies, based on the management of global networks of closely integrated foreign based subsidiaries. Both groups have tried and to a large extent succeeded in directing the benefits of globalisation towards lowering unit costs and shortening development cycles. Their success is evident in the pressure brought on many of their less global competitors, many of which have turned their attention towards developing their own approaches to competing within the restructured global automobile industry.

BOX 5.1

A new type of infrastructure

A more recent influence whose full impact has yet to be evaluated stems from the rapid adoption of the internet by companies such as Ford, General Motors and Renault. These automobile producers are using the internet to drastically lower supply prices as well as to revolutionise their marketing operations. This allows them to establish their own proprietary electronic markets, one for suppliers and one for customers (see also Chapter 11).

On the supply side, both Ford and GM have opened web pages on the internet which invite suppliers around the world to use the pages to bid for contracts to provide the companies with parts and materials. These global electronic markets replace the formerly time consuming and costly process of individually identifying and negotiating with individual suppliers around the world. The internet makes it much easier to open up supply relationships with companies that were perhaps unheard of and would have remained so under the old system. Offers and prices may be settled (or revised) almost instantaneously and continuously. Greater international competition to supply automotive parts and components will greatly reduce their cost.

Another web page market for customers will enable the company to contact customers directly and to negotiate prices, perhaps individually. It will also enable the company to undertake new initiatives, such as producing cars to order, as happens with some computers today, more flexible pricing and greater capability to respond to customer requirements regarding options.

Can more locally oriented companies and smaller competitors survive against such competition? Yes they can, but much will depend on how they adopt and position themselves within the new global industries. ■

SUMMARY

- Developing the competencies that are behind global competitive advantage will require major changes in the firm's infrastructure, i.e. its organisation, skills, resources and support systems.
- The Ford Motor Company provides an example of such change. Ford began its international operations based on competencies it had developed in its local home market. Early Ford cars that were virtually identical to those which the company sold domestically were well received abroad.
- Responding to foreign competition and the increasingly urgent needs of international markets, Ford developed locations abroad for the design and production of its automobiles. Dependence on the parent company diminished. Ford's competencies in Europe came to be based largely on local skills and capabilities.

- For a good many years, such efforts at localisation were fragmented along national lines. Regionalisation of Ford's European operations took a major step forward in 1967 with the establishment of Ford of Europe headquarters. Subsequent years saw the development and consolidation of Ford as a regional company.
- To transform itself into a global company Ford had to reconstruct itself. Developing the infrastructure to make it into a global player with global competencies required a series of steps. These included a new organisation structure launched in 1994 which integrated the firm's major worldwide operations. Also, the development of global information systems as well as new supply relationships, development of new functional skills, new planning systems, common worldwide manufacturing standards, new manufacturing systems and other changes.
- Specific moves aimed at developing particular features, skills and capabilities should not obscure the strategic considerations behind globalisation. Becoming a global player enabled Ford to focus its resources differently, mobilising its worldwide resources behind specific global objectives.
- There is no single 'right' path towards globalisation. A look at the different players in the automotive industry indicates the diversity. Instead of following the Ford formula, General Motors chose to make one of its overseas subsidiaries the focal point of its globalisation drive. Both companies have had setbacks on their paths towards globalisation.
- The Japanese automobile producers began their internationalisation at a different point of time and with different competencies. In recent years, there has been a tendency towards convergence among the major car producers, towards the development of global competencies. The internet is a major new factor which will influence this trend.

NOTES AND REFERENCES

1. I am indebted to the many managers of Ford of Europe and particularly Mr Robert Lutz, who provided free access to the research material which forms the basis for much of this chapter.
2. *Ford Facts – History of Ford Sales in Europe*, Ford Motor Company.
3. Donner, F. G. (1967), *The World-Wide Industrial Enterprise*, McGraw Hill, pp. 20, 21.
4. *Ford Facts*.
5. Seidler, E. (1976), *Let's Call it Fiesta*, Patrick Stephens Ltd., pp. 159–84.
6. *Financial Times*, 3 April 1995, p. 11.
7. *Financial Times*, 3 April 1995, p. 11.
8. *Fortune*, 28 June 1993, pp. 72, 73.
9. *Fortune*, 28 June 1993, p. 73.
10. *The Wall Street Journal Europe*, 10 May 1995, p. 5; *Financial Times*, 12 May 1995.
11. *Business Week*, 3 April 1995, p. 5.
12. *The Wall Street Journal Europe*, 22 November 1994, p. A1.
13. *Financial Times*, 26 May 1994, p. 27.
14. *Business Week*, 8 April 1996, p. 28.
15. *Financial Times*, 1 July 1997, p. 20.
16. *Financial Times*, 15 June 1999, p. 32.

6 Positioning in global industries

Whatever competencies a firm may have, they are of little use unless they are incorporated into a coherent strategy. The heart of any competitive strategy begins with the firm's competitive positioning, that is, its relationship to its main rivals. This refers particularly to its relationship in terms of those characteristics which influence its ability to compete against them. Whether in sport or in business, any attempt to gain competitive advantage requires some knowledge, however imperfect, of the competitive positioning of the various players.

For firms in industries undergoing globalisation, this relationship is particularly volatile. As companies extend their known environment, new rivals with new capabilities and competencies appear on the horizon, becoming part of the competitive contest. In the light of these changes, the firm's positioning has to be constantly re-examined and assessed on a world scale, to identify what it is and what it should be.

PASSIVE REPOSITIONING

All firms are constantly being repositioned. Even firms that have done nothing to alter their own characteristics find that their relationship to their rivals has changed if those firms perceived as their rivals have undergone major changes in size, products, technology or other competitive characteristics.

The Spanish firm, INI, got a preview of this when Spain became a member of the European Union. As the leading firm in a number of key industries, the Spanish conglomerate discovered that becoming part of a larger business environment introduced new rivals into its home market. These brought with them new capabilities and competitive strengths. INI soon found that its position of leadership in terms of size and technology in certain key industries suddenly disappeared when compared with the larger and more technically advanced newcomers. Within the new, larger European competitive environment, INI had been repositioned. It suddenly found itself both smaller and less technologically advanced than its rivals.

The company subsequently embarked on a series of alliances aimed at repositioning itself by increasing its access to both advanced technology and the economies of large scale production. Many companies in industries undergoing globalisation find themselves today in much the same situation.

RETHINKING THE FIRM'S POSITIONING

For the global firm, and indeed any firm within an industry undergoing globalisation, strategic thinking that is locally oriented is not only mistaken but dangerously misleading. Moving from local to global rivalry requires a new interpretation of the firm's relationship to its competitors.

The need for such rethinking is often triggered by the emergence of a single global player. In the aircraft industry the success of Boeing on a world scale presented a clear challenge to the more locally focused European passenger aircraft producers.

BOX 6.1

Response to a new global rival

The European producers of passenger aircraft had previously considered themselves as major players, within their own spheres of competition. These consisted mainly of their respective national markets plus associated export territories. With the emergence of Boeing as a global competitor they found themselves repositioned. Compared to the new rival invading their respective home territories, they found themselves lacking, having neither the product range, the efficiencies of scale nor the marketing network required to compete. Realising this, four of the largest European local producers, British Aerospace, Deutsche Aerospace, Aerospatiale and CASA of Spain pooled their resources and coordinated their several diverse operations into a single global entity, Airbus Industrie. They effectively repositioned themselves, forming a new organisation, representing a single global player able to rival Boeing on a world scale.

Shipping firms in many Western countries received a similar shock with the advent of South Korean shipbuilders and their encroachment into what they had formerly seen as their own territory. The advantages enjoyed by Korean shipbuilders in labour costs and scale of production forced the European shipbuilders to rethink their positioning. Eventually they repositioned their products, moving away from bulk cargo towards specialised ships, such as roll-on roll-off carriers and cruise ships. ■

A GLOBAL VIEW OF POSITIONING

Once an industry begins globalising, the number of rivals will change, generally increasing as the perception of what constitutes the playing field is extended worldwide. Positioning as defined against local rivals is made obsolete. Companies in any part of the world become potential rivals. Certain players may become more vulnerable, particularly those now facing global competitors for the first time.

Does this really matter? Yes it does. One may insist that nothing has changed – but in fact it has. First, there is the question of management accurately interpreting its competitive situation. Managers who persist in considering only local rivals when, in fact, the major threats and opportunities are global, place themselves at a major competitive disadvantage.

In the American automobile industry the three traditional local rival producers, General Motors, Ford and Chrysler, once had a local view of the world. They competed and were aware of competitors in many countries, but rivals were interpreted locally, each country considered individually. Recognition of the global nature of their rivals came late, too late to save them from a steep decline in market share in their own domestic market.

Once they started thinking globally, they found they had to consider at least 20 additional rivals scattered around the world. Each firm's position versus 'the competition' was affected.

A change in positioning also alters management's self-perception of the firm and its capabilities. A change from a local to a global perspective will alter not only the firm's relationship to its rivals, it will directly influence management's thinking about itself. The firm that sees itself as a minor player vis-à-vis its rivals will have a quite different view of its possibilities and strategy compared with the firm that sees itself as top of the league. The latter is able to take initiatives and adopt strategies in relation to price leadership, bluffing, acquisitions, partnerships, etc., which draw their credibility and persuasiveness from its power and standing compared with the other players. Less powerful competitors will base their strategies on a realistic notion of their relative strengths and weaknesses. Globalisation implies these are constantly changing.

The changed perception of the firm's positioning which attends globalisation also affects customers. It is no secret that public recognition of firms that are leaders in their industry can affect customers' attitudes and buying behaviour. Hence the advertising campaigns undertaken recently by many leading companies, to declare themselves to be 'world class'.

The change of a firm towards a global positioning is also of interest to governments. National political bodies are increasingly concerned with the competitiveness of their national companies relative to international competitors.

Stung by charges that its anti-trust policies were producing firms smaller and with fewer resources than some of their international rivals, the United States government has made major changes in its approach to anti-trust, adopting policies somewhat less restrictive of inter-firm collaboration, particularly as regards industries open to foreign competition. In the late 1980s the US government, worried about Japanese competitiveness in microchips, provided financial backing for a consortium (Sematech) of leading American producers of such products to improve their production methods. A few years earlier such collaboration between rival American producers would have been subject to heavy fines. The European Union has special legislation permitting alliances between European firms competing with their products outside the European Union.

Companies that are purely local and wish to remain so are also affected. In an industry embarking on globalisation, they too will find that they are just as much influenced by this change as the more internationally oriented firms; sometimes more, since they are often the first target of an emerging global competitor. Furthermore, local firms that wish to understand their new global rivals will have little option but to take a global view themselves of their industries, seeing the world through the same eyes as their global competitors. Those that continue to view rivalry locally, on a country-by-country basis, will fail to understand both the motivation and objectives of such rivals, why they do what they do and what they may do next.

POSITIONING IN GLOBAL INDUSTRIES

The objective of any positioning strategy is to relate the firm to its rivals and markets in ways which will enable it to defend itself and to secure competitive advantage. The aim of the positioning decision should be to help the firm attain this objective through identifying a position within the global industry that will enable it to:

- exploit potential strengths and develop competencies that are consistent with the firm's resources and capabilities and that will help it to secure global competitive advantage;
- provide new barriers to rivals. The more readily and easily a particular positioning can be duplicated, the more likely it will gradually lose its effectiveness.

Positioning criteria

The classic distinction most often used to identify the positioning of companies engaged in rivalry is relative size. Academic writers on the subject as well as business practitioners have pointed out the role of size-related differences in competition as between the bigger, more powerful 'majors' and the smaller, more specialised contestants. In seeking a competitive advantage, these two distinct classes of competitor will move to capitalise on their respective strengths. The larger major players of the industry will attempt to position themselves so as to exploit the production efficiencies and market power that are potentially associated with bigness. Smaller players will seek to make use of the flexibility and speed in decision making more readily accessible to smaller organisations, while at the same time avoiding head-to-head competition with the larger more powerful majors by positioning themselves in the more specialised niche areas of the market.

The differences of size between competitors are most usefully measured in terms of relative sales, usually market share. Helmut Maucher, chairman of Nestlé has been quoted as saying that his ideal position is 60% share of the market.[1] Jack Welch, chief executive of the American General Electric Company, is famous for his insistence that his businesses must strive to be first or second in their field.

Today it is necessary to qualify such statements further. 'First' or 'second' in what geographic context? What constitutes the playing field? Are the comparisons with local rivals only or are they made with reference to rivals anywhere in the world? A firm considered to be a major player within a particular country or region may be far from 'major' when considered against competitors anywhere in the world. Many firms thought to be quite large locally may in fact be relatively small when compared with competitors in other countries.

Nearly all the European producers of computers were at one time considered to be among the largest firms within their own countries. The globalisation of the computer industry changed all that. Measured against global rivals, most such European players were found to be quite small – many of them too small to survive in a global industry context without major changes. The same in investment banking. Considered as large players within their domestic markets, European investment banks were forced to reconsider their positioning when faced with competition from larger foreign investment firms. A period of mergers, acquisitions and restructuring followed.

Global vs. local positioning

In an earlier era, when rivalry was more locally limited, positioning was simply assumed to refer to the firm's position against other local players. Globalisation has changed that, introducing a new positioning dimension – geography. More specifically, the geographic scope over which the firm engages in rivalry against its competitors is now a vital consideration.

The issue is not simply one of geographic coverage. Global players are different. Their ability to coordinate their activities on a global scale gives them access to quite different strengths, potential advantages and strategic options. Whether a company is global or local has quite different implications for competitive strategy and the relationship of the firm to its rivals.

This means that in determining positioning within a global industry, it is important to consider not only whether the firm is a large major player or a smaller, more specialised niche competitor, but also whether such relative size comparisons are being made against global rivals coordinating their operations around the world or locally limited competitors. Both dimensions have to be considered. A local firm, competing within a larger national market such as the United States, may be larger than certain global players. Size is not the same as the geographic scope over which the firm coordinates its rivalry. Furthermore, size must also be defined in connection with reference to a particular product group and industry. Multi-business firms may attain great size without reaping size related benefits.

GLOBAL POSITIONING

There are four general positioning options for companies competing in global industries. These are indicated in Figure 6.1 and further described below.

Global market share

(Large) (Small)

	Global	Major global player	Global niche player
Geographic scope of rivalry			
	Local	Major local player	Local niche player

FIGURE 6.1   Global industry positioning options

Major global player positioning

Firms positioned as major global players are typically the giants in their respective industries. They engage in rivalry on a world scale, competing globally for a significant share of the world markets for their products/services. Important parts of their global activities are closely coordinated. This category includes firms such as Sony, Citibank, Merrill Lynch, Nike and Federal Express. Multinationals operating in the more traditional mould, as networks of loosely coordinated nationally focused subsidiaries, do not qualify as global. Their individual subsidiaries are to be considered as local players.

Features of major global player positioning
The following features are associated with major global player positioning:

● A major global player must have a significant share of the global market. This will vary from industry sector to industry sector, depending on the degree of concentration within the industry. In the fragmented pharmaceutical sector 5% global market share is sufficient to qualify. In other, more highly concentrated industries such as aircraft engine production, ranking as a global player may require 15–20% of the global market to qualify.

● To attain and maintain this high global market share, firms that qualify as major global players may be expected to compete and maintain a significant presence in the larger national/regional markets of the world for their particular product or service. This means that their products, prices, production and organisation will be geared for high volume. These are the firms most likely to stress global product standardisation. The more they can standardise across different national markets, the better their prospects of capturing global efficiencies of scale, scope and market power. To the degree that this positioning proves successful in capturing these and other global sources of competitive advantage, it provides these players with a competitive edge.

Advantages of major global player positioning
Companies positioned as major global players are able to draw on their greater scope to develop global competencies. With proper planning and execution their ability to coordinate their activities globally gives them access to efficiencies of world scale

production and potentially lower costs. In some industries they are also in a position to secure the advantages of offering a global service as well as advantages associated with global purchasing, market power, image and other advantages (see Chapter 4).

Research and development costs for such firms will frequently be high in absolute terms but low on a per unit basis, reflecting the ability of such companies to defray their research costs over a larger global volume of sales. Here again, such advantage does not accrue automatically. It requires worldwide coordination of research and development activities.

The scope and scale of their operations and their ability to coordinate them globally provides such companies with a powerful entry barrier against smaller, less globally coordinated players.

Risks and disadvantages

Companies positioned as major global players also encounter certain disadvantages:

Political visibility.   Every strength is also a potential weakness. The global scale and positioning of such companies can and frequently does make them politically vulnerable. Major global players are of necessity involved in many different markets under diverse political regimes. By virtue of their size and power they will have high visibility. Their involvement in one country may in itself cause offence to others, as in the case of the Arab boycott of firms operating in Israel.

Their projects also tend to be large; anything which disrupts their smooth operation will attract unfavourable attention. In addition their global reach and close involvement in projects of many different countries projects a degree of economic power that some governments find disconcerting.

Their practice of thinking and coordinating globally can also disrupt local sensitivities, posing as it does a possible conflict of interests. A company closing down plants in one country in order to secure lower costs or other advantage elsewhere, may be expected to encounter political opposition. This will be all the more potent if the firm is large and seen to be 'foreign'.

To be sure, the global firm will counter such adverse political tendencies by pointing out that the advantages they confer in terms of jobs, exports, investment and technology, offer a net advantage to governments which outweighs the negatives. Some governments will still prove sceptical.

Costs and risks of global coordination.   Coordination on a global scale, the externally visible sign of a global player, also carries its unique costs and risks. In an era of downsizing and movement towards flatter organisations, organising such coordination efficiently and effectively presents a major challenge.

Most notably, the risk of system-wide stoppages is increased. Global interdependence means that a strike or port closure in one part of the world may, and probably will, affect operations elsewhere – possibly across the firm's entire global network.

The greatest cost of globalisation may well relate to the morale and motivation of local managers. Global coordination brings with it certain constraints on the freedom of local managers. Certain decisions at the local level cannot be made independently, but have to take into account global objectives. This means that decisions that were once made entirely by locally based managers have to be referred elsewhere so that they can be coordinated with others. This risks the alienation and loss of morale among managers used to a high degree of autonomy. Local staff may feel that local interests are being sacrificed to support company operations in distant parts of the world at the expense of their own interests.

General Motors encountered something of this nature when it suddenly decided to transfer the head of its German Opel company back to the United States where it was felt he was most needed. This move was followed by the resignation of the chairman of the company's German supervisory board. Considerable unrest in their German operations followed as well as comment in the press to the effect that there was too much centralised control (from outside the country) and that Opel needed more autonomy.[2]

The need to coordinate globally also requires a global perspective, particularly on the part of top management. In order to ensure that such managers are fully informed, there may be a temptation to install bureaucratic procedures and multiple 'review' levels which slow down decision making. Flexibility and the ability to respond speedily to fast moving events, particularly local events, may be reduced.

Firms positioned as major global players are also those that stand to gain maximum advantage from global product standardisation. Along with its rewards, such standard-isation exposes the global player to the risk of major investment in products that fail to attain universal customer appeal. In attempting to satisfy high volume consumer markets on a global basis, certain niches are inevitably neglected. These may prove to be the breeding ground for the new, more effective competitors that will someday depose the major global player.

It is evident that firms positioned as major global players are relatively few. Other types of competitors not only survive, but many of them prosper. Such players are able to carve out alternative positions which have their own advantages.

Global niche player positioning

Only a few companies in each industry sector will be able to assemble the massive resources required to qualify as major players on a global scale. A successful niche player is one that has found a special narrow segment of the world market which it is able to focus on to advantage. As with other global players, such firms perceive and implement rivalry globally, operating many of their activities around the world in a coordinated manner. Many more players will have access to the lesser resources required to target a global niche.

Compared with the larger major players in the same industry, global niche players seek to access many of the competitive advantages of operating as a global company but with a lower resource commitment. They are in effect specialist firms operating globally. They target a smaller, specialised segment of the world market. Such specialisation opens up the possibilities and advantages of globalisation even to small firms.

Chematur Engineering is a Swedish firm employing a total of only 120 people. Yet it operates around the world, specialising in niches related to environmental issues.

Its product portfolio includes hydrogen peroxide, a chemical replacing the more environmentally harmful chlorine bleach in the production of paper. Another of its niche specialties is a process for recovering volatile chemicals from manufacturing residue.[3]

Features of global niche player positioning

The following features characterise global niche positioning:

- **Global specialisation**. Specialisation focused about a global market segment is the main requirement of this positioning. Though global, the target is narrow and a 'niche', relative to the overall market viewed globally. Toshiba, with its focus on laptops, competes for a global niche in computers.
- **Product differentiation**. A niche product will be differentiated not only in terms of its target market, but also by the skills and production methods required to produce and market it.

  Customised chips, microprocessors especially designed for particular applications, represent a niche which requires special design, production and marketing skills quite different from those used by the major global players, such as Intel and Texas Instruments, who concentrate on ready made chips aimed at the much larger mass market for this type of product.
- **Complementarity**. Global niche players seek complementarity with major global players (as well as avoiding them) rather than confrontation. A major mistake of the Apple Computer company was the early rejection of complementarity between Apple computers and those of the much larger IBM. Many smaller niche players that took just the opposite approach, i.e. the numerous IBM clone producers, reaped the advantages of such complementarity.
- **Alliances**. Motivated by the same drive to develop effective defence against global rivals such firms actively pursue alliances with other players in all three positioning categories. No small part of the movement towards international alliances, so prevalent in today's business world, is due to niche players seeking to reposition themselves within the new global competitive environment.

Advantages of global niche player positioning

Focusing on a global niche enables such firms to avoid head-on confrontation with larger and more powerful major players. As in some sports, a good big player can usually beat a good small player.

Within their niche, global niche players have access to many of the same competitive advantages of major global players. Their focus on a particular segment of the global market enables them to concentrate their resources to achieve advantages of global volume (within the niche specialty), network and distribution advantages, purchasing power and so on. But given their smaller scale, the degree to which they are able to reap such size related advantages, particularly those associated with efficiencies of scale, may be expected to be less than those of the major global players. Also, their market power, the ability to focus resources and influence events in a particular world market, will generally be less than that of the majors.

Compared with their larger rivals, global nichers are better able to focus their management efforts. This will contribute to greater flexibility and speed in decision making as well as closer first hand contact and knowledge of 'the business'.

Michael Bloomberg used his close knowledge and first hand experience as a bond trader to establish Bloomberg Financial Markets, a company providing a user friendly financial news service especially directed at bond traders through leased terminals. His service has proved successful in this global market niche, competing against much larger established major players such as Dow Jones, Reuters and Telerate.

Political advantages. Such specialist companies will often be at the forefront of technology. This together with their opportunities for using their international connections to generate exports and employment will enable them to offer governments attractive opportunities for furthering their objectives. In comparison with the generally larger companies positioned as major global players, such niche companies will often be less visible and politically less sensitive as 'foreign' rivals to local domestic companies.

Entry barriers. The chief defence of such firms is their specialisation on a niche in world markets which is usually too small and too specialised to attract firms positioned as major global players.

SGS-Thomson, the French electronics company, was able to develop a world lead and substantial profits by focusing its efforts on the development and production of microprocessors to decode video signals. It thus avoided head-on confrontation with major global players in higher volume products, such as memory chips.

Their global scope is a major differentiating factor and barrier against firms positioned as local players. The national player will only be able to bring its full force to bear against part of their operations – those within its own national territory. Local players, so long as they retain this positioning, will not be able to duplicate the strengths that such firms draw from their ability to coordinate globally.

Risks and disadvantages

Positioning as a global niche player also entails certain risks and disadvantages.

The niche itself may change. This may be due to its very success. A niche will typically have been chosen in the first place because it appeared promising, offering a prospect for growth. At some point the niche may become so successful, that it grows far beyond its original or expected size. In other words it outgrows its niche status. It becomes a mass market attracting the major players.

Global niche players may then find that their particular niche has been invaded by larger players. This has been the case with many companies offering products which were initially considered as specialty goods, then subsequently experienced rapid growth. Helicopters were initially considered an exotic niche in the aircraft market. This enabled Sikorsky, a relatively unknown company at one time, to thrive for a while relatively undisturbed by competition from the larger players. Eventually demand grew to the point where major players such as Bell Aircraft and Boeing also entered the competition.

A number of firms producing customised microchips have had the same experience. Initially, the demand for such circuits was so small as to prove unattractive to the larger major players. The smaller producers who spotted the niche and went into it were initially successful. However, growth in demand for these types of circuits subsequently escalated to the point where it attracted much larger major global players who invaded the niche providing stiff competition and reducing the profit margins of the smaller companies, driving some of them out of the niche altogether.

Technology may also change, undermining the exclusivity of the skills used to produce and/or market the niche product. In some cases such technological change has enabled larger players to produce the niche product with much the same processes and machinery they have been using for their much higher volume products, undermining the exclusivity and barriers to entry which served earlier to protect the niche.

Demand for the generic product or service may decline. This may have the effect of encouraging former 'outsiders' producing non-niche products (within the same industry sector) to invade the niche.

European firms specialising in luxury ships such as cruise liners and ferries have encountered increasing competition from South Korean shipbuilders that were not formerly direct competitors in this niche. Declining ship prices have spurred South Korean shipbuilders to embark on what is for them a new type of ship.

Political costs. Although less politically visible than the global major players, the situation of global niche companies is still one of operating abroad as a 'foreign' firm with close links to markets and resources in other countries and the added costs and risks of global integration.

Decision making. In addition, such players face many of the same risks and disadvantages associated with global decision making procedures and structure as outlined above for the major global players, though to a lesser degree. Global niche players also require procedures whereby certain decisions are made far from the scene where they are to be implemented, sometimes alienating local managers. They too face the possibility of a longer reaction time to changing local conditions and a risk that a stoppage of their operations in one part of the world may affect their global network.

Major local player positioning

Many firms, even those within global industries, will seek to remain local. Local players have access to a quite different mix of capabilities. Properly positioned, they are able to mount a strong defence against inroads into their markets by global players and compete successfully against them within their local environment. But in industries undergoing globalisation, the balance of advantage as between one type of positioning and another may shift. In an increasing number of cases, change has been to the advantage of the global firms.

To be successful, local firms increasingly have to take into account their new global rivals and position themselves accordingly, making maximum use of the advantages associated with their local positioning.

Features of major local player positioning

Companies positioned as major players locally have the following features:

- A focus on a sizeable share of the local market. Such firms are typically 'big', measured only in terms of their share of the local market. For example, there are many local banks that qualify as major local players, in that they are quite large compared with other local banks. The same organisation may be, and usually is, quite small as compared with the total corporate operations of a global competitor. However, it may well be the case that the local operations of a local firm are larger than the local operations of a global player.

   The designation 'local player' may also refer to the local operations of multi-national firms, if they are of the multi-domestic variety. The international sub-sidiaries of multi-domestic type multinationals are in effect a collection of local players. Note that in these cases, references to scale do not refer to the scale of company operations under common ownership but rather to the scale of the multinational firm's business in a particular country.

- Close familiarity and contact with local customers, and marketing institutions. Such firms are likely to have superior knowledge and contact with local trends and preferences. Global players, despite their improved capabilities enabling them to assemble information from around the world, may still be one step behind the local player in this respect. Local firms are able to focus daily on the trends, peculiarities and eccentricities of a single local business environment.

- Close ties with government. Such firms are large enough to matter in the local economy. They are the ones most likely to have close ties to government and local institutions, such as trade unions and local industry associations. As 'home' companies they are in a position to lobby for restrictions against foreign products and firms, erecting entry barriers to global firms perceived as 'foreigners'.

- Local image. They are also in a position to engage in extensive promotion of their image as a local firm, building on the preference of local buyers for local products.

Advantages of major local player positioning

The above characteristics make available certain competitive strengths for players with this positioning. Their local ties and connections, better knowledge of local customers, the market, suppliers, local institutions, all these provide areas of potential competitive advantage. Local firms are also better placed to identify with local (national) interests and to deal with situations special to the local environment.

Greater local focus. Companies positioned as global players must keep track of numerous foreign markets, governments and conditions. Inevitably, they are less able to focus their full resources and decision making on the needs of a particular local territory. They frequently have to consider trade-offs, i.e. sacrificing an optimal situation in one location to secure a possibly greater benefit in another. In developing globally standardised products, for example, such firms will frequently have to make product compromises, sacrifices of certain product benefits which appeal to one set of national customers in the interests of greater market effectiveness globally. Local firms are able to concentrate their full resources locally.

The Kao company of Japan produces a range of laundry detergents, household cleaners, bleach and shampoos which brings it into direct confrontation with the product lines of major global rivals such as Unilever and Procter & Gamble.[4]

As a local competitor, Kao has access to certain formidable defences and advantages. While its more global competitors struggle to comprehend Japan's complex distribution system comprising thousands of small fragmented outlets, Kao's chain of company owned distributors provide it with fast reliable information on what is happening in the Japanese market place. Kao is able to pull together such information from its own distributors plus hundreds of cooperative local retailers to identify buying patterns and preferences which give it exceptional insight into changing market trends.

Despite strong competition from global players such as Procter & Gamble, Kao has maintained a strong grip on its domestic Japanese market. It has positioned itself successfully as a major local player. It remains a profitable and growing local company.

Speed and flexibility. A tight, locally focused organisation is able to give such firms a speed of response and flexibility difficult for global players to match.

A political edge. There are also certain government incentives and rewards in remaining local. Governments, as indicated earlier, have reason to feel more comfortable with firms whose decisions are made locally with reference to local conditions. Trade treaties notwithstanding, incentives and material support are frequently available for those companies that can be developed as local champions, representing and forwarding the interests and technology of the country in which they are located.

Their closer relations and knowledge of local governments may provide local players with additional protective measures, including outright protectionism, government contracts and insider information. Government support, financial and otherwise, for certain local companies, including airlines, banks, computer firms, telecommunications and many others is too well documented to require further elaboration.

Entry barrier protection. Close association with a particular nation state (or region) is able to provide such local players with potential entry barriers against foreign global competitors. Foreign entrants will find it difficult (but not impossible) to duplicate their general familiarity with the local business environment, including their closeness to customers, political contacts and other advantages.

At the same time the larger scale of their operation provides a barrier that smaller local firms may find difficult to duplicate.

Of course, none of the above provides a defence against a global competitor that is also locally based. In such cases the local firm will search for advantage in terms of its tighter focus (relative to the home based and other global companies) with reference to local customers, conditions and trends.

Risks and disadvantages

It is the major local players that are most at risk from global rivalry. The scale of their operations makes them a tempting target for global companies. Furthermore, many global players are rapidly improving their ability to identify closely with the local market, almost matching local players in this respect. Although they retain certain disadvantages, as outlined above, they are often able to offset these. For example, they may offer governments wary of their global interconnections certain advantages which these can bring, such as increased exports and employment. The benefits of their often greater research capability is another consideration.

In many products and services, innovation has increased the advantages and indeed the requirement for large size. Global players taking advantage of potentially larger volumes offered by world markets and global products pose a threat to local players that is often difficult to counter. This is spelt out at greater length in the case study presented in the following chapter.

Local niche player positioning

This category refers to the innumerable smaller companies, including small producers (e.g. crafts), service companies, small restaurants, builders and bakeries, that have developed their own niche in the local market. Companies in this niche feature even closer association (compared with major local players) with the local environment and customers, even to the point of familiarity with the circumstances of individual clients. Unlike the major locals, they have only a small market share. With low or non-existent efficiencies of high volume, such firms specialise in closely meeting the particular needs of their particular niche.

Advantages of local niche player positioning

With a tight focus on their local specialty, such companies have the same local advantages as discussed above for major local players, often to a greater degree. Being smaller they are often even closer to their customers, in some cases on first name terms. They have even greater potential for fast action to quickly and flexibly adjust to changes in their immediate locality. In addition, they are often characterised by close geographic proximity (neighbourhood shops) and the personal contact this provides. They tend to be less constrained by the legal and institutional restrictions which often apply to larger firms.

The small size of their niche provides an effective entry barrier, their best defence against major players, both local and global.

Risks

As with all niches, there is always the danger of invasion by larger competitors. This may be due to a change in technology. For example, the use of vending machines to replace sales of cigarettes, confectionery, newspapers and other items previously sold by small shop owners. Such invasion may also come about following the development by larger firms of managerial techniques which cope successfully with small scale operations, as in the case of fast food franchises, such as McDonald's, replacing locally owned and managed shops with those at least partly managed by large local and even global players.

Worst of all worlds

The fact that there are certain trends that favour globalisation are plain for all to see. But becoming a global player requires more than a decision at the top to move into one of the positions in Figure 6.1. Such diagrams are useful in setting out the broad options; they oversimplify to make a point. However, reality is seldom this simple – a matter of black and white choices. Managers see a world of various shades of grey. When has the firm completed the actions required to reposition itself? Have they been effective? Will the new position achieve the desired results? There are no pat answers, certainly not in advance of the fact.

Implementation that does not quite achieve the desired shift can land the firm in the notorious 'in-between' position identified first by Peter Drucker. Referring to differences in size, Drucker has pointed out that real profits tend to be made at the extremes, either by large firms enjoying a dominant market share or small specialist firms which have identified and adjusted to a good niche.[5] The problem is with companies that do not qualify for one or the other. They have neither the advantages of large size nor the advantages associated with small firm specialisation.

Firms in global industries face another such 'in-between' possibility. For them there is the added possibility that the firm is neither global enough to reap the advantages of global companies nor local enough to acquire the advantages of local positioning.

Refinements

The above discussion sets out the basic positioning options in global industries. These may be further refined to take into account additional positioning criteria, as may be considered useful in relation to the firm's overall strategy. In some industries, an additional distinction which may be relevant is that between 'high cost' and 'low cost' producers, or a distinction between firms producing 'basic products' versus those with a product line that might be classed as 'sophisticated' and so on.

Mixed positioning

With the present diversity of local business environments, some companies will find that they cannot position themselves uniformly in every part of the world where they operate. Particularly where there are high border barriers, as in the case of countries where exchange controls and tariffs impede cross-border flows, some global players will find their local operations positioned differently. Because of the difficulties of integrating local units in such countries into their worldwide network, their operations there may be positioned as local players.

The following chapter looks more closely at how some companies have attempted to reposition themselves.

SUMMARY

- Firms in industries undergoing globalisation experience major changes in their relationship to their rivals. That is to say, their competitive positioning changes and has to be rethought.
- Once an industry begins globalising the number of rivals will change as the perception of what constitutes the playing field is extended worldwide. The changed positioning may affect not only the way the firm thinks about itself but also how its customers, as well as governments, perceive it.

- The objective of a positioning strategy is to relate the firm to its rivals and market in a way which will enable it to defend itself and to secure competitive advantage. It should help the firm exploit potential strengths and develop competencies as well as provide barriers to rivals and support the firm's overall strategy.
- One classic competitive positioning criterion is the size of the firm. The major players are in a different position and typically have different strategies from smaller rivals. Today, another major competitive positioning criterion is the scope of the firm's rivalry. That is, the distinction between firms that engage in global rivalry and those that conduct their rivalry locally.
- There are four general positioning options open for companies competing in global industries. 'Major global player positioning' is one of these. Companies with this positioning will have a significant share of the world market with a presence in the major world markets of the industry. Their basis for competitive advantage derives from benefits associated with their size and scope.
- Some firms will be positioned as 'global niche players'. These seek to capture many of the same advantages of the major global players but with a lower resource commitment. They are specialists operating globally. They concentrate on global niches which are too small and too specialised to attract the major global players.
- A positioning option that will suit some firms that do not wish to go global is that of 'major local player'. These are companies which are 'big' when measured in terms of their local market. Indeed some of them may be big even when measured against global competitors. Their closeness to local markets and governments often provides them with opportunities as well as defence mechanisms.
- Smaller firms may find that their best option is that of 'local niche player'. Here again, size and specialisation are able to provide entry barriers against larger rivals, both local and global. Closeness to local customers provides a basis for superior speed and flexibility.
- All of the above positioning options have their risks as well as advantages. The danger is one of falling in-between. That is, a position which is neither one thing nor another, providing none of the advantages but all of the risks.

NOTES AND REFERENCES

1. *The European*, 17–23 March 1995, p. 18.
2. *The Wall Street Journal Europe*, 26 October 1998, p. 1.
3. *Financial Times*, 3 April 1995, p. 11.
4. *The Economist*, 30 March 1996, pp. 68, 69.
5. Drucker, P. (1981), *Managing in Turbulent Times*, London: Pan Books Ltd, pp. 62–5.

7 Repositioning the local firm

GLOBAL REPOSITIONING

Once companies begin adopting global strategies, those that have remained local competitors find themselves facing a new type of rival. The new global players, many of them armed with competencies derived from their greater scale and scope, will inevitably seek to make inroads against local firms. Some will succeed. The game changes rapidly from a local to a global competitive contest.

As this sort of rivalry unfolds in one industry sector after another, it is becoming ever clearer that there are certain trends that favour the more global players. Technical advances in communication and information technology mean that the costs of becoming a global player are rapidly diminishing. Also contributing are widespread reductions in tariff barriers, deregulation and the increasing adoption of worldwide standards for various products, services and procedures.

Global companies are thus in a better position to capitalise on their potential advantages and competencies, to research and develop successful new global products, to provide worldwide services to their customers and to develop worldwide brands and corporate reputations.

In some industry sectors, such as aircraft, aircraft engines, large ocean-going vessels, computers, telecommunications, etc., local players have been rapidly reduced and in some cases eliminated. In the past a number of the largest local players have been able to fall back on the support of their governments. Government assistance, particularly in Europe, has enabled many large national companies to remain relatively immune from external rivalry. Companies considered strategic have been supported as national champions, receiving government protection in the form of tariffs, financial subsidies and other forms of assistance which has ensured their survival.

But given the present size of some of the many global players, the price of such support has escalated to the point where this is no longer feasible. This is a significant new development, which has not always been fully appreciated. During the era of local firms and local industries, governments were seldom constrained from pursuing their objectives by the magnitude of the investment required. Backing a national firm to ensure its success and survival was a decision government could readily take. Such backing usually involved a cost to the government but there was seldom a question of not being able to afford it. However, today the resources required to defend local firms against the competitive challenge of foreign rivals can prove to be beyond the means of many, if not most, governments. Across a growing number of products and services, the sheer magnitude of investment required to develop a company into a global enterprise can reach levels which exceed the resources available even to national governments. It required the combined efforts of several major countries to develop a European competitor to Boeing.

Added to this is the fact that certain agencies, such as the European Union, have ruled that government subsidies to support national companies are considered anti-competitive and are prohibited. Many companies that in the past would have bene-fited by support from their local government in their fight against global competition now find themselves cut off from such assistance.

The local trap

It is understandable in the light of these developments, that local firms may find themselves in a sort of trap. Their local competitive position becomes increasingly untenable due to pressure from emerging global companies. At the same time, the particular strengths and capabilities they have developed locally may not be well suited to responding to the thrust of the new rivals. Local firms may find that their present defences, developed to meet the rivalry of local firms, are less effective against the quite different methods and capabilities of the global players. At the same time, a 'me too' strategy, copying the methods and capabilities of their global rivals is not always practicable.

The Japanese Kao company has succeeded in its home market as a local player – but it now finds itself under increasing pressure from larger global firms, such as Unilever and Procter & Gamble.[1] Though the latter have not managed to push Kao from its position as the dominant firm in its Japanese business, it is clear that they are making increasing inroads into its domestic Japanese market. Partly as a response to this, Kao seeks to expand abroad – to become itself a global player – but the strengths it has so successfully employed in succeeding at home have not proved readily trans-ferable to other parts of the world.

As we saw in the previous chapter, Kao's strengths lie in its close relationship with distributors and retailers in Japan and its intimate knowledge of the Japanese market. These strengths would be very difficult if not impossible to reproduce abroad. Unlike certain product and technical attributes, such as superior product design or a formula for a successful pharmaceutical, these strengths are not readily transferable.

The same applies to the fast and flexible form of organisation Kao has developed specifically tailored to its operations in Japan. Its domestic organisation structure, relying on minimal support staff, is not suited to the much larger information gathering and coordination task required of the global firm.

Furthermore, Kao has not been able to surmount the cultural problems of integrating foreign managers and workers into its domestically oriented organisation. Psychologically, the success it has achieved locally makes it more difficult to contemplate the drastic restructuring required to become a global player. Undertaking such a task, becoming a global player, would risk undermining some of the qualities and strengths which have been responsible for its success locally. Meanwhile, its more global competitors continue to develop their competencies and capabilities, becoming ever more familiar with the once strange Japanese markets and narrowing the lead Kao enjoys there.

Local players alert to such change, will attempt to adjust to the new situation by strengthening their defences, raising protective barriers against the incursions of global players. Others may choose to become global players themselves. Whatever the precise form of the reaction, successful adjustment to industry globalisation sooner or later requires a change of the firm's competitive positioning, that is, the relationship to its competitors which influences its ability to defend itself and to acquire customers.

REPOSITIONING IN GLOBAL INDUSTRIES

Once global rivals appear, the players and the positioning of all firms in the industry will be altered. Local companies that find themselves in these emerging global industries have two broad options. They may capitalise on their particular local strengths, improving their contact with the local market, the speed and flexibility of their response, and other local strengths as described in the previous chapter to build up their defence against global companies, or they can 'join them', becoming global players themselves. Both require change but the latter option, particularly, will require a major transformation.

Repositioning the company as a global competitor will require a sharp break with the familiar past, a conscious decision on the part of management to alter fundamentally the direction of the firm. It entails certain costs and risks not incurred by companies that choose to remain local. It is not a path which all local firms will want to follow. But for an increasing number of such companies 'going global' will be a realistic option.

What it takes

Local firms that wish to become global players will find that the lure of habit, routine and business experience all work against the sort of changes required. Breaking with the 'think local' mentality is the first requirement.

Secondly, the resources required to reposition the firm as a global player, even in a global niche, are very considerable. In addition to material resources, technical, financial and managerial inputs far over and above those previously used by the local players will be needed.

Furthermore the price of entry into the global arena increases as new players enter the game. In most industry sectors, the first entrants have already established themselves; they have progressed on the learning curve of managing a global company.

They have capitalised on their advantages as 'first movers' to form alliances with the best partners on offer and to target the prime customers. Their increasing numbers and competence raises the entry price for followers.

Eventually the entry price reaches a point beyond the resources of the local player. Even if the firm determines that its local positioning is no longer tenable, it may have lost the option of changing to a global positioning.

Because of the generally high resource requirements, as well as other reasons, alliances which mutually benefit the various partners and other forms of inter-firm cooperation appear to be a necessary part of any successful repositioning.

Even more important than the resources is the manner of their employment. The larger size of global players is often mentioned in the same breath as their economies of scale and other competitive advantages. However, the two do not necessarily go together. It does not follow that large global size leads automatically to the capabilities and competitive advantages potentially available to global companies.

Simply increasing the scale of the company's operations may not yield the economies of scale and other benefits sometimes enjoyed by global firms. The Ford example cited in earlier chapters illustrates the great lengths in terms of reorganisation and restructuring across the entire gamut of the firm's operations which are required to access such global capabilities.

Managerial resources, particularly managers with the breadth of vision and multi-national experience required to manage globally, are the greatest limiting factor. Simply because worldwide information and coordination are now more economic does not change the fact that there is a shortage of managers with the background and skills required to use these capabilities effectively.

A complete change towards marketing and markets is also required. International markets are no longer an extra, to be subcontracted out to an exporter or even an internal marketing department. They are, taken together, the firm's new domestic market. Priorities, activities and the organisation itself have to be rethought accordingly.

GLOBALISATION IN THE COMPUTER INDUSTRY

How do companies go about this transformation? For a local company to implement such a change in its positioning represents a major decision, usually requiring the pressure of an impending crisis. In industries undergoing globalisation, such crises are not in short supply. The case example below provides an insight into how one local firm went about repositioning itself within a computer industry that was rapidly undergoing globalisation.

IBM was the first of the computer firms to go global. Having established itself first as a local competitor in a number of international markets, IBM moved to integrate its global operations in a way which gave it access to many of the advantages of a major global player (as outlined in the previous chapter). Many of its local competitors were slow to recognise the competitive threat this presented. Some firms, including Digital and Fujitsu, subsequently sought to match IBM. But most computer companies initially remained positioned as local competitors, seeking to counter the more global producers by reinforcing their local defensive positions. Even though they also had extensive international sales and operations, the multi-domestic focus of these individual national markets positioned them as local players.

This was especially true of the European computer firms – companies such as the Italian computer firm Olivetti, Siemens of Germany, Groupe Bull of France and Tulip in Holland. All of these were closely associated with their local environment and positioned at the time as major local competitors. The bulk of their sales were within the European region and focused primarily on their own domestic national markets.

These firms were also perceived as national industry leaders by their respective national governments, which provided them with substantial financial support. Hence the term 'national champions' used to describe them. Another firm formerly in this category was the British company ICL (International Computers Ltd).

The rise of a national champion

From its inception, the British firm ICL had strong local links to its local home market, the United Kingdom, as well as strong political support from a government concerned to maintain and reinforce British technical expertise in computers. The British government gave clear preference to ICL in awarding government contracts for new computer systems purchased by government agencies (which accounted for the majority of computer sales during that era). ICL also had a close relationship with its local suppliers, several of which had an equity interest in the company. Strong links with local university research departments contributed to a highly effective research effort, making the most of ICL's research budget. Its local orientation enabled ICL to focus closely on the needs of local British based customers, tailoring its computer systems to their needs.

Taken together these local links provided the British firm with formidable defensive barriers, enabling it not only to survive but also to prosper during its early years in its competition against IBM. The fact that the latter was a much larger global player with an international network made little impact on ICL during this period. Its strengths within the local national environment enabled the firm to compete vigorously for sales in its home territory, developing and marketing a complete range of computers, which it was able to market profitably while enjoying 25% annual growth. It was able to compete successfully against IBM, despite the fact that the products of the latter often sold on the open market at prices below those of ICL.

However, during the early 1980s, ICL's favourable competitive situation began to erode. Besides its major operations in North America, Japan and elsewhere, IBM operated 15 manufacturing plants and nine research and development centres in Europe alone. Its operations, particularly research and development, were coordinated internationally to avoid duplication and reduce unit costs. IBM's budget for R&D at that time exceeded ICL's total revenue. This gave it an enormous advantage not only in terms of unit cost, but also in its ability to support more rapid model change. Drawing on its worldwide sales and operations, IBM was able to sustain rapid product development at a pace the local firm found difficult to match. As the pace of technological change accelerated, ICL encountered difficulties in making the necessary investment required to keep abreast of new model development.

Building on its global size, IBM was eventually able to lower its costs relative to ICL's to the point where even the British government baulked at paying the extra price for computer systems required by the local firm. Furthermore, local government supporting purchases of ICL computers, was jeopardised by new European Union legislation prohibiting government preferential treatment of this sort.

In addition, ICL's local national focus exposed the company to the 'all the eggs in the same basket' type of risk. As the British economy moved into recession in the 1980s ICL finances moved rapidly into the red, requiring government financial support. Recognising the dire economic situation of the firm, the British government eventually extended substantial financial assistance to ICL to allow it the necessary time to restructure itself, while taking in return a 25% equity in the firm.

Moving to a global niche positioning

Faced with an impending crisis, the management of ICL embarked on a new strategy which in effect shifted the firm out of its local player positioning. The following changes were made to implement this shift in positioning.

- To begin with, ICL products were made plug-compatible with IBM's, in effect abandoning efforts to develop all of its own local products as well as shifting ICL's product line away from its previous non-compatibility with IBM products. Compatibility of ICL's new products with those of IBM made it much easier for customers to purchase products from both firms.
- A series of decisions and initiatives were undertaken aimed at expanding the firm's operations globally. Previously, it had been estimated that only 3% of ICL's sales were made outside its home market.
- ICL formed a partnership agreement with Fujitsu, a major global Japanese computer firm. This partnership enabled ICL to rely on the Japanese firm to supply it with large mainframe computers, an area where ICL had found it difficult to maintain the pace of expenditure required to update the product in line with IBM's new product offerings. As part of the overall arrangement ICL sold Fujitsu mainframes in Europe under its own brand name. This enabled the British firm to focus its own computer product development more narrowly while at the same time strengthening its global marketing capability.
- A series of additional joint ventures and alliances with international firms in other parts of the world were also undertaken, facilitating ICL's international expansion as well as contributing to its product line. Having abandoned the production of mainframes, ICL focused on becoming a producer of smaller, specialised computer systems for retailers, government offices and banks. Its marketing efforts were redirected to take advantage of market opportunities in many other parts of the world. In short, ICL repositioned itself as a global niche player.

The change in ICL's positioning had a favourable impact on its finances. ICL moved back from the brink of bankruptcy and returned to profitability.

Other European computer firms such as Olivetti, Siemens-Nixdorf and Groupe Bull were similarly positioned at about the same time as major local players. As the computer industry has continued to globalise, these other European computer firms faced the same competition and struggled with many of the same problems faced by ICL. But unlike ICL they remained local players focusing on their own countries and regions for a much longer period of time while their competitive position continued to deteriorate. Subsequently, efforts have been made by them to become more global, but is it too late?

Groupe Bull, with the majority of its equity owned by the French government, has gone through several restructurings encountering severe losses despite having received over 2 billion dollars in government aid. The stated aim has been to enable the firm to become less dependent on government support and to become a global player (hence the acquisition in 1990 of the US computer firm, Zenith). None of this has worked. More drastic restructuring has been suggested, including new alliances and privatisation. Further government assistance is constrained by European Union regulations.

Olivetti has experienced a series of annual losses. Finally abandoning efforts to position itself as a major local player with a full product range, it has attempted to restructure itself into a much more specialised firm – targeted at several specialised local niches, but with very limited success.

Siemens-Nixdorf's performance in computers has also been unsatisfactory, even though it has performed somewhat better than either Olivetti or Groupe Bull. As one of the largest firms in the world with over 350,000 employees worldwide, it may be supposed that such a giant would be positioned as a major global player, but this is not the case.

Though Siemens has sales and facilities distributed throughout the world, the focus of its activities is essentially national/regional. Over two-thirds of its sales are in Europe with over 40% of total sales in its German domestic market. Siemens remains positioned as a local player in computers, but heavily involved in many different industry sectors, nearly all of them undergoing rapid globalisation. Less than 15% of total Siemens sales fall into the 'information systems' category (which includes computers). Its sales in this category have been stagnating or experiencing slow growth during an era when worldwide sales of computers have been undergoing rapid increases.

Rising entry barriers

The computer industry case outlined above illustrates some of the options and issues faced by managers of companies seeking to reposition themselves globally. With the exception of ICL, all of the European computer firms continue to operate as local players. Sales of all European based computer firms have remained largely concentrated in that region and particularly within their home markets. All of these companies have found that their local player positioning has become increasingly untenable, progressively undermined by the encroachment of global players.

Having initially developed skills and capabilities aimed at reinforcing their local positioning, it appears difficult, if not impossible, at the current stage of the computer industry's movement towards globalisation for these predominantly local firms to assemble the necessary resources and the quite different skills needed to reposition themselves globally. Rapidly changing technology and ever escalating requirements for investment in R&D and new product development are pushing entry barriers into the global league ever higher.

Was ICL's repositioning as a global company successful? That depends on your point of view. ICL was eventually acquired by its Japanese ally Fujitsu which had helped it in its globalisation efforts. It is no longer an independent British based company let alone a national champion. But in an increasingly global industry how relevant is the locus of ownership? The fact is that ICL remains a profitable and viable organisation. It continues to provide many highly skilled jobs, making a major contribution to the development of British skills and production capability in this key industry. There is little doubt that its performance is now better than most of its more local competitors.

Switching positions

There will also be occasions when some companies may find it advantageous to abandon a global positioning, switching to a more local orientation. Some time ago, the Chrysler corporation found it difficult to maintain its position as a global player. Divesting itself of major foreign production facilities, mainly in Europe, the company repositioned itself as a local player, focused on North America. This was followed a few years later by a return to profitability.

Chrysler was subsequently merged with the German automotive producer, Daimler-Benz. The latter had been gradually moving away from its global niche position in the luxury car market. The Daimler-Benz product range had expanded to the point where it was challenging, but not quite matching, the size and scale of operations of major global competitors such as Toyota and General Motors. The merger with Chrysler, forming DaimlerChrysler, moved the combined companies firmly into a major global player positioning.

SUMMARY

- Advances in communications and IT mean the costs of becoming a global player are diminishing. Some local firms will find themselves in a sort of trap. Their position as local players becomes increasingly untenable against new global competitors while at the same time they may find that it is difficult and even impracticable for them to become global players. Whatever the response, firms in industries which are globalising cannot remain static.
- Local companies in emerging global industries have two broad options. They may develop their local strengths to position themselves as local players in a global industry. Alternatively, they may become global players themselves. This requires major changes in management's mentality as well as resources.
- The case of the British computer firm ICL serves to illustrate the changes required for a local firm to transform itself into a global player. Initially, ICL's local orientation enabled it to focus closely on meeting the needs of local British organisations. It prospered for a number of years as a major local player in computers.

- Competition from more global competitors and particularly IBM brought the firm under increasing competitive pressure. It had difficulty in keeping up the investment in R&D required to match its more global competitor. Partly as a result, its prices also became less competitive. Moving towards bankruptcy, the company was forced to consider drastic change, altering its positioning as a local player.
- In the process of changing itself into a more global company, ICL made a number of major changes. Its product line was made plug-compatible with that of IBM, repositioning its products and making them less directly competitive with those of IBM.
- ICL also extended its operations internationally. It narrowed its own product line development, forming an alliance with Fujitsu to supply it with mainframe computers. ICL focused on becoming a producer of smaller, more specialised computer systems.
- Was ICL's repositioning as a more specialised, global niche player successful? The firm was eventfully acquired by Fujitsu but it continued to operate with greater success than the majority of other European computer firms that started out in much the same position.
- There may also be occasions when a company positioned as a global player may not be able to meet the requirements of that positioning and has to revert towards a more local orientation.

NOTES AND REFERENCES

1. *The Economist*, 30 March 1996, pp. 68, 69.

8 Developing products for global markets

Global companies interpret the playing field quite differently from their local counterparts. This applies with special force to the way they see their markets. Global players take a worldwide perspective – but this does not imply that such companies view the world as a single market.

On the contrary, such companies have a particular need to develop special skills in identifying the many national differences and local features that are crucial to success in marketing to the 'world market'. But marketing managers in such companies must also be able to integrate these numerous, quite diverse local market situations into a world view of what constitutes the global market for their product. In short, global marketing managers must have the ability to see beyond disparate local market situations, viewing them collectively as an interdependent, global whole. This local/global way of viewing markets distinguishes global marketing from that of local players.

It also distinguishes it from traditional exporters and multinationals. Even though such companies operated in many different countries, their tendency was to treat each national market individually. Their marketing remained locally oriented, lacking the world view and global integration referred to above.

A new perception of the customer

Global marketing begins with a fundamental change in the perception of the customer. Peter Drucker defined marketing as the whole business as seen from the point of view of the customer.[1] But for companies marketing their products and services in countries characterised by differences in language, tradition, laws, culture and economic development, the identity of their customers, who they are and how they see the firm is far from obvious.

An essential first step in identifying the global customer is to abandon the distinction between 'foreign' and 'domestic'. As obvious as that may sound, the habit of classifying customers and markets in terms of particular geographic areas called 'countries' has become so deeply engrained in our psyche that seeing them globally is not something that comes naturally. Even within companies that have been marketing their products and/or services globally for some considerable time, there is still a psychological barrier.

This country-by-country view of the world is supported first by force of habit, which often begins in the schoolroom. It is also reinforced by the fact that market information, the raw data that enables us to identify, quantify and interpret markets is made available by government statistical offices on a national basis. Within the international/global company itself, the organisation structure may reflect traditional geographic divisions. Management responsibilities and tasks are frequently defined according to national or regional geographic units, such as 'our managing director in country X'. Arriving at a perception of the local/global market is not therefore something that comes naturally. It requires a new mental model.

Rethinking markets and customers

It may be hard to imagine today but the earlier appearance of the national corporation called for a similar perceptual change and re-examination of just 'who is the customer?'. Identifying and reorienting the marketing of national companies to the new national customer required new ways of researching and interpreting customers nationally rather than locally. The subject and study of marketing itself as a distinct specialisation was both initiated and developed by the requirement of the new national companies to reorient their thinking, to identify their new national customers. Those that were able to break the habits of the past, to develop new ways of seeing their markets nationally, gained an important competitive advantage. Segmenting the market nationally enabled its pioneers to 'see' it in a broader perspective. Products were targeted at national rather than local customer segments.

In the 1920s, companies in North America pioneered the application of market segmentation on a national level. Revolutionary at the time, this led these firms to view the market in a different light. It enabled them to evolve new marketing strategies featuring products targeted at specific segments of the national market. This gave such companies an important marketing advantage over the competitors who took a more local view of marketing.

The same type of rethinking is required today. Accepted concepts have to be re-examined with a view to the global customer. Nowhere is this more urgent than in the design and development of new products.

DEVELOPING GLOBAL PRODUCTS

A successful global product (the term 'product' is used here and elsewhere to include services) is one that achieves universal acceptance, appealing to large numbers of customers around the world in much the same standardised form. This requires that the developers of the product are able to arrive at a design or formula that bridges the many international differences which characterise world markets.

When successful, such products offer certain advantages to their companies not available to local players. These include not only the familiar economies of large (global) scale, but further advantages in distribution and branding. Much less noticed but perhaps even more important are potential savings in terms of management's time and focus. Executives engaged in global marketing of products across many diverse markets find their task more manageable when dealing with relatively few products. Companies that develop product variants for each market soon find that the sheer number and variety of such products enormously complicate and even obstruct management's ability to comprehend the firm's global product line in relation to its customers. Reducing the number of products through global standardisation, marketing essentially the same products around the world, opens the possibility of major savings in management time and production costs.

Developing a globally accepted product may come about quite accidentally, in the sense that its design and development was not initially intended to appeal to customers globally. Most of today's global products were originally developed and targeted towards a single national market. They were designed and intended for a particular country or region, typically the firm's home market. Their success locally laid the foundations for their subsequent launch in the same form internationally. This usually began with exports.

Exports comprise a sort of test marketing. In those few instances where such products were successful with little or no variation to their domestic design, they became global products. Export success was followed by additional investment that promoted the foreign market penetration of such products in a standardised form.

This was the usual route. Develop and launch locally; if it works in one country, try it elsewhere. This method has produced a number of remarkable success stories, including various banking services, insurance, certain software products, McDonald's hamburgers and so on. But there is also ample evidence of a far greater number of failures and partial failures produced by this 'try it and see' approach. American producers of genetically modified seeds and foods were taken aback by the negative reaction to their products in Europe. This not only affected their sales locally in the European market, the greater sensitivity of European consumers to such products and their negative reaction has shown signs of spreading to the United States domestic market. Most such failures, facing declining sales, are less visible than the success stories and less often mentioned.

BOX 8.1

Developing new products for foreign markets

Figure 8.1 illustrates four different policies pursued in developing products that are marketed internationally. The second and third development options are the most common. In both of these cases the basic product is tested in the sense that it is marketed in one national market before being transferred elsewhere. Both of these approaches reap the benefit of prior market experience and the opportunity to utilise the lessons gained thereby in developing the product. ▶

However, since development in these cases is initially focused on a given national market, they may also result in products that are not readily transferable or even viable in other markets. The final option is global product development. ■

1. **National development**
   Product developed individually for each national market

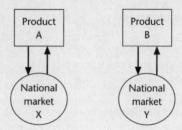

2. **Domestic development**
   Product developed for a specific national market (typically the firm's domestic or 'home' market) and exported or produced elsewhere without change

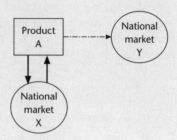

3. **Sequential development**
   Product developed to suit one national market, subsequently modified to suit conditions in a foreign market

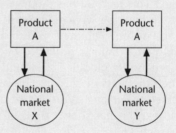

4. **Global development**
   Product developed from the outset for world markets

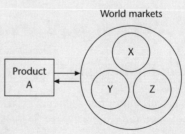

FIGURE 8.1 Product development policies

Source: From Leontiades, J. C. (1985), *Multinational Corporate Strategy*, Lexington Books.

Global product development

An increasing number of companies today set out purposely to develop global products. That is, products and services designed from the outset to be marketed in most countries of the world with very little change. Market research and development are carried out on a global basis – searching for the design or formula that will appeal to customers worldwide. Is this realistic? Bridging customer differences at any level is difficult, just try preparing a menu for five or six guests with different tastes. How realistic is it to even attempt to set out purposely to develop global products? Is it possible to anticipate the requirements of so many customers in widely different parts of the world?

The development of any new product inevitably represents a compromise. This is just as true of products aimed at a particular national market as it is of those which aim at marketing success globally. With the exception of those few items, such as tailor-made suits, designed for specific individuals, all products attempt to bridge individual differences in consumer preferences and buying power. It is predictable therefore that even the successful new product will not be everyone's ideal. Certain product features will appeal to some prospective users but not to others. Some will prefer a drink that is sweet, others one that is dry, some will favour modern design, others traditional.

For the above reasons and despite the growing faith in globalisation, there is a considerable body of opinion among marketing practitioners, that attempts purposely to develop such products are, to say the least, premature. One expert in marketing products internationally argues strongly against the purposeful development of products designed from the outset for global marketing.

If the vital task in evaluating and launching a new product is to cut down the risks, it must follow that to cut down on possible negatives in a number of different countries at once is either completely impossible or represents a sure recipe to introduce the lowest common denominator, i.e a product which is so neutral that it will not attract any attention in any country.[2]

In other words, the risk is high that such attempts will lead to products falling between two stools. Having been designed to appeal to a wide range of different tastes and market conditions, they will fail to appeal either locally or globally.

Recent developments

More recently two developments have appeared which work against the above view and favour the development of global products. First, there are genuine signs that many markets around the world are converging. Consumer preferences are becoming more similar in certain important respects. The same improvements in communications which have contributed to the new global reach of management and competition on a world scale have undoubtedly influenced consumer tastes. Exposed to many of the same films, sports events, famous personalities and fashion shows, it is not surprising that customers are expressing preferences for many of the same products and services. Greatly increased opportunities for travel and tourism have also influenced consumers to try new products. Large numbers of us have taken to new foods, clothing and other products previously considered foreign.

Rising levels of income have also enabled millions of consumers in formerly less economically developed countries to express preferences for products previously attainable only by those in the more affluent developed world. Such changes have brought about a greater similarity between customers widely separated by geography, language and background than ever before. National consumer preferences, using this term to include both the desire on the part of consumers for a particular product as well as the power to exercise this by purchasing the item in question, are becoming more similar. But they do not, nor are they likely to, completely converge. Differences in consumer preferences reflecting differences in income, tastes, habits and institutional infrastructure from one region to another will remain. This does not rule out the development of standardised global products.

With market convergence, differences between customers in different parts of the world become smaller. It therefore becomes increasingly possible to design global products. But this does not ensure success. No amount of convergence will eliminate all differences from one local market to another. Purposeful development of global products will require careful research and no small degree of imagination and persistence. The challenge for global product development is to design those products that target international similarities while circumventing those areas where there are strong consumer differences – all the while not sacrificing features which give such products their appeal and uniqueness.

To illustrate, let's consider a map of consumer preferences as indicated in Figure 8.2. Let's assume for purposes of illustration that the world market for a particular product is limited to three countries and that all consumers have sufficient income to purchase it. The product in question has two major characteristics, size and performance. The arrows indicate that there is a growing convergence of consumer preferences for these characteristics in national markets A, B and C. Over a certain area of the map, the preferences of consumers in the world market overlap (preferences of consumers from all three countries are similar within the cross-hatched area of Figure 8.2). Customers within this group share similar preferences for this product irrespective of their nationality. These are the potential 'world customers' for the product.

But despite this convergence, the preference map also indicates that many consumers in these countries do not share this similarity of tastes. There is still a considerable degree of diversity. Some consumers in all three countries have preferences which are dissimilar.

How do firms cope with these differences? The 'try it and see' approach of the early exporters was to launch domestic products in different world markets in the hope that they might succeed. Those that did not succeed as global products might still find success in particular national foreign markets, either A, B or C on the map. Still others (falling into the shaded areas of Figure 8.2) might be suitable as regional products.

The hit and miss approach, trying products internationally on the strength of their successful performance in a local market with little prior research, is still widely practised. It is particularly attractive to smaller companies since the additional investment required for product development is minimal.

However, the trend today is to minimise the risk of failure through market research. For most global players, there is more at stake than the risk of financial loss attached to the failure of a particular product. Greatly improved information and dissemination

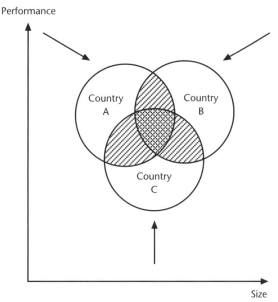

FIGURE 8.2 Market convergence. Product preferences of consumers in three countries

of news ensures that any such failure is reported well outside the national territory in which it took place. Company reputation suffers, the damage quite possibly extending to other products and regions. Hence the increased reliance on international research to guide the purposeful development of products designed from the outset to appeal to world customers.

DEVELOPING AND MARKETING GLOBAL PRODUCTS

For the company aiming to develop a global product, the task is first, to identify the customer groups in the various markets around the world whose preferences have converged sufficiently so that they are potentially 'in the market' for the same type of product. Secondly, it is to carry out research that evaluates these preferences, arriving at a specific set of product features that will appeal to these groups in the various world markets. Finally, such features will be incorporated into a product which does in fact appeal to these global customers and can be sold at a profit. (For an example of such development see Chapter 5.)

Timing

Even if the markets are converging, and the company has developed the right product, there is still the problem of timing. Global product development which lags the convergence of world markets risks losing the initiative to competitors. Launching a product aimed at global markets prematurely, before the markets have converged sufficiently to generate the required demand, can be disastrous. In such cases, one may then be tempted to draw the conclusion that a particular product which works in one market or region will not be accepted elsewhere, when in fact the problem is a matter of timing.

A classic example of premature product launch into a new market is the failed launch of pre-mixed cake mixes onto the British market. The product was designed so that any housewife could produce a professional type of cake. The fact that it failed in England after success in the United States was held up as an example of differences in consumer preferences. The published view was that these differences were of a cultural nature.[3] British consumers were supposedly more traditional, more old fashioned, less willing to try new products. The differences cited were held to be of a long term nature and the product was withdrawn. Certainly there was little indication that the same type of product would one day be widely successful. But some years later, the same national market proved very receptive to a wide variety of similar pre-mixed products.

Surprises in timing may also work in the other direction. Some developing countries adopted mobile telephones much quicker than expected and indeed quicker than some of the wealthier countries. Their less advanced telecommunications systems provided a spur to the early adoption of the new technology.

Segmentation

National and regional boundaries are of course a form of segmentation that has value as a first approximation. But within any country potential customers will still be characterised by wide differences in marketing related characteristics.

Global marketing managers need to develop a global overview of their product's positioning in world markets. Within each country, they must identify their target segment, which customer group or groups serves as the main focus for the firm's marketing efforts. Target segments may be identified using different criteria for each local market (country or region). For example, potential consumers in some countries may be segmented according to age, profession, buying habits and so on. But using different criteria in each local market will make it difficult to relate the various markets to each other or to identify the firm's overall global product positioning.

In Figure 8.3, the product which is being marketed is income sensitive. Below a certain level of per capita income, experience indicates potential consumers cannot afford to buy it. But after a certain income level, consumers in certain of the wealthier countries prefer more luxurious, higher priced competitive products. Accordingly, the firm's customers in its various world markets, A, B, C and D, are segmented according to their level of income. The cross-hatched area identifies the high potential target segment in the four countries, those customers whose income levels indicate they are in the market for this product. The proportion and number of the population thus targeted varies widely across the four countries. This is not unexpected given their differences in per capita income.

Market research has shown that products purchased by the middle and even lower income groups in the wealthier countries may fall outside the purchasing power of these same categories in the poorer developing countries.[4] A product which is readily affordable by a broad section of the American population may have to be limited in

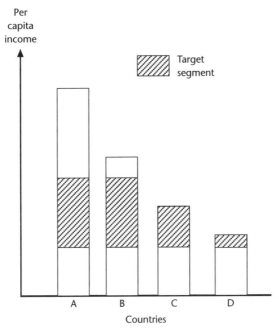

FIGURE 8.3 Targeting global customers

less affluent countries to a much smaller segment of the population, those in the higher income brackets, as in countries C and D of Figure 8.3. It is well to keep in mind, however, that given the large populations in some of the countries with lower incomes, such as China and India, the segment illustrated in country D may be numerically larger and more rewarding than the target segments indicated in countries A, B and C.

Market share

The global player also requires a fresh approach to market share. The fact that market share is important is supported by both industry leaders and a substantial body of research. But market share has in the past most often been measured nationally, company sales viewed as a percentage of total national industry sales. For the global company a global measure of market share is essential, first of all for tracking its own global performance against competitors. However, since competitive conditions and markets differ from one country to another, it is also important to measure the firm's market performance locally. Finally, the relationship of market share to profitability (see Figure 8.4) has long been cited as a justification for share-increasing strategies. Managers pursuing such strategies can no longer assume that the relevant market share for this purpose is measured on a national basis. A company which has a small market share in a particular country may still enjoy a very large percentage of the world market and vice versa. IBM may be the largest computer company globally but there are a number of national markets where its market share is small. Which market

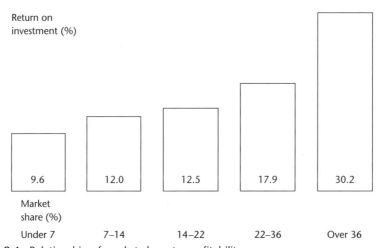

Return on
investment (%)

9.6	12.0	12.5	17.9	30.2

Market
share (%)

Under 7   7–14   14–22   22–36   Over 36

FIGURE 8.4 Relationship of market share to profitability

Source: From Schoeffler, S., Buzzell, R. D. and Heany, D. F. (1974), Impact of strategic planning on profitability, *Harvard Business Review*, March–April.

share measure is applicable? Companies will now have to consider whether the relevant market share for their purposes is local (national or regional) or global. The global enterprise tracking the firm's performance requires both. The competitive relationship between the firm and its rivals, including market share, should be assessed globally as well as locally.[5]

Marketing functions

All of the major marketing concepts and functions are similarly altered by the globalisation of the firm and the changed definition of 'the customer'. Pricing, applied globally, has to take into account, not only the usual influences of exchange rates and tariffs but also the effect of pricing on the firm's worldwide image and competitive position.

Moreover, the price placed on the product is closely associated with product acceptability and product design. If there are efficiencies associated with large scale production, as there appear to be, then the cost benefits of globally standardised products enabling the global company to offer lower priced products may also influence consumer acceptance.

Global products which are not immediately attractive on the basis of taste preference, i.e. those falling outside the cross-hatched area in Figure 8.2, may still prove attractive to customers if they result in production efficiencies and a significantly lower price.

The American General Electric Company was not at all certain it would find a market in Japan for its refrigerators. These standard American refrigerators were much larger than those customarily purchased for the smaller Japanese homes. But priced at half the cost of Japanese refrigerators, they sold very well.[6]

Promotion, if developed separately for each country can prove expensive and wasteful. An advertising campaign that has proved successful in one country sometimes proves successful in others. But differences in customer attitudes as well as local legislation and media have often spoiled attempts at global advertising campaigns.

The globalisation of distribution offers its own marketing challenges. Customers buying products in one country are transhipping them to other countries where they can be sold at a higher price. For example, pharmaceuticals bought in Hong Kong at relatively low prices are shipped elsewhere, often to their country of origin, where they can be sold at a profit. The right price, promotion and distribution arrived at within this more global frame of reference will usually be quite different from that constructed for local markets considered individually. For the global company, the entire marketing mix changes.

The message is clear. Global marketing must make allowance for local variations in culture, taste, economic demand and institutional structure. But such diversity is purposeful and coordinated. Not only should the right hand know what the left in another part of the world is doing – but both must operate within a framework of global marketing objectives based on a world overview of markets and customers.

INTERNAL MARKETING CHANGES

Although external visible changes towards globalisation have received the most attention, equally important but less visible are the internal changes taking place within companies. Management's steadily improving global reach, the ability to communicate swiftly and easily with markets around the world, has reduced the costs of accessing and evaluating international market information. As a result, managers are now better able to carry out the market research required to take advantage of the growing convergence of markets described above. As in the case of Ford's global product efforts discussed earlier, they are better equipped today with the tools and techniques required purposely to design products that appeal globally. Also not to be overlooked is the greatly increased level of international marketing expertise due to the experience that companies have accumulated.

Companies do learn. Lessons gained from both successes and failures have been incorporated into improving planning systems and market organisations as well as the expertise of many marketing managers. Using new programmes and analytical tools, companies are much more capable today of interpreting customers' likes and dislikes on an international scale. They no longer have to rely on 'try it and see'. This growing internal fund of experience in countries outside the firm's home market has raised the level of international marketing competence, enabling a growing (though still relatively small) number of companies to identify, develop, launch and market global products successfully.

Managers responsible for global marketing are also moving to new planning systems that make better use of the marketing knowledge of local marketing managers. When local managers were insulated by communication and transport difficulties from the other parts of the organisation, there was little option but to allow each local unit to develop its own marketing plan in isolation. This decentralised approach to planning meant that any overall 'global' marketing plan was simply the collected local plans, see Figure 8.5(a).

Today managers responsible for firms' worldwide marketing are increasingly able to interact with local managers. A two way flow of information is encouraged. Local

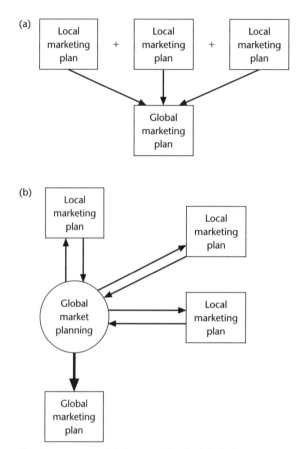

FIGURE 8.5 Two planning systems: (a) Decentralised global planning process; (b) Globally integrated planning process

views are gathered and compared. Local managers are better informed concerning the marketing experience, policies and programmes of the organisation in other parts of the world. Managers responsible for the firm's global marketing policies and programmes are better informed concerning the problems and opportunities facing managers in local markets. Information from this interaction informs both the local as well as the global marketing plan, Figure 8.5(b).

MANAGING MARKET DIVERSITY

The changes noted above have all involved a greater degree of cross-national co-ordination. The role of the coordinators, typically some form of regional or global headquarters, has correspondingly increased with the move towards globalisation. Global marketing itself has often been associated with standardisation, globally standardised products and worldwide media campaigns. But this is not necessarily the wave of the future.

The same improvements in global reach that have contributed to the improvements in the research and design of these global products have also provided the basis for an improved ability to identify and react to local market situations around the world. Responding to global market diversity becomes easier and less costly. With growing competition, greater consumer sophistication and increased purchasing power, the importance of such local differences and the tailoring of company products to local needs will increase.

In other words, both supply and demand trends point to greater concentration by global players on the particular needs of local markets. The pressure on marketing managers to gain a competitive edge by catering to local differences may be expected to increase, even where the differences themselves diminish. For some companies and industries marketing global products, the pendulum may have already swung too far. Firms that have developed globally standardised products and are already well advanced along this path will have to reassess their product strategies and associated marketing plans.

Localisation with a difference

This sharper focus on local customer requirements does not imply a return to the more traditional country-by-country approach so widely practised in the past. The local marketing of the global player will be quite different. Locally diverse marketing programmes will be part of a more comprehensive global marketing plan. Global players, even those most closely associated with standardisation, are already responding to the pressures and possibilities for greater adjustment to local market conditions. Their aim is to reap the best of both worlds, localisation and globalisation. This is illustrated in the use of product strategies and cost saving initiatives such as those we describe below.

Global 'core' products

A promising method for catering to market diversity without sacrificing the gains of globalisation is the development of products with a globally standardised 'core'. The core of the product, i.e. the portion containing its basic features, is produced in a standardised form and for all world markets. This secures the efficiencies of global scale production for the product components comprising the core.

The product core is augmented with peripheral attachments and modifications that may vary from one country or region to another, adapting the total product to local market conditions.

Goss Graphic Systems, a manufacturer of printing presses, designs its products around a common platform which remains the same wherever marketed. But add-on features can be changed to suit the special requirements of various local market situations, including those of the emerging markets.[7]

This product core method is particularly effective for products which are able to reap substantial benefits from efficiencies of scale but are targeted at global customers with varying characteristics and product needs.

A local/global product mix

Another approach is to mix the global firm's standardised products with local products developed and designed for a particular national or regional market. In expanding into different national markets companies tend to accumulate a number of purely local products. Such local products can be marketed alongside global products as part of the firm's overall product mix. This 'local product tail', as it is sometimes referred to, can make a valuable contribution, supplementing the firm's global product lines and enabling it to better cater for local customer needs. Pharmaceutical firms frequently market global drug products alongside medicines special to a particular national market.

Localisation programmes

In Ireland, several thousand people work at 'localising' the standard software of the various foreign software companies located there. Language is of course a part of this localisation, Microsoft's Windows 95 were released in 20 languages. But localisation also extends to tailoring software images, colour and style as well as adapting units of measurement and financial symbols to suit the different national sensitivities of the markets where the software will be purchased.[8]

THE MOVE TO GLOBAL MARKETING

Companies that have become accustomed to interpreting their foreign markets individually, are sometimes taken aback to discover that what appears to be a perfectly rational marketing programme when viewed nationally does not appear that way when viewed globally.

Cadbury Schweppes, the British producer of confectionery and various soft drinks, encountered just such a situation. In the mid-1970s, two of its executives made a tour of all of the firm's various foreign subsidiaries, something which up to that time had not been done on any regular basis.[9]

They found that the Cadbury companies abroad were marketing much the same products as the parent company domestically. However, there were major differences in their marketing practice that caused concern. This was true not only between the parent company and its overseas affiliates but also between the foreign affiliates themselves. Products were promoted, packaged and branded differently from country to country. The company's logo, which corporate management considered to be a major marketing asset, was displayed, designed and used quite differently from one country to another. The packaging of its products and the colour and design on its wrappers also varied internationally as did the name of the product. Advertising campaigns in all of the firm's overseas territories were prepared using methods which differed from those that the parent company had developed at considerable expense. The advertising message itself differed, as did the advertising budgets of the various Cadbury affiliates calculated as a percentage of sales. New products were launched in diverse national markets with no apparent thought regarding the wider implications of the timing of such introductions.

Did this diversity simply represent local management initiative, a constructive adaptation to local conditions? Is there, after all, any need for any coordination between the company's various operations worldwide? If conditions from one national market to another differ, why shouldn't the firm's marketing programmes there also differ?

The parent company was prepared to admit the need for local variation in response to national differences. At the same time there also appeared to be good reasons for a certain degree of coordination and standardisation of marketing programmes and practices from one country to another.

For example, one executive pointed out that although there were good reasons why advertising campaigns might vary from country to country, the firm's products were remarkably consistent internationally in terms of their positioning to similar target customers. Questions also arose concerning the adverse impact of such international variation on the company's global image.

Furthermore, a review of the company's international operations had revealed that its competitors were beating it to market with its own products. The same communications that gave management the capability of managing at a distance also made it possible for competitors to observe a competitor's products in one national location, copy and launch them in another. Cadbury found that competitors were simply copying products which it had developed and proved successful in Britain and then introducing them into certain foreign markets before it could do so. The company review concluded that its marketing programmes in its various foreign markets had fragmented beyond anything that made sense.

To begin its move towards more globally coherent orientation Cadbury called an international marketing conference, bringing its various local managers together to discuss these issues and how such a framework could be achieved. Its marketing managers from around the world agreed on the need for the development of a common approach to marketing planning, execution and documentation.

This was only the first step on a long and bumpy road. The initial welcome which met the parent company's efforts towards a more global marketing approach was sometimes replaced by friction and even outright opposition from its managers abroad. Coordinating the operations of Cadbury's various international affiliates inevitably stepped on some toes. Local managers, while initially agreeing on the need for a degree of cohesion and uniformity in the firm's global marketing, were not always willing to make the sacrifices in their freedom to make their own decisions and to go their own way that this required.

Cadbury proceeded to launch a series of initiatives aimed at bringing about greater coordination in its international marketing effort. Planning was one such area. Previously it had been entirely a bottom-up, financially oriented process. The firm's overall plan was described by the group planning manager as 'long range budgeting', consisting mainly of the collected budgets of the various operating units (see Figure 8.5).

A more strategic approach was instigated based on a planning exercise that introduced a more proactive role on the part of the corporate planning office. The aim was to bring together information from all of the operating units, giving a global perspective of the firm's operations and a basis for dialogue between the corporate office and the company's various operating units. The plans of the local units could be discussed with the corporate office before they were finalised. They could then be related to the firm's overall global objectives and, in that context, possibly modified.

Another initiative was the attempt to introduce commonality in advertising. This had mixed success. Most such attempts foundered on the failure to get agreement from Cadbury's various international operating units. On closer inspection, the positioning of the firm's products was not as similar as first supposed. In some countries, customers might consider a particular confectionery primarily as nourishment, in others a novelty type product. A more successful approach was to develop a common theme. This preserved a certain degree of global uniformity while allowing considerable scope for local variation to suit individual national markets.

Developing a uniform logo was another of Cadbury's initiatives aimed at achieving a more globally coherent image and policies. A major tool in this respect was Cadbury's 'Design Guide'. This came in the form of a manual setting out the design, colour and format to be used when displaying the company logo in any part of the world. Here again there were difficulties which had to be overcome. Once the issue was addressed it became clear that there was a substantial administrative load involved in supervising such change. The Cadbury logo appeared (in many forms) in thousands of locations. Uniformity was desirable but the expense and effort required were not welcomed by hard pressed managers in Cadbury's local operating units.

Coordination on such a scale and across national boundaries required a number of changes in the firm's organisation. One of the most significant was the establishment of an international marketing department. The chairman of the company, Dominic Cadbury, defined the mission of the new department as: 'to assist the chief executive in pulling together marketing strategies around the world and to identify opportunities'. A major function would be the coordination of new product introduction into the firm's various local markets.

The international marketing department achieved a degree of success in coordinating the firm's advertising and product programmes. However, the department eventually encountered difficulties. Not all of the powerful executives heading the firm's various national subsidiaries welcomed its assistance. Eventually it was superseded by another, more far reaching organisational change.

Cadbury's entire worldwide operations were subsequently reorganised and focused around two global product groups, confectionery and beverages, referred to as 'product streams'. Each global product stream had its own chief executive with global responsibility for that product category, including the coordination of new product introduction. The product streams were further divided into national business units, each reporting to the chief executive of their respective product stream. The new structure replaced the company's former multi-domestic organisation which presided over a collection of quasi-autonomous operating units, each with its own marketing programme.

GLOBAL MARKETING

The task of global marketing is to avoid the sort of fragmentation which is often associated with international marketing as described above.

The marketing success of the global enterprise depends on its ability to balance both local and global requirements. It has to be able to compete against local companies which concentrate all of their energies on the requirements of the special needs and peculiarities of a single local market. At the same time, consumers around the world are becoming more demanding. In the future, these global firms will be faced with the task of meeting the often conflicting aims of global markets characterised by both convergence and diversity while stretching to attain the advantages associated with globalisation. The pre-globalisation approach of treating each country individually, a separate domestic market with little reference to the firm's global position or other countries, is giving way to a more comprehensive world view of markets and marketing.

Global marketing aims to identify and target the growing similarities in consumer tastes and preferences while at the same time recognising and taking account of the many differences that still divide customers around the world. The successful global player will aim for a balance that reaps the best of both worlds – the advantages of globalisation together with responsiveness to local customer needs and characteristics.

SUMMARY

- Global marketing aims to identify and target the growing similarities in consumer tastes while at the same time taking account of the many real differences that still differentiate customers around the world. Global marketing begins with a new perception of the customer. An essential first step is abandoning the distinction between 'foreign' and 'domestic'.
- In the past, developing products that appealed to customers globally typically depended on a 'try it and see' approach. There was a high failure rate.
- Two developments make the successful design of such products more practicable today. First, there are signs that consumer preferences are indeed becoming more similar even though major international differences remain. Secondly, there is more effective use today of international market research.
- In developing globally standardised products, the first task is to identify potential customers in the various markets whose preferences are sufficiently similar. Timing is important as is global market segmentation.
- There is increasing pressure to cater to local differences. For global players, the major marketing functions, such as pricing, promotion and distribution, should allow for local diversity within an overall framework of global marketing objectives.
- A number of methods, such as product localisation, are being used by such firms to cater to local market diversity without sacrificing the gains of globalisation. Experience indicates that moving towards global marketing involves more than marketing. Reorganisation to bring about the necessary coordination may also be required.

NOTES AND REFERENCES

1. Drucker, P. (1968), *The Practice of Management*, London: Pan Books, p. 54.
2. Kraushar, P. M. (1977), *New Products and Diversification*, Tiptree, Essex: Anchor Press, pp. 182, 183.
3. Sommers, M. and Kernana, J. (1967), Why products flourish here, fizzle there, *Columbia Journal of World Business*, March–April, p. 93.
4. Leontiades, J. C. (1978), Patterns in international markets and market strategy, in M. Ghertman and J. C. Leontiades (Eds), *European Research in International Business*, Amsterdam: North Holland, pp. 239–62.
5. Leontiades, J. C. (1984), Market share and corporate strategy in international industries, *The Journal of Business Strategy*, vol. 5, no. 1, pp. 30–7.
6. *The Wall Street Journal Europe*, 1 November 1995, p. 5.
7. *Financial Times*, 13 February 1998, p. 10.
8. *Financial Times*, 24 June 1996, p. IV.
9. I am grateful to the managers of Cadbury Schweppes for their extensive cooperation in connection with this research.

Chapter

9 Emerging markets

Games seldom stay the same – keeping up with change is part of the contest. In coming years companies marketing their products globally will find that their greatest challenge lies in the emerging markets of the world, those rapidly growing markets, many from the so-called developing countries.

For the past two hundred years world trade and economic activity have been dominated by the group of countries bordering the North Atlantic Basin. Europe and North America were the seat of the industrial age and the main beneficiaries of the much higher levels of productivity and income that came with it. The countries of these regions were considered to be the economically developed, Western industrial countries. They also comprised the major markets of the world.

The great majority of the world's 170-odd countries and the bulk of its population remained outside this elite industrial group. Until the early 1900s, their links to the Western industrial countries followed the colonial pattern of trade. The non-industrial countries exported raw materials to Britain, France, Portugal, the Netherlands and other countries of the industrialised West. In return they imported from them manufactured products. As recently as the early 1950s almost half of Great Britain's exports were directed towards its former colonies.

Even today, the nations officially listed by the International Monetary Fund as industrial countries are confined to North America, Western Europe, Australia and New Zealand. Japan is the only exception. Japan was the first country without European roots to break into this exclusive club. But even after it emerged from World War II as a major competitor, it was still years before Japan became a major market for Western firms. For a number of reasons, Western firms were (and many still are) unsuccessful at penetrating Japanese markets.

It is not surprising then that the attention of major international companies came to be focused about the markets of the high income, Western industrial countries.

These were the locus of the larger and more dynamic consumer markets. It was here that Western business firms directed their major investments and marketing initiatives. Yes, they also invested and conducted marketing operations in the less developed, non-industrial countries but these were accorded a lower priority.

The countries of the industrialised West, those bordering the North Atlantic Basin, represented the largest concentrations of purchasing power and the focus of the major markets and the major companies of the world. The bulk of new products and services were developed for those countries and marketed there. Such products were designed to suit Western markets and Western tastes. Those were also the countries where the managers of the international/multinational firms felt most comfortable. They provided a relatively familiar working environment. Certainly there were individual national differences. France is not the same as Sweden. Despite a common language, Britain and the United States have major differences. But there is also a certain similarity between the Western powers, much of it based on a broadly common level of affluence as well as certain shared political and economic institutions. Western managers working outside their home country were better able both to understand and to adjust to the national markets of these countries.

HISTORICAL CHANGE

The economic differences between developing and developed countries were not always those we see today. At about the time of Shakespeare, the per capita incomes in the developing countries were not very different from those in the West (see Figure 9.1). But countries in the West experienced faster growth rates, particularly with the onset of the industrial era in the early 1800s, than those outside the West. The faster growth rate of the West continued during the post-World War II era (1950–1973) particularly in Western Europe. However, it is noteworthy that economic growth in China, several South East Asian countries and Eastern Europe ('other Europe' as shown in Figure 9.1) was above that of North America. More recently, China and certain Asian countries have achieved economic growth rates faster than both North America and Western Europe.

However, the per capita income levels in the non-Western countries (excluding Japan) remained far below those of the average Western countries. This situation had persisted for so long that many thought the economies and hence the markets of such countries were destined to lag behind those of the West.

Reference to the so-called 'ladder of industrialisation', was used to illustrate a popular view among some economists that these countries, referred to as less developed or more diplomatically developing countries, were destined to pursue a pattern of development that would follow in the footsteps of the more economically advanced countries – one rung at a time. Their economic development would progress starting with simple manufactures such as textiles, then moving on to more complex products, such as the less sophisticated machine tools and consumer goods. Ultimately developing their skills and resources to the point where they were able to produce more technologically advanced products.

The large populations of the nations in the non-Western developing country category were not seen as an asset. It has never been a secret that these countries contained

Average annual compound growth rate of per capita GDP			
Year	1820–1950	1950–73	1973–95
The West	1.27	3.64	1.80
West Europe	1.06	3.89	1.72
North America	1.58	2.45	1.54
Japan	0.81	8.01	2.53
The Rest	0.50	2.89	1.38
Other Europe	1.06	3.82	−0.75
Latin America	1.01	2.50	0.62
China	−0.24	2.87	5.37
Other Asia	0.32	2.78	2.49
Africa	0.56	2.01	−0.32
World	0.88	2.90	1.11

GDP per capita in billions of 1990 international dollars			
Year	1500	1820	1995
The West	$624	$1,149	$19,990
West Europe	670	1,269	17,456
North America	400	1,233	22,933
Japan	525	675	19,720
The Rest	$532	$594	$2,971
Other Europe	597	803	5,147
Latin America	415	671	5,031
China	600	600	2,653
Other Asia	525	560	2,768
Africa	400	400	1,221
World	$545	$675	$5,188

FIGURE 9.1   GDP: Growth rates per capita (capitalist epoch)

Note: These estimates draw on material for 1500–1995 in A. Maddison, 1995, *Monitoring the World Economy* and *Chinese Economic Performance in the Long Run*, 1998, published by the OECD Development Centre, Paris. The time series for GDP were merged with estimates of 1990 GDP derived by use of purchasing power conversions rather than exchange rates and called here 'international dollars'.

the bulk of the world's population. But large populations do not necessarily translate into large markets. The experience during much of recent history has been quite the reverse. Most of these large populations were outside the market economy. They contributed little to effective purchasing power. Large populations and rapid population growth obstructed the accumulation of capital, a critical feature of rapid economic development and the rise of major concentrations of purchasing power. It seemed logical that these countries would experience incremental economic growth, moving slowly in the wake of the more advanced economies.

Such thinking has been proved wrong. Several countries in South East Asia and elsewhere have shown that it is possible to leap-frog entire stages of economic progress, moving quickly towards the top of the ladder and surpassing in the process many countries in the more advanced, developed country category. Following the lead of Japan, Singapore, Hong Kong, Taiwan and South Korea have broken the traditional mould, they are no longer slow moving, underdeveloped economies. Far from it. They have clearly demonstrated an ability to develop their economies with surprising speed to levels comparable with those of many Western countries. Even their names, at one time unfamiliar to Western ears, are now known as the site not only of new markets but also formidable new competitors able to take on Western firms on their own ground.

These nations have demonstrated that it is possible for countries outside the West to develop the necessary political and economic infrastructure required for rapid economic growth. This, along with rapidly rising wages in the developed countries and improving corporate mobility has enabled them to attract capital and technology from abroad. International companies have been attracted, using them as a base for the production of some of their most advanced products.

In an astonishingly short space of time economies based on agriculture and crude manufactures have given way to sophisticated market economies and the emergence of a significant number of industrial companies able to compete on an equal footing with their counterparts in the West. Rising income levels have accompanied their greatly improved productivity.

These newly developed nations can no longer be described as developing. New names have been coined, such as Newly Industrialised Countries (NICs) or Mid Developing Countries. Whatever the name used to describe them, they have been transformed into the sorts of markets which most global players are eager to cultivate. This does not apply to all previously developing countries. Some of the developing countries have indeed 'emerged', others remain non-industrial and less economically developed. Just why some have been able to break the economic barriers of the past and others have not is still a subject of debate. What is evident is that there is a ferment of economic activity and growth in territories that were at one time economically insignificant.

Not far behind the first wave of such newly emerged economic powers, analogous signs of rapid economic development began to appear in Thailand, Malaysia, Indonesia, Mexico, Brazil and China. Other countries such as India and Argentina appear poised to follow this upward trend. It is this rapid growth in previously stagnant economies that qualifies the markets in these countries as 'emerging'.

Their population size now takes on a new significance. China and India alone have a combined population more than three times the total of North America plus Western Europe. Populations of this size, set on the path of rapid economic development, represent the beginnings of a historic change in the economic balance of power. This is shifting away from its traditional focus about the industrial nations around the North Atlantic, moving towards the emerging market countries, some of them in Latin America, many of them bordering the Pacific Basin.

THE EASTERN BLOC COUNTRIES

Another group of emerging markets derives from the great changes which have taken place in the former Eastern Bloc. Unlike the developing countries discussed above, Czechoslovakia, Hungary, East Germany and Poland along with other countries of Eastern Europe together with the former Soviet Union had achieved a high level of industrial development. But until recently they were part of the Warsaw Pact trade group dominated by the former Soviet Union. Currency exchange rates were fixed by the state. Markets in the sense of free exchange between suppliers and consumers were virtually non-existent. Opportunities for business with countries outside the Eastern Bloc were severely restricted. In other words, these countries were not part of the global market economy.

Emerging from the economic collapse of the Soviet Union all of these former Eastern Bloc countries have been the subject of a far reaching restructuring. Starting from a low base, the consumer markets of these countries have developed rapidly. They have become more open and market oriented. In this sense, these countries have emerged. However, their emergence is quite different from that of the developing countries discussed earlier. The markets of South East Asia and Latin America emerged from previously non-industrial, low-income economies. Their economic transformation featured the replacement of primitive means of production with more modern methods.

Most of the former Eastern Bloc countries have a long tradition of industrial production and technological achievement – in many cases equal or superior to some of their Western counterparts. In an earlier era, many of these countries had enjoyed standards comparable to their more advanced Western counterparts. A number of them were classed among Europe's leading economic powers. Emergence in their case was in fact re-emergence. Markets for the free exchange of goods and services were reintroduced where previously there had been only centrally planned production and distribution systems.

To a substantial degree these new markets have now been opened up to foreign investors outside the former Eastern Bloc. Entry barriers have been lifted. Foreign companies now invest and compete for customers in the new market environment. The newly industrialising countries of Asia and Latin America together with the newly opened economies of the former Eastern Bloc comprise the world's 'emerging market' countries. The changes taking place here have greatly altered management's view of the opportunities these countries offer. For global players, the message is one that requires little elaboration. The emerging market countries will one day comprise the bulk of the world's purchasing power. They will be the home of the bulk of their future customers. Moreover, the impact of these emerging markets on future global rivalry is likely to prove decisive in terms of the competitive positioning of the various players. Companies that succeed in marketing their products to countries like China, Brazil and India stand to gain a decisive lead on companies sticking to the old priorities, continuing to focus on traditional Western markets. No company that aims to become a major player in the global league can afford to neglect the opportunities here.

THE INTERNATIONAL PRODUCT CYCLE

The appearance of these rapidly emerging markets together with globalisation has made obsolete that favourite of academics, the international product cycle. When the various countries were relatively isolated, one from the other, it did not make much difference if new products were introduced in some markets several years after their appearance in other parts of the world. There was even a theory explaining why this should be so. Developed by Raymond Vernon, this theory offered guidance not only on the timing and location of new product introduction internationally but also where these products should be produced.[1]

Vernon points out that most new products are introduced in the markets of the 'advanced' developed countries (early versions of his theory gave particular emphasis to the United States). There are reasons for this. First, the larger size of the market and the high per capita income of consumers in these countries provide a receptive sales environment. Customers there may be expected to have both the sophisticated tastes to appreciate product innovations as well as the income to pay the higher price new products usually command during the early stages of their development.

Furthermore, in this initial stage, production of the new products is generally located in the same country in which they are marketed. Geographic proximity is typically required since the newly introduced product requires certain alterations and adjustments. These changes are best made if there is close communication between those marketing the product and those responsible for its development and production. In short, the final development of the product is greatly facilitated if both its initial production and marketing take place in the same geographic location, that is, within the same national territory. For the reasons already mentioned, this is likely to be one of the larger more advanced countries. Hence, both the first production location and the initial target market of new products is likely to be in one of these countries.

The innovating firm will begin to export the new product from this initial location. Ultimately, the product itself becomes more developed and standardised. This leads to increased pressure from competitors. Standardisation also facilitates transfer of production to developing countries, which due to their lower wages are attractive locations for new plant. In the final stage of this process, some of the 'new' products produced in developing countries are exported to the developed countries, completing the cycle (see Figure 9.2).

Many new products have actually followed such a pattern. Introduced and produced first in economically developed countries, a whole host of products, from pharmaceuticals to sewing machines, have followed this cycle. But better communications and faster reaction time have now undermined this concept.

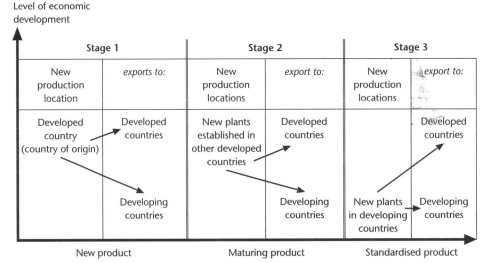

FIGURE 9.2 International product life cycle

GLOBAL REACH AND THE PRODUCT LIFE CYCLE

The improved ability to monitor and manage operations at great distances means that the link between where a product is produced and where it is launched has been broken. Geographic proximity to the market place is no longer required by product developers. Products produced and developed in one country can be launched in the distant market of another. Improved communication ensures that in developing new products the necessary feedback from the market place to those responsible for final refinements and development can be delivered quickly and effectively irrespective of distance.

Whatever the validity of Vernon's concept for an earlier era, the need for production facilities to be in the same national location as the launch market for the new product has disappeared or is rapidly disappearing. Physical presence in the same country is not required, even when the product is new. Geographic distance, while still presenting a barrier, has lost much of its power to influence locational decisions of this sort.

Another factor contributing to this change is a new perception regarding labour productivity. Not very long ago it was widely held that labour in developing countries was very much less productive than that in the more advanced economies. There was a link, it seemed obvious, between the higher productivity in this latter group of countries and their higher income levels. Labour in the less developed countries produced less, hence was thought to be less productive. To be sure, the cost of an hour of labour in these countries was lower, but once the lower labour productivity there was taken into account, there seemed to be little prospect of a net gain from locating production facilities there.

Since then the myth of higher labour productivity in the more affluent countries has been shown to be just that, a myth. Companies employing labour in the less economically developed countries have proved that employees there can reach productivity levels equal or better than those in the advanced economies, if they are similarly equipped. Capital, technology and management have been shown to be the key variables, not the labour force.

This upgrading of their production capability has radically changed the position of the developing countries in international trade. New products produced in such countries for the first time are now marketed to more advanced industrial countries. Initially concentrated on clothing and simple manufactures, this now includes more complex products.

A number of developing countries have clearly set themselves the objective of becoming producers of high technology products. Malaysia has set out to attract foreign capital to a development (the 'multimedia super corridor') which it hopes will become the Silicon Valley of Asia. Towards this end it has established an advisory panel which includes representatives from Sony, IBM, Oracle, Apple, Compaq, Sun Microsystems and others. Microsoft has set up its regional headquarters in the Malaysian capital. Malaysia will have to work hard to overtake its neighbour Singapore, which had already embarked on a similar strategy.[2] Israel is another example. It has been so successful in developing its technological exports that it long ago passed from the ranks of the developing countries.

A common thread in the endeavours of developing countries to develop their more technological industries has been an effort to attract the assistance of foreign companies. Many such firms have recognised this as an opportunity. Rather than wait to meet the products of developing countries' companies as competitors, many companies from the West have joined with them in alliances which will be mutually beneficial, contributing to their own resources and capabilities as well as those of the companies in the developing countries. Often the partners in such alliances are linked together by supplier–buyer relationships forming supply chains which have attained global dimensions.

Global supply chains

Many of the more sophisticated goods produced in these countries do not appear in consumer markets. Major companies increasingly use developing country products in their own internal production processes. An ability to capitalise on this type of international specialisation is one of the major advantages of a global company. Such companies are able to coordinate their supply chain globally. They draw their supplies wherever costs are lower and integrate goods, materials and services from sources around the world into their own global supply chains. Sometimes they employ their own production facilities in these countries as part of this process. Other arrangements include joint ventures, licensing or other contractual agreements with local producers.

The types of goods from developing countries used by such companies in their own supply chains have also changed. At one time such imports were mainly confined to raw materials and simple manufactures readily available on the open market according to standardised specifications. With difficult communications and slow transportation, integrating more specialised items into their internal production processes posed difficulties. A computer board designed and produced in Singapore will require the sort of close communication between new product development and market requirements (in other countries) mentioned by Vernon in his international product life cycle. But this close communication is now available through various electronic channels including the internet.

Today, companies with a global reach are increasingly able to source some of their most sophisticated intermediate product requirements from production sources in these countries. The production processes of such companies include imports of components for computers, machine tools, automobiles and household electronics. Nor are these supplies limited to manufactured goods. Services sourced in developing countries, such as information processing, and aircraft maintenance, are increasingly included in the supply chain of such companies (see Figure 9.3).

Competitive imitation

An even more pressing reason for abandoning the international product cycle approach to new product introduction is the growing threat of imitation. The improved ability of competitors to monitor markets around the world means that companies can no longer afford the luxury of gradually perfecting products in one market or region then

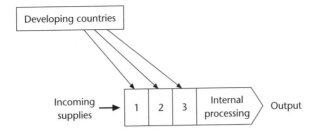

1. Raw material and commodities

2. Simple manufactured goods and equipment

3. Sophisticated manufactured goods, equipment and services

FIGURE 9.3 Developing countries and the global supply chain

launching them, perhaps years later, into other markets. Competitors with a global scanning and information processing capability are able to identify a promising product in one part of the world, copy it and launch it into other markets while the company that originated the new product is still preoccupied with perfecting it. Patents and other proprietary knowledge offer only limited protection, as the Cadbury Schweppes company found out in the case described in the previous chapter, i.e., its confectionery products were identified, imitated and launched internationally by competitors into other markets. These imitators are not necessarily global companies. Many local firms, in emerging markets and elsewhere, are adept at product imitation.

As barriers, particularly information barriers, between countries disappear, such imitation is happening more frequently, and the stakes are considerably higher. A nimble imitator need not be content with seizing a local market. With globalisation, capturing a good share of the world market with a product invented by another company has become a realistic proposition.

Global players have responded by introducing products more quickly across world markets. The gradual dissemination of new products from country to country, as per the international product cycle, has gradually given way to the global 'roll out' – the launch of globally standardised products quickly and in a planned sequence into markets around the world.[3]

This has not proved to be a complete solution. Although in theory global products are designed and planned to meet the needs of consumers worldwide, the fact is that the design of any globally standardised product represents a compromise. Any new product design will inevitably appeal to some consumers and some countries more than others. For obvious reasons, it made sense in the past to adopt designs which were biased towards the needs and preferences of consumers in the larger Western markets.

These same standardised products were also marketed in the developed and emerging market countries, but here their appeal was much narrower. Given the lower incomes and different tastes, such products appealed only to market niches consisting of customers with purchasing power and other characteristics analogous to those in the developed countries. Hence, products which were able to reach the mass of consumers in the richer countries often attained only a small proportion of consumers in the developing economies.

Research confirms that many products purchased by the great majority of households in the high income countries are purchased by only a small minority of the population in developing country markets. Washing machines, for example, are sold around the world. However, they are purchased by only a small percentage of the population in developing countries such as India. The same pattern is repeated in other developing countries across a wide variety of products, including most electronic and household items.[4]

As the emerging markets continue to develop, this will gradually change. Companies will no longer be able to structure their marketing programmes on the assumption that the richest and largest markets are in the traditional developed countries of the world. Increasingly they will find that many of the largest markets for certain products are in the former developing countries. Also that the potential for future sales growth is greatest in these countries.

This represents a dramatic change. In the past both of these features, size as well as future potential, favoured the developed countries. This fact shaped international marketing and investment decisions. In particular, it is the potential for future growth, linked to the size of their larger populations, that will be decisive in swinging management's priorities towards products and marketing programmes aimed at meeting the needs of the newly emerging market countries.

Global companies cannot afford to wait until this potential becomes fact. They cannot afford to tolerate marketing policies which treat these countries as residual markets, launching products designed primarily for the traditional industrial countries and suited only for capturing minor niches in the markets of newly emerging countries. Companies planning to take advantage of these new markets have to act well in advance, even before the emerging markets have fully emerged. They have to prepare now, launching products and marketing programmes aimed at developing the brands, company image, organisation structure and support systems, required to service the new markets.

ORGANISING FOR GLOBAL MARKETING

To better equip themselves for taking advantage of the opportunities represented by the emerging markets, global players will have to consider major changes not only in their marketing efforts, but also in the organisation structures which support these.

The purpose of the firm's organisation structure is to focus its resources and skills, taking into account the company's purpose and objectives as well as its external operating environment. For companies operating outside their domestic market, this has traditionally led to structures which gave particular prominence to distance and geography. International organisations were structured first and foremost along national lines. The various national markets with their border barriers and differences formed the basic unit of the international organisation. At another level of the hierarchy, these national units were usually aggregated into larger regional geographic areas consisting of closely adjacent countries. When travel and communication were difficult, there was an obvious logic to organisation compartments based on geographic proximity.

The diminishing importance of distance has led to a reassessment of organisations and particularly the emphasis on geographic areas. The same capabilities which enable companies today to transcend the old barriers of distance and borders have brought about a shift in the thinking on how best to organise global and international companies.

One reaction, particularly of the more global companies, has been to reorganise about features which pay less heed to geography, such as global product divisions, i.e. the head of a particular line having global responsibility over a particular product line irrespective of geographic location (see also Chapter 11).

This is not to say that geography and geographic distinctions are now eliminated. Companies continue to include geographic units as major elements of their structures, even though they tend to play a less dominant role. Global product divisions, for example, may themselves be subdivided into national and/or regional sub-compartments.

The geographic regions usually employed in organisation structures, such as 'Latin America', 'Europe', 'the Middle East' were based on closely adjacent states. But the use of the traditional regional areas in organising the global company is more a reflection of past habit and practice than current utility. With improvements in travel and communication the organisational significance of geographic proximity is changing.

Much more important today are geographic units based on a similarity of market needs and other features. The old distinction between developed and less developed countries was a step in this direction. Even when this had not been formally incorporated into the firm's organisation structure, companies operating internationally made a practical distinction in their planning as between markets in the poorer, less economically developed countries and those in the economically affluent countries. The theory of the international product cycle also reflected this distinction between rich and poor.

With distance and national boundaries becoming less relevant, the simple dichotomy between developed and developing countries is no longer applicable. For the reasons stated above, it makes little sense today to lump the emerging market countries together with developing countries which have not yet emerged. Emerging market countries represent a quite different and distinct group, with their own special needs and marketing requirements. They do not as yet have the per capita income levels of the developed countries (although some, such as Singapore, may by now have reached these levels). Neither do the emerging market countries share many of the features usually associated with developing countries. Countries such as China and India, able to launch their own space satellites and to develop their own atomic power, cannot be classed as technologically backward.

Nor are such countries necessarily deficient in management. Emerging market countries continue to require skilled managers, but the great majority of their needs can now be met by their own citizens, many of whom have graduated from the best Western universities. These can be supplemented as required by the ever more mobile consulting firms, willing and able to provide whatever expertise may be needed to whatever country requires it.

Neither are emerging markets necessarily characterised by a shortage of capital. At one point South Korea even felt the need to restrict the inflow of foreign capital. Foreign capital has of course proved important in aiding the economies of these developing countries, as is also the case with the developed countries.

Most significant of all, from the marketing point of view, these countries are characterised by rapid economic growth, including growth in consumer purchasing power beginning from very low levels of per capita income. This gives them their own special set of attributes, they are neither developed nor developing. They differ from both the less economically developed countries as well as the developed economies in terms of customer characteristics, product tastes and general marketing requirements. Global players that hope to capitalise on the new opportunities in these markets will have to adopt organisation structures that focus management resources and attention on the special needs and characteristics of this group.

National markets will continue to play a significant role in organisation structure. Customer and market related differences, from one country to another, cultural, economic and institutional, mean that national boundaries still provide significant lines of demarcation which global players must take into account.

There will still be a need to think also in terms of larger geographic units. But we may expect that, increasingly, such larger units will not comprise geographic areas in the sense of the familiar regions made up of closely adjacent countries. More often, the larger geographic units of the organisation will be country groupings, made up of countries in widely different parts of the world but with certain features in common.

Global companies and other companies that are similarly oriented will need to distinguish between at least three such multi-country groups. In the future, the markets of the economically advanced countries will increasingly be seen as a distinct group, with certain unique market features. Developing countries that have not yet emerged will comprise another such geographic market group. The emerging market countries, still another.

At the global level the task of marketing managers will be to integrate and co-ordinate the various marketing programmes and activities of the company within and across these three major geographic groups.

SUMMARY

- For the past two hundred years world trade and economic activity have been dominated by the industrialised countries around the North Atlantic Basin. The bulk of new products have been developed for these countries. Their markets represented the world's greatest concentrations of purchasing power.
- For a time it was accepted that the economies of countries outside this industrial elite would improve only slowly, following in the footsteps of the Western nations. Such thinking has proved wrong.
- Several countries in South East Asia and elsewhere have shown that it is possible to leapfrog ahead. They have produced sophisticated economies and companies able to compete on an equal footing with the West. Their emerging markets

represent the beginnings of a historic change in the balance of economic power, away from the North Atlantic.

- The former Eastern Bloc countries are also part of the emerging market group. But they are emerging from a quite different economic background. Unlike the developing countries, these nations have a history of sophisticated industrial development and technical achievement. They are emerging from the collapse of the Soviet Union's economic system.

- The emergence of these new economic powers has also made obsolete the notion of an international product cycle. In the past, many products launched into international markets did indeed follow the general pattern predicted by this concept. But better labour productivity, improved communications and the growing threat of imitation have undermined the validity of such a cycle.

- Many global companies are able to lower their costs by sourcing the production of even their most sophisticated products in developing countries, incorporating them into their supply chain. Such sourcing also includes services such as information processing.

- With rising incomes, a much larger proportion of the population of developing countries have become potential consumers, joining the market economy. Their large population size now takes on a new significance. Global companies can no longer proceed on the basis of marketing policies which regard these markets as residual consumers.

NOTES AND REFERENCES

1. Vernon, R. and Wells, L. T. Jr. (1991), *The Manager in the International Economy*, 6th edn, Prentice Hall International, pp. 5, 6, 83–6.
2. *Financial Times*, 26 February 1997, p. 4.
3. Leroy, G. P. (1976), *Multinational Product Strategy*, Praeger.
4. Leontiades, J. C. (1978), Patterns in international markets and market strategy, in M. Ghertman and J. C. Leontiades (Eds), *European Research in International Business*, Amsterdam: North Holland, pp. 239–62.

10 The headquarters role

The quickest way to lose the game is for the various members of the team to each go their own way. Teams engaged in sports, as well as companies, require some degree of coordination. For companies moving towards globalisation, this is a key issue.

If the global firm has any intrinsic characteristic which differentiate it from the traditional international business company, it is the fact that its various activities around the world are subject to a degree of coordination.

Let us recall the two basic internal capabilities of a global company:

1. **Global vision**. To be a global player, a company must have the necessary resources and systems that enable it to interpret markets, competition and those factors affecting them, such as supply sources, political change and currency movements on a global basis. In other words, it must have a world picture of the playing field. There is a great difference between the company with a global view, a grasp of world trends and market patterns and a company with an international perspective, i.e. knowledge of many different countries and regions considered separately. To achieve a global perspective requires that the firm be organised and equipped to acquire, interpret and distribute information from around the world.

2. **Global action**. A global player must also have the capability of acting globally, implementing strategies that extend beyond national and regional boundaries. Global activity in the sense of isolated operations conducted in many parts of the world is not enough. If it is to capitalise on the opportunities thrown up by a global perspective, a global player must also be able to exercise a degree of global coordination over its activities.

THE ROLE OF THE CENTRE

In order to deliver on both of the above capabilities, management must have quick access to information from around the world as well as the necessary decision making power and lines of communication which enable it to implement globally coordinated action. Coordination on this scale will not happen accidentally or by separate units of the company acting independently. It requires some form of centralised information gathering and decision making body. This is typically the role of headquarters. Within any company, there is usually at least one unit of the organisation, that is, corporate headquarters, charged with carrying out this coordinating function. In the global firm, managers and staff are appointed to various such units (usually there is more than one) to carry out the necessary worldwide coordinating functions.

But just what is required to implement such coordination and how it is best done have been subjects of much debate. The key issue in such debate has been the relationship of the coordinating centre or centres to the periphery. That is, the relationship between some form of central headquarters and locally based managers responsible for carrying out the firm's business in the various countries in which it operates. The issues here have been a topic of considerable controversy, particularly with respect to the multinational company and the coordination of its foreign based subsidiaries. Furthermore, it is not difficult to show that many of the same issues discussed here with reference to multinational companies are also applicable as between exporters and their relations with local agents.

In dealing with the centre/periphery relationship, companies have sought to locate the best balance between coordination from the centre and the freedom of local management to make its own local decisions. In striking this balance, both the local unit as well as the global headquarters may claim to have certain strengths which the other does not.

The local manager, operating on the spot, has a closer and more detailed view of local developments and events which are vital to the firm's operations. But to ask a manager located in, say, Brazil to help coordinate the firm's various operations in Japan, Singapore, Greece or Canada is unrealistic. Managers in charge of local operations for a particular national or regional territory will have all they can do to keep abreast of the requirements of the local business.

Developing the overview which gives the global company its vision requires the participation of some form of coordinating centre, i.e. a headquarters charged with this responsibility and equipped with the necessary staff and communications to carry it out.

What is the proper division of labour between the two? Managers at the headquarters centre, viewing the firm's operations globally may claim that they have a better perspective on the big picture. They are better able to see threats and opportunities in parts of the world that are beyond the vision of the local manager focused on operations in a particular country or region. Locally based managers have a more intimate and immediate perception of local events. They are better placed to 'feel' the local environment, the trends, the shades of feeling that are difficult to communicate in written or electronic form.

Both have their particular strengths. The question is one of arriving at the best balance, between local and global perspectives. The difficulty of achieving such a balance is reflected in the many changes that occur in the relationship between headquarters and the various local units. These also underline the many different forms this relationship can take.

THREE HEADQUARTERS ROLES

The various roles of headquarters outlined below are used to illustrate the major choices open to management in establishing this relationship, i.e. the role of the coordinating centre vis-à-vis that of its local operating units.

The headquarters as banker

Management's responsibility to shareholders requires a certain minimum of supervisory and information gathering activity by a central headquarters acting on behalf of the firm's top management. This minimalist banker role requires that the diverse company operating units supply the coordinating centre with information on their sales, profits and other financial data used to monitor their performance. Such information enables headquarters to assess the financial performance of the firm's international operations against budget targets. Are costs in line with expectations? Are revenue targets being met? Is liquidity in line with good accounting practice?

It also serves as the basis for resource allocation decisions – portfolio type decisions made centrally on where new investment on the part of the parent company is warranted and where (which countries') poor performance may indicate potential areas of disinvestment.

The banker role has the advantage of minimal interference with the firm's locally based managers. Even with all the recent technical advances, the firm's local managers in a particular country are inevitably closer to the customer and have a more complete grasp of local conditions than a more remote headquarters. Living in the local environment, they are insiders. By giving them virtually full decision making power, this role enables them to take advantage of their closeness and feel for the local conditions. They are able to respond quickly and flexibly to local markets and competition.

Headquarters will require these local units to supply certain information on their financial performance but, otherwise, the freedom of local managers to make their own decisions is not affected. In other words, the centre intrudes as little as possible into the actual running of the firm's various international operations.

In this role, headquarters is not equipped to maintain close day-to-day contact with markets and competition in different parts of the world. It has neither the ability to 'see' global trends and opportunities nor the authority, other than in financial matters, to take the sort of action that requires global coordination.

The Italian firm Alleviate at one time stated that its policy with reference to its various businesses in North America was one of local autonomy – 'Our aim is to leave them independent under local management'.[1] Consistent with this view, strategy at the centre was mainly limited to portfolio decisions concerned with resource allocation and associated activities such as: identifying new investment opportunities, monitoring business performance of the locally based international units and reducing company commitment in cases where performance was below acceptable limits or the business activities of the local units were not considered to be in line with company objectives.

BOX 10.1

An emphasis on financial analysis

Throughout most of its history, Arnold Weinstock managed one of Britain's largest companies, GEC Ltd. From a tiny London office, supported only by a few assistants, he pulled the disparate companies which made up the GEC enterprise together into one of Europe's most successful firms.

Each of GEC's many component firms was headed by a general manager who reported directly to Lord Weinstock. Each manager was in charge of a business and enjoyed considerable freedom to make whatever decisions he or she thought appropriate. Relations with other parts of the firm outside this business were not part of the manager's responsibility. The performance of each such company was personally reviewed periodically by Lord Weinstock and assessed individually. A trained statistician, Weinstock judged the performance of the various businesses against a set of financial ratios, such as return on capital, working capital to sales, inventory and liquidity. Profits above a certain level were sent to the central headquarters which in turn determined what new investment would be made in the various businesses and new business opportunities.

For many years, the formula worked, catapulting GEC into the ranks of the top performing companies and the accumulation of a cash mountain of some 18 billion dollars. It is still a giant of the industry. More recently, the company's share price has underperformed that of some of its rivals, notably that of General Electric of the United States. Some observers have noted that GEC has not assumed a leading role in any of the new technologies, such as computers, integrated circuits, software, mobile telephones, etc. ■

The federal headquarters

Headquarters in this type of role is much more active. It fulfils all of the above banker role functions. Over and above this it acts as facilitator – providing the basis for international coordinated activity on a discretionary, ad hoc, basis. For example, it may sponsor conferences at which managers from various parts of the world are able to meet periodically and exchange information and ideas. Parent company staff are able to update the firm's foreign based managers on recent company innovations and product developments. Whether this information is used remains at the discretion of local managers.

This type of headquarters may also provide assistance to local units in the form of information on global marketing trends, news on competitor moves and strategies, new industry technical developments, suggestions and ideas on cost and sales improvement, global marketing campaigns and so on. It may also provide material assistance in the form of specialist technical staff and advice, assistance to foreign units with new product development and implementing new types of marketing programmes as well as training. The company's various international businesses are invited to make use of such information and assistance, as they choose. International coordination in the form of global advertising campaigns, joint marketing strategies, timing of product launches, etc., are encouraged but not mandatory.

The centre relies on persuasion, information and communication to mobilise the efforts of its locally based managers. Decision making power, however, remains firmly in the hands of local managers. Under this system local managers are still clearly accountable for their performance, while the centre makes available new ideas, methods and other suggestions which may assist them.

The global headquarters

In this role, the centre takes on added powers, going beyond discretionary coordination. In the global enterprise, there are certain activities and functions requiring global coordination that cannot be carried out on an ad hoc basis.

If, for example, components from one country are sent to be combined with parts produced in another part of the world into a common product, the various flows have to be closely coordinated. In this capacity, headquarters may require and not just persuade, the local managers of its various international operations to follow specific plans of action and timing which ensure that such coordination is successful.

Analogously, the firm seeking to develop global competencies, such as implementing a service which gives a uniform standard of assistance to customers around the world, will find that it must coordinate its operations globally.

Headquarters in this role must be equipped with the necessary staff to both gather and interpret information on a global basis. Within a small, localised organisation, such as the corner grocery store, informal systems and direct observation may yield sufficient information on which to base strategy and other management decisions. In the case of companies with geographically dispersed activities and interests in different parts of the world only a small portion of the information management needs to know to implement global coordination is available at first hand. Purposely developed information systems are necessary to gather, filter and channel the required data. This includes not only financial information but a wide range of data on competition, political, product and marketing trends. Information on markets, competitors, technical data, professional advice and services. Information flows both to and from the headquarters to its various foreign based operations.

Headquarters in this role is much more proactive. If successful, it can ensure a degree of global coordination not attainable under the previous two roles. But its very involvement in decisions affecting local managers carries certain drawbacks. In particular, some of the advantages of the local responsiveness, local accountability, speed and flexibility associated with the banker headquarters role may be lost. The discretion of local managers to make their own coordinating decisions, a feature of the federal role, is also lacking.

There is no single best role or best balance. The right balance varies with the firm's own strategy and objectives and the type of company it wants to be. It also varies over time with changing circumstances and particularly, with changes in management's global reach. Figure 10.1 summarises the positive and negative features of the three roles.

Banker role

Positive features:
- Clear local accountability and control
- Small headquarters staff (small expense)
- Few layers of management between local and global management
- Contributes to the early development of general managers

Negative features:
- Minimal lateral cooperation between local units
- Short term focus on annual results
- Inability to mobilise overall company resources
- Minimal or non-existent global strategy

Federal role

Positive features:
- Clear local accountability and control
- Offers opportunity for sharing and coordination with other local units
- Provides local managers with insight into opportunities beyond the scope of their local unit operations
- Contributes to the early development of general managers

Negative features:
- Voluntary nature of local cooperation makes global planning and strategy difficult and uncertain
- Difficult to reconcile accountability for local performance with global cooperation and coordination

Global role

Positive features:
- Able to mobilise resources and ideas of local units across the entire company behind global objectives and strategies
- Able to monitor the global competitive and market environment
- Able to identify market and competitive initiatives not visible at local level
- Able to develop global competencies
- Local managers gain international experience

Negative features:
- Loss of clear accountability at local level
- Loss of unrestricted freedom of local managers to make local decisions
- Higher cost
- May be subject to some loss of flexibility and speed of decision making

---

FIGURE 10.1 Characteristics of the three headquarters roles

THE REAL ROLE OF HEADQUARTERS

The role of any headquarters is to add value. Personnel employed in the headquarters may be busy going here and there carrying out numerous tasks but if at the end of the day these activities do not add value they are not worth doing.

For example, it has been proved that the total value represented by some companies is greater when they have been split into their component parts and then sold as separate businesses. Whatever coordination was implemented from the corporate centre of such companies was clearly not adding value. If it had been, the whole should have been worth more than the sum of its parts. Where headquarters does add value, the removal of the coordination it provides will result in tangible loss.

To add value a headquarters should be doing something (or doing it better) that the various operating units of the company cannot do on their own. Whether this adds value depends not only on the added income or revenue that may be attained, but also on the cost of the coordination itself. Like most things in business, a cost benefit analysis is called for. Both costs and benefits depend on the type of enterprise, its strategy and aims.

A conglomerate comprising highly independent businesses can probably get along very well with a small headquarters, fashioned along the general lines of the banker model. Certainly there are global companies that manage with only a small headquarters staff. However, implementing a global service network able to service customers uniformly in any part of the world, for example, will require a staff equipped with the necessary information gathering capability and the power to coordinate service standards as well as flows of information, finance and resources. Does this mean a large headquarters?

Percy Barnevic, chief executive officer of ABB Asea Brown Boveri, would say 'no'. His company, one of the leaders in globalisation with operations divided into something like 1200 companies, functions very well with a global headquarters of only 100 professionals. The company's division into large numbers of small units operating with considerable autonomy and a dedication to decentralisation are part of the secret. Alongside the autonomy of the operating units is the fact that the firm's country managers 'must respect ABB's global objectives'. They have to cooperate with global managers. Mr Barnevic does not hide the contradictions which must be overcome in being simultaneously big and little, centralised and decentralised.[2]

The optimal headquarters role is likely to change as the forces underlying both the costs and benefits of the global headquarters change over time. Most recently, these forces have been changing in favour of coordination on a global scale, i.e. in the direction of the global headquarters role. The greater similarity of tastes and preferences (convergence) taking place between consumers in different countries has undoubtedly added to the potential benefits of headquarters coordination, as in the case of producing globally standardised products and services.

GLOBAL COORDINATION COSTS

Changes in technology have greatly reduced the costs of global coordination. The costs of global reach have declined drastically and every indication is that this will continue. However, there are also costs associated with global coordination which still remain substantial and should not be underestimated. They deserve careful consideration.

Loss of morale and motivation

The greatest cost associated with global coordination is the possible loss of motivation and morale of locally based managers due to what may be perceived as the intrusion of the headquarters into local affairs. Companies switching from the banker or federal role to a more global headquarters orientation may expect that their locally based managers will face a difficult period of adjustment. Some may feel that they have lost their authority and freedom of action.

This is further aggravated when the headquarters managers and staff are seen to be insensitive and out of touch with local conditions. The main issue, however, is the shift of certain decisions which were formerly carried out locally to central headquarters.

Unless carefully managed, this sort of cost can obviate all the advantages of globalisation. No matter what the benefits of global coordination, it cannot deliver the goods if the bulk of the firm's managers become alienated.

General Motors encountered major difficulties at its German Opel subsidiary when its drive towards globalisation met stiff resistance from locally based managers. In response to GM's efforts to coordinate decision making from its international headquarters, there were outcries to the effect that 'Opel needs more independence'. Local managers were upset at what they saw to be an effort by GM to centralise control of the company's worldwide product development. The prestigious chairman of Opel's supervisory board resigned, further embarrassing the company.[3]

For many companies going global the adverse impact of this sort of friction is an all too painful reality. Research shows that active opposition to such coordination is not an isolated event.[4] Firms in this situation have to plan if they hope to minimise it. For example, it is quite possible for local managers to interpret attempts to move towards the global headquarters role as a one way street, i.e. a loss of their authority and opportunities. But there are also benefits. It is possible, through training and planning, to point these out and make maximum use of the new job opportunities opened up by globalisation.

One possibility for reducing the scope for such alienation lies in the new career paths on offer. Managers who at one time were limited to job opportunities in a particular location have, within the context of the global corporation, greater chances for taking advantage of new career opportunities in other parts of the company in other locations. Globalisation generally opens up new career paths, breaking down former career path constraints.

Another approach lies in demonstrating the capability and associated benefits of a global headquarters in providing assistance to local units. The same improvement in communications and information technology which is sometimes seen as undermining the authority of local managers also makes possible much greater support for these same managers in the way of information, technical and marketing assistance. The headquarters relationship with local units must become a two way street.

BOX 10.2
Information support from headquarters

International Paint Ltd is in the business of providing marine paint to ships and sea based structures. The parent company has developed a computerised information system which tracks ship repairs and painting around the world. Trained inspectors monitor the main dry docks of world shipping. They record the condition and needs of ships brought in for repainting using standardised procedures. Information on ship maintenance is then reported back to central headquarters which uses the raw data to interpret and project global ship painting requirements, identifying individual ships.

This information is fed back to the firm's various international affiliates, assisting them in interpreting the extent and nature of future demand requirements. Information thus provided also serves as a powerful marketing tool, enabling company representatives to approach potential customers with useful advice on their needs, just as they are due to make decisions on repairs and painting. ■

Loss of accountability

An important associated cost is loss of accountability. Where headquarters actively coordinates the activities of local units it automatically assumes a responsibility for the outcomes, the results of such coordination. With increasing cross-national integration the ability clearly to identify which manager is responsible for which result is made more difficult (see also Chapter 12).

Increased coordinating costs

Even with improvements in technology the costs of communication, travel and global coordination are not negligible. Integrating the various threads of the firm's far flung operations – keeping close touch with events unfolding in many parts of the world – represents an expense as well as a burden on the travel budgets (and stomachs) of headquarters managers attempting to maintain even limited personal contact with local developments in different parts of the world. There are certain global communication barriers that cannot be fully overcome, even with the most advanced technology. Differences in time zones are an example.

Risks

Coordinating the firm's activities on a global scale also introduces certain risks which translate into costs. Global coordination of production processes means that problems, such as a work stoppage, technical fault, adverse exchange rate movements, even revolutions, in one part of the organisation's distant operations, may affect the entire global enterprise. Management may attempt to minimise such risks by providing duplicate and triplicate facilities. The fact remains that compared with the independent operations characteristic of the banker type headquarters, the interdependence inherent in global coordination increases such risk.

In Europe the labour strikes that used to characterise many seaports and recent blockages of the Channel Tunnel by farmers and others graphically illustrate the threat of stoppages. Companies with closely coordinated production facilities on either side of the English Channel run the risk that their operations on both sides will cease functioning.

Political costs

There is a perception by many governments that companies that are a part of closely integrated global networks are less sensitive to local needs. Such companies may be at a disadvantage in seeking government contracts or other forms of government related assistance. Companies involved in defence contracts and other nationally sensitive areas are particularly subject to such political costs.

Human costs

Although mobility from one country to another has physically become much easier, frequent geographic change can have a real cost in terms of psychological stress and family relations. Such mobility is accepted by some managers better than others. Certainly, there are even those who see advantages in moving periodically from one country to another, enjoying the challenge and the opportunity to come into contact with new cultures and different nationalities. On balance, however, an increase in geographic relocation should be counted as part of the costs of a global enterprise – even though difficult to quantify.

PLANNING

To what degree the above costs, particularly those associated with alienation of local managers, are actually realised will depend very much on the way the headquarters function itself is managed. Whether 'headquarters' is perceived as an intrusive nuisance, getting in the way of the actual running of the business or something constructive which adds value depends very much on how it approaches the interpersonal aspects of global coordination. As indicated earlier, any contribution headquarters can make to assist local units in managing their businesses, whether it be in the form of information on potential customers, technical advice or other forms of assistance will make for a positive relationship. An emphasis on methods and processes which enrol the participation of local, foreign based, management in negotiation and dialogue with headquarters is seen as particularly useful.

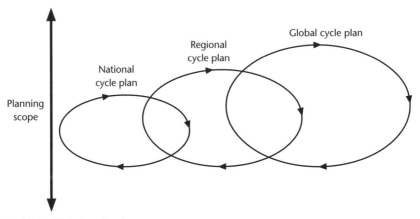

FIGURE 10.2 Global cycle plan

Source: From Leontiades, J. C. (1985), *Multinational Corporate Strategy*, Lexington Books.

The planning process

The planning process can provide the basis for such a dialogue. A growing number of firms are using planning cycles to develop a shared global vision and as a basis for global coordination (Figure 10.2). The term 'cycle' refers to the fact that plans are reviewed and revised annually.

To begin the process, global headquarters indicates in broad terms the firm's global objectives over the next planning period. Units at the local national level take these as starting points on which to base their own plans. Certain local units will be better able than others to comply with the stated objectives. National planning proposals feed into the early stages of regional planning. There will be feedback and exchange between local and regional plans. Similarly, regional plans in their preliminary stage feed into the early stages of global planning. Again there is discussion and adjustment of plans leading to the final global plan. The process depends on communication, negotiation and give and take between the different units involved. Planning is used as an instrument for bringing about coordination through communication and mutual agreement. It encourages dialogue and understanding between the different parts of the organisation.

Properly done, such a planning procedure involves the firm's national and regional managers around the world in a series of discussions with global headquarters staff. Negotiated planning of this sort is superior to both the centralised, top-down approach to planning as well as the simplistic bottom-up method. Unlike the latter, the global plan in such cases is not simply the sum of local plans developed in isolation, as was so frequently the case in international companies. The give and take inherent in the process described is aimed at bringing together the thinking as well as the local plans of the firm's various units into a coordinated overall global plan.

The timing of the planning cycles in different parts of the firm is synchronised so that the results of local plans are finished early enough to feed into the development of regional plans, the latter used as input into an overall global plan.

Decentralised headquarters

The decentralisation of the headquarters function itself can also make a difference. For the sake of simplicity the above discussion has focused on a headquarters as a single coordinating unit, the 'corporate headquarters'. This has, in fact, been the usual practice. But global coordination need not depend on any single unit of the organisation. The use of multiple headquarters, as opposed to a single parent company headquarters, serves to decentralise the headquarters function and to reduce the alienation so often associated with 'orders' emanating from a single, overpowerful central headquarters.

Global coordination involving multiple headquarters units located in different countries removes the association of any particular country as the source of global 'orders' together with the negative feelings that this may give rise to. The company's local French subsidiary may be assigned the task of coordinating global strategy for the production and marketing of product X. Another headquarters may have the role of coordinating product Y. Still other headquarters units in different countries may be assigned similar global coordinating roles in other specialised areas. Such multiple coordinating units located in different national or regional centres are also able to incorporate a wider range of the firm's personnel resources and expertise into the coordinating function.

With today's much improved communication capability even a single coordinating headquarters unit might have its personnel spread geographically over several countries, its members exchanging information and making decisions through electronic means – a 'virtual headquarters'.

Companies, particularly those engaged in globalisation, have been innovative in developing different types of headquarters units, such as those described below, aimed at bringing about the coordination they feel they require.

Competence centres

A local unit (e.g. a subsidiary) which has been particularly effective in producing a particular product or component may be designated as a leader or competence centre. Such centres serve as models for other parts of the firm, coordinating the flow of advice and special knowledge to other local subsidiaries on how to produce and market specified products. For example, a particular international affiliate may be designated as the competence centre for one of Unilever's soap products. Other parts of the company producing the same product will take their lead from this competence centre – which provides them with advice and coordinates the firm's global strategy for producing and marketing this particular product worldwide. Another affiliate of the same company, in a different part of the world, may serve as a competence centre for another product line. Competence centres may also advise on marketing and other functional areas. They may be made responsible for developing new methods and techniques for their particular competence.

This type of international specialisation, assigning to the part of the firm's organisation which excels in a particular area a lead role, makes maximum use of special locally available competence while contributing to the development of management talent within the global organisation.

Global product mandates

Another variation on this type of decentralised coordination is the so-called global product mandate – the arrangement which designates a particular plant or business of the firm as exclusive supplier of a specific product or service for all other parts of the company. Global firms trying to obtain maximum benefit from efficiencies of scale may designate many such production centres, each focusing on the production of a particular product or component to meet the company's worldwide requirements.

Global project teams

Project teams able to move between the company's operations in different parts of the world often serve as mobile coordinating units. Such teams are receiving increasing attention as a means of integrating the skills, background and cultural differences of managers from diverse countries and regions. Usually established on a temporary basis to carry out a specific assignment, they provide an effective means of cutting across the established power structure – in effect circumventing the formal hierarchy and bringing together participants from diverse parts of the company. The use of teams formed on a temporary basis to carry out a specific task enables the company to go outside the established organisation structure, selecting and combining managers and experts from diverse parts of the firm with the skills and experience especially suited to the job at hand.

The style and impact of global coordination will also depend on the mix of the various coordinating mechanisms employed by management, as outlined in the following chapter.

SUMMARY

- A global company must have quick access to information around the world and the ability to act on it in a coordinated way. This requires a centralised unit able to receive and process information, i.e. a headquarters. There is considerable debate as to what form this should take. What is the appropriate relationship between such a centre and locally based managers?

- There are three distinct headquarters roles which may be used to illustrate the options open to global players. The headquarters as banker is one such option. There is also the federal headquarters role and the global headquarters role.

- More generally, the role of any headquarters is to add value. For the global company, this does not necessarily require a large headquarters staff. Technology has greatly reduced the costs of headquarters coordination, but significant costs remain.

- The greatest potential cost of global coordination is the loss of morale and motivation among local managers. Measures which reduce such costs include developing new career paths for local managers and the use of headquarters to provide concrete assistance to local units.

- A planning process which involves headquarters in an interactive dialogue with local units can also contribute to a constructive headquarters relationship. Other methods include the decentralising of the headquarters function, the use of competence centres, global product mandates and international project teams.

NOTES AND REFERENCES

1. *Financial Times*, 8 November 1982, p. 12.
2. Taylor, W. (1991), The logic of global business, *Harvard Business Review*, March–April, pp. 91–105.
3. *The Wall Street Journal Europe*, 26 October 1998, p. 1.
4. Prahalad, C. K. and Doz, Y. L. (1981), Strategic control – the dilemma in headquarters–subsidiary relationship, in L. Otterbeck (Ed.), *The Management of Headquarters–Subsidiary Relationships in Multinational Corporations*, Aldershot: Gower, pp. 187–203.

11 Organising for global operations: structure and other coordinating mechanisms

One of the more well established beliefs in management is that a company's organisation structure follows its strategy. If this is true, then it means that companies pursuing globalisation as part of their strategy will have to change their organisation structures accordingly.

In fact, companies operating internationally have for years modified their structures to suit the particular requirements of international operations. Most evident in the case of both European and American multinationals has been the tendency of such companies to organise themselves along geographic lines. The firm's business in country A was considered as a distinct part of the organisation, quite separate from the business in country B. The multi-domestic type of multinational company represented the extreme form of this emphasis on geography, with authority and responsibility allocated to nearly autonomous subsidiaries.

This traditional structure does not fit well with the increasingly global outlook and cross-border activities that characterise today's world of business. As discussed earlier in this text, the practice of treating national units of the firm as virtually self-contained businesses drew much its justification from the poor communications environment that characterised the early development of companies operating internationally. Today's low cost, instant communications through the internet and other electronic media forms have removed such constraints. Strategies have changed. There is greater emphasis on cross-border rivalry, marketing, mergers and other initiatives. The result is a major re-examination by companies regarding their preferred form of organisation structure. In company after company, we have witnessed a series of reorganisations. Something that used to happen every decade or so, reorganising the firm, has become much more frequent. Nowhere is this more apparent than in companies with a major commitment to international/global operations.

To appreciate the nature of such change and its implications for the organisation of global companies, it will be helpful to consider the structure of the earlier international firms. In this chapter we shall first examine the formal organisation structure of such companies, that is, the organisational hierarchy as reflected in the familiar flowchart diagrams.

EARLY ORGANISATION STRUCTURE

The organisation structure of international firms was often an extension of the firm's domestic structure. For example, companies which began their international experience through exports looked on the network of agencies marketing the firm's products outside the home market as simply a continuation of their domestic distribution facilities. Exporting is still sometimes referred to as 'extended distribution'. The firm's export department was not infrequently simply an extension of its sales department. But as sales grew and the company gained experience, more specialised organisation forms appeared.

The international division

There was a particular need for major changes in organisation in companies investing abroad, the multinationals. The generally larger scale of their foreign operations and commitments called for an organisation form which allowed greater priority and focus on the firm's international activities. American multinationals approached organisation from a background of experience in their large domestic market. In that context many of the larger American firms already had extensive experience with the divisional form of organisation.[1] With this as a background, adapting the divisional structure to their international operations was a natural step.

The divisional form of organisation structure divides the firm's various operations into a number of largely self-contained units. Headed by a general manager, each division is equipped with its own staff and support services. In its most popular form, each division is organised around a particular product (using this term to include services) or product group.

Distinctions between one division and another could also be made according to other criteria, including function. The general managers of the various divisions would be supported by the division's own staff specialists in finance, marketing, research and whatever other specialist services were required. Within large scale organisations, the cost of such support services and staff was acceptable. The divisionalised form is a particularly flexible structure which has proved itself well suited to many types of firms and situations.

For multinational companies the division structure provided a convenient organisation form readily adaptable to international operations. All international operations were typically grouped into a single 'international division'. Within the multinational

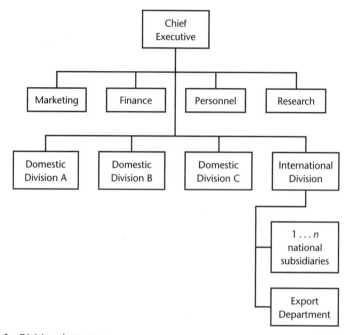

FIGURE 11.1 Divisional structure

Source: From Leontiades, J. C. (1985), *Multinational Corporate Strategy*, Lexington Books.

company, the main building block of the international division was the national subsidiary, each of the firm's subsidiaries established as a separate company operating under the laws of the country where it was domiciled. The simplest form of this structure is to be found in the single product company with each subsidiary having national jurisdiction (Figure 11.1).

The international division had the advantage of focusing the firm's international assets and expertise under a unified management team dedicated to international operations. It also performed the very important function of keeping the productive assets of this group separate from the competing demands of the generally larger and more numerous domestic divisions. Despite this, the international division still remained the junior partner, almost invariably outnumbered by a greater number of domestic divisions within the same firm, with their own domestic priorities. This meant at the very top management levels, i.e. meetings of the various division heads, overall decision making power was weighted in favour of the domestic divisions. These were naturally concerned first and foremost with their own problems, that is to say domestic concerns and priorities.

Where there was a conflict of interest between divisions, such as the allocation of investment funds or the allocation of scarce product supply during periods of rapidly rising demand, there was an in-built tendency to favour domestic concerns and interests above those of the international division.

Nevertheless, this type of organisation has shown itself to be remarkably flexible and suited to a wide range of situations and strategies. The international division structure has proved very adaptable, offering many possibilities for supplementing the formal chart relationships between the various units with other means for bringing about the required coordination.[2] It remains today one of the most widely used structural types, particularly by American companies. It is still used by many companies moving towards globalisation.

The European approach

European companies, starting their international expansion from smaller domestic markets favoured the less elaborate 'mother–daughter' structure.[3] The typical European multinational began as a domestic company organised according to function. As the company extended its operation to other countries, it simply established new, smaller versions of the parent company, as shown in Figure 11.2. These 'daughters' reported directly to the president of the parent company. These structures developed quite naturally, the relatively short distances between the various countries facilitating travel and direct contact with the parent company.

Personal visits by the chief executive to the daughter companies were the major means of monitoring and managing the firm's international operations. Relations between the daughter companies and the parent relied heavily on such visits. If the chief executive of a French parent firm, visits the company's new operations in nearby countries such as Switzerland or Germany the fact that these are foreign based daughter companies presents few special problems. The foreign subsidiary might actually be closer and more convenient than certain of the parent company's domestic operations.

The mother–daughter structure has much to commend it, especially for companies with a small number of foreign based daughter companies. A small staff and the absence

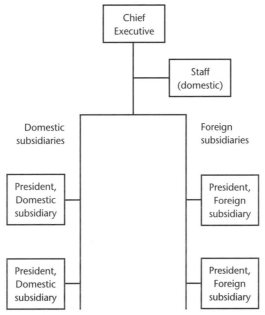

FIGURE 11.2 Mother–daughter structure
Source: From Leontiades, J. C. (1985), *Multinational Corporate Strategy*, Lexington Books.

of multiple layers of management between the chief executive of the company and locally based, front line managers, contributes to a lean responsive organisation. Also, the fact that both domestic and international units report directly to the same executive facilitates coordination.

Unlike the international division structure, the president in such organisations usually lacks the assistance of a specialised international staff to collect, interpret and process information from the firm's various operating companies. The chief executive gathers information and issues instructions by travelling to the various international operations, meeting directly with the managers of the firm's various local units, in much the same way as with the firm's domestic operations. The chief executive is responsible for overseeing both the domestic and foreign operations of the company. It is a highly personal form of structure, with much face-to-face contact and few organisational layers between the top of the hierarchy and personnel involved directly with operations.

But as the firm expands, a company of this sort may easily encompass 30 to 50 daughter companies scattered across 20 or 30 countries as well as many domestic operations. To maintain personal contact through (necessarily) brief flying visits, provides little time for evaluating and understanding the local situations of the various daughter companies. The chief executive visiting the firm's foreign based operations will be called upon to interpret and discuss operational and strategic matters which relate to many distinct businesses, each focused about a particular country with its own distinctly different political, legal and cultural environment. Such a visiting executive from the mother company, exercising authority but with little knowledge of the local situation and with little responsibility for results (this remained with local management), may all too easily be seen by local managers as an intruder.

Significantly, the larger European multinationals such as Ciba-Geigy, Nestlé and Philips have led the trend away from the mother–daughter type of organisation towards more global structures.

TOWARDS GLOBAL STRUCTURES

Globalisation with its emphasis on cross-border coordination and vision has caused firms to rethink their existing organisation structures. There has appeared a search and a willingness to consider alternatives to the emphasis formerly placed on the nation state as the primary building block of international organisations. How does the global firm reconcile the need for worldwide coordination of its activities with the fact that it must adjust and remain responsive to many diverse operating environments? This is the same issue addressed in the previous chapter in relation to the role of headquarters. The following sections take up this theme in the broader context of the firm's overall organisation structure.

Global coordination and decentralisation

Current thinking on organisations in general stresses the usefulness of flat organisations and local empowerment. There is a perceived need to provide maximum authority and freedom of decision making to the manager who is on the spot, close to the customer. A need to reduce the restrictive effect of hierarchical management pyramids.[4] These findings exist uncomfortably, side by side, with the equally urgent requirement by global companies for worldwide coordination.

Reconciling the one with the other, local authority for the man on the spot with the need for wider coordination, has been the cause of much debate in the literature. One of the more popular themes has been that organisations sharply reduce or even abandon hierarchical type structures altogether.[5] Despite considerable appeal, the most radical suggestion (eliminating hierarchy) has so far found little representation in fact. Even the organisations held up as examples of non-hierarchical businesses, such as universities and consulting firms, still retain structures that are not only hierarchical but need to be so in order to function. Indeed, those with first hand experience in such organisations are among the first to deny that they have to any substantial degree eliminated the role of hierarchy.

Companies operating globally face a particularly difficult task. Even those that favour local autonomy will encounter situations where a degree of coordination is considered desirable, but as the head of a major service company exclaimed 'How do you get 22,000 people around the globe to face the same direction at the same time?'[6]

If there is to be some form of hierarchy – and all evidence points to this fact – then it seems logical that management should attempt to identify and avoid its better known and more obvious problems. Perhaps the most famous of these has to do with 'overcentralisation', excessive power at the centre, towards the top of the organisational hierarchy. Any proposed change in the firm's organisation soon raises a debate over the issue of centralisation versus decentralisation and the apparent conflict between the two.

BOX 11.1

An attempted solution

The debate is one with a lengthy history. Alfred P. Sloan, the well known industrialist and writer, felt he had found the answer. Sloan was looking for a formula that would provide a structure that would neither be too weak, with too little hierarchical coordination, nor too rigid and command oriented. He summed up his solution in his famous and deceptively simple prescription of 'decentralized operations with central control'.[7] This aimed to provide coordination across the entire enterprise (central control) but with maximum flexibility at the local level (decentralised operations). Many years later, looking back, Sloan noted the inherent contradiction in his prescription. The first requirement is inconsistent with the second. Operations cannot be fully decentralised if there is to be central control. There is always a compromise between the two – which is more or less where we started from. ■

Unfortunately, the discussion and focus on centralisation versus decentralisation has proved to be sterile. The very terms are confusing and often misleading. For example, a shift of certain responsibilities away from the corporate central head office, say in New York, to a regional coordinating headquarters in, say, Geneva may appear to management at the centre as a move towards decentralisation. Responsibility and authority have moved away from the centre to a more peripheral unit. However, to the national units of the company, the fact that such responsibility and authority is now exercised by regional managers who are much closer and have a more detailed knowledge of their own (local) situation, will very likely appear to them as reducing their own freedom to act and decide for themselves, in other words a step towards greater centralisation.

Similarly, devolving authority to a cross-national team charged with carrying forward a specific global project for the firm may appear as a move towards decentralisation to those at the corporate centre. The same move may strike the firm's local business units (receiving visits from the team) as a change towards greater interference from the centre.

While the centralisation/decentralisation terminology is best avoided, there are nevertheless, real issues to be addressed in developing organisation structures that reconcile the need for global coordination with freedom for local managers to make decisions that make best use of their local knowledge and speed of response.

THE SEARCH FOR ALTERNATIVES

There are no pat formulas. However, it is possible to identify a few useful guidelines for structuring the global organisation. For the early multinationals, an international organisation structure consisting of nationally focused local units with a high degree of autonomy, was probably a necessity. But for a global company, any structure based on units that divide and separate the various parts of the firm according to national or regional boundaries represents a contradiction.

The global organisation should avoid distinctions based on categories such as 'domestic' and 'international' or 'home' and 'foreign'. In the context of the global enterprise, these are outmoded concepts. The aim should be an organisation which places all parts of the company on an equal footing, avoiding distinctions and divisions based purely on location and nationality.

One should also keep in mind that every organisation structure has its own particular advantages and disadvantages. Management has to decide which of these represents the best balance of advantage with reference to their firm's own particular situation. The technological change which has brought about global rivalry and the rise of the global corporation has shifted the balance of advantage towards organisation structures which do not stop at national borders. Previous chapters have outlined the competitive and marketing advantages of global coordination which advances in communication have recently made much more accessible at a lower cost. Pursuing such advantages, the global company today should aim for a structure which turns geographic differences into an asset, utilising the various international operations of the firm in a coordinated manner irrespective of national or other geographic/political boundaries.

The search for alternative organisation structures which incorporate some or all of these qualities has led a number of firms to move away from the more traditional organisations discussed above towards so-called global organisation structures – such as those we describe below.

Global area structures

Global area structures move the organisation away from the nation state as the basic building block, segmenting it according to major geographic regions. As indicated in Figure 11.3, each major region has its own area executive and headquarters.

Below the chief executive of each area, a further segmentation of the organisation may be based on national units. For example, as in the figure, the head of each national unit reports to the area executive. National boundaries in this type of organisation have not disappeared, but they are now secondary, each national manager reporting to an area executive responsible for coordinating national activities within the region. The overall chief executive of the corporation oversees fewer geographic compartments and is better able to keep close contact with the fewer managers in charge of the various geographic areas. The danger of course is that division of the company by national units, as in the older organisation forms, is simply replaced by another (regional) geographic dividing line.

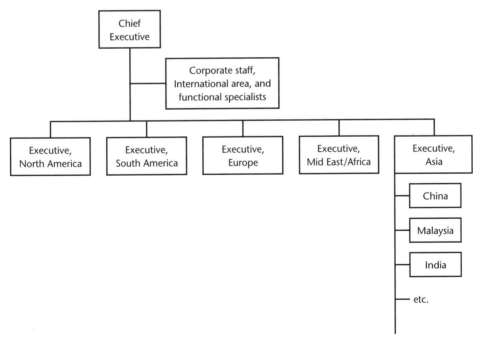

FIGURE 11.3 Global area structure
Source: From Leontiades, J. C. (1985), *Multinational Corporate Strategy*, Lexington Books.

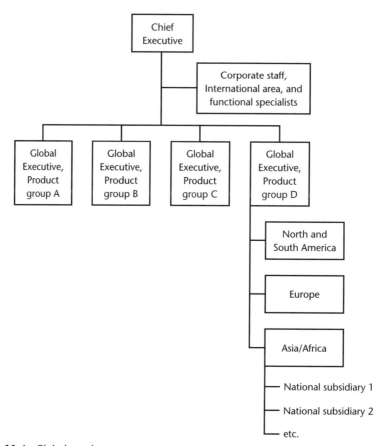

FIGURE 11.4 Global product structure
Source: From Leontiades, J. C. (1985), *Multinational Corporate Strategy*, Lexington Books.

Global product structures

Companies with global ambitions are increasingly organising themselves around global business units. The most popular version of this type is product based. The company is organised about its major products or services (Figure 11.4). Each major product (or service) group of the company is headed by a global product manager with worldwide responsibility for that group. The global company organised in this fashion is in effect made up of a number of global businesses, each with its own management and staff dedicated to the worldwide management of a particular product or service group.

Compared with the global area structure, this form of organisation moves authority away from a regional focus and places it in the hands of executives with worldwide responsibility and perspective. The aim is better coordination on a world scale. The managers of the firm's global businesses have the ability to view their markets and competitors on a worldwide basis and to take action accordingly.

The global product structure appears much better suited to the needs of global companies. However, research shows that the hoped for benefits are not always achieved.[8] Much depends on factors other than organisation structure – including the availability of managers with the necessary global perspective and international experience to head up such groups. In practice, the very seniority of the position may act against appointing the best person for the job. Companies adopting such a structure may find that the most senior managers in line for promotion to global manager positions are those whose experience has been almost entirely within the firm's domestic operations, the very managers with the least international experience.

Apart from its greater geographic scope, the global product organisation is very similar to divisionalised domestic organisations focused about products or services. Perhaps this is not so strange after all, since companies adopting such structures are in effect attempting to treat the whole world as 'domestic'.

FEATURES OF GLOBAL STRUCTURES

Global structures share a number of characteristics. Most important is the lack of any built-in structural separation between the domestic and foreign parts of the organisation. The lack of such a distinction avoids the usual majority of domestic units at the top level of the organisation (as in the case of the international division). Reinforcing this, the global organisation may also feature multiple international headquarters, particularly in the global area type of structure, situated in different parts of the world.

Probably the most widespread use of global structures has been to shift the orientation of the organisation away from the more traditional focus on geographic units and particularly the nation state. Within such structures, national geographic units may indeed appear on the organisation chart but they are now of diminished importance. Not surprisingly, this loss of position (and power) by national units within the organisational pecking order has not always gone unopposed.

Some years ago Royal Dutch Shell replaced its geographic based structure with a new global product organisation formed around five worldwide product and business activities. The aim was to reduce the power and potential for conflict between different regional divisions of Shell and to promote 'convergence and co-operation' between the firm's local companies.

The local national units within this new structure were intended to remain strong, able to act decisively but also coordinated behind global strategies. But as so often happens, things did not work out that way. A few years later Shell implemented another major change, this time reducing the power of the heads of its major national units in Britain, France, the Netherlands and Germany, referred to by Shell as 'country barons'. These had apparently resisted the previous changes in the group's structure.[9]

When Louis Gerstner undertook the task of transforming IBM into a more global corporation, one of his first tasks was to reorganise IBM's European operations. The new structure moved power away from local managers, each ruling over a national IBM unit, towards industry based units without border constraints.

Under the old structure, global customers for IBM products found it impossible to deal with the firm as a single entity. Separate arrangements had to be made with the firm's various national/regional businesses. The goal of the new structure was greater global coordination and control over sales, marketing and product development.[10]

The new organisation structure realigned the company around 14 worldwide teams, each organised to service a particular industry sector. Geographic coordination remained but was no longer dominant. The activities of the various teams were coordinated within the firm's various geographic regions by regional sales managers. The global organisation may also be structured around certain global functions, such as a global marketing unit, global R&D, and global production.

A more recent variation of the global organisation uses market related distinctions to form the main elements of the company's global structure. Investment banks, insurance companies and consulting firms are among the companies that organise themselves first and foremost about global customer groups with, for example, one part of a bank organised to service retail customers worldwide while another is organised to service corporate customers.

American Express recently reorganised itself about three global groups. One of the new global groups is to focus on managing 'establishment services'. This relates to merchants who handle the firm's credit and charge cards. Another organisational group 'travel services' is focused on travel and corporate card clients. Still another group deals with 'consumer marketing and product development'.[11]

AN EVOLUTIONARY PATH

More often than not, major organisational change takes an evolutionary path. In such cases the organisation seems to evolve, adopting a series of incremental changes as management gropes for the right structure.

The organisational change which led Cadbury Schweppes to adopt a global product structure followed just such an evolutionary change.[12] In attempting to stop the fragmentation of its international operating units, each going their separate way, Cadbury first established a regional type organisation. Shortly thereafter four international departments were formed, reporting to and advising the company's chief executive on international marketing, finance, technical matters and personnel. Of these, the international marketing department was the most active in coordinating the firm's global operations. Its task, according to the department head, was to 'assist the chief executive in pulling together marketing strategies around the world and to identify opportunities'. This included establishing the firm's brands as strong international brands, establishing an international company image and the coordination of worldwide product launches.

A few years later another reorganisation followed. The parent firm formed two separate companies. The first, Schweppes International Limited, became 'responsible for determining international policies for drinks and for guiding and supervising international drinks development within the group policies laid down by the main board'. Not long afterwards an analogous company was formed exercising the same functions for confectionery and foods. Boards of directors were appointed for the new companies whose role vis-à-vis the parent organisation was largely advisory. Specifically, they were to advise the managing director of Cadbury Schweppes 'on the conduct and development' of operations throughout the world and to coordinate activities relative to the firm's two main product groups, confectionery and drinks.

Several years later, still another change. The international marketing department and the other international departments were eliminated. Their functions were divided between the chief executive and in a move towards decentralisation certain functions and responsibilities were assigned directly to the firm's various operating units.

These arrangements were short lived. In the subsequent months further changes in the interest of developing a 'global perspective' of the firm's worldwide chocolate and drinks businesses were announced. A managing director of international confectionery was appointed with responsibility for coordinating the firm's confectionery operations worldwide. A similar appointment to coordinate beverages, the firm's other major product group, was also made. These greatly strengthened the firm's previous tentative moves towards a global product structure.

The new appointees were given direct line authority (unlike the advisory international departments) over their respective operations. This initially excluded some of the firm's largest operations but gradually these, too, were incorporated into Cadbury's new global product organisation.

Matrix structures

Every organisation structure is a compromise between particular strengths and weaknesses. With every alteration, priorities are changed. Some parts of the organisation are strengthened, usually at the expense of others which are weakened. Global structures strive to place greater emphasis on those features that contribute to greater global vision and coordination but in doing so they are prone to sacrifice sensitivity and focus on some other area, such as the local environment. In an effort to avoid this, to get the best of all worlds, some companies adopt structures that give equal priority to more than one dimension of the organisation. The most frequently used type of matrix coordinates the firm's operations along two dimensions, usually by product as well as by geographic area. A manager in such a matrix structure will report to two different bosses, each with equal authority. For example, the same manager may report to the chief of a particular geographic area as well as the executive in charge of a particular product. Figure 11.5 illustrates the general principle.

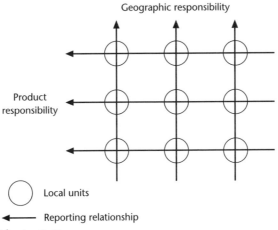

FIGURE 11.5 Matrix structure

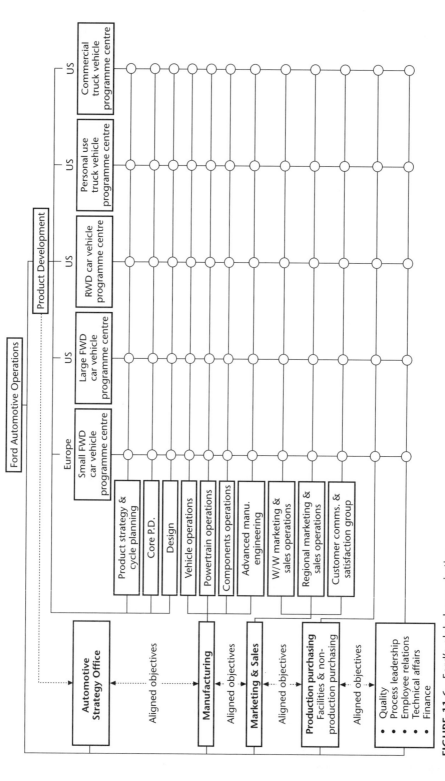

FIGURE 11.6 Ford's global organisation

Source: From *Financial Times*, 23/24 April 1994, p. 11.

BOX 11.2

A customer focused matrix

In 1994, Ericsson's chief executive noted that the company had a tendency to behave like 'seven different companies' within the various countries in which it operated. In an effort aimed at getting more coordination among its various international businesses, the firm reorganised itself in the form of a matrix. The aim was to better coordinate its activities both within the various countries in which it operated and within global product divisions focused around its various products.

Under the new structure, unit managers reported both to global product managers responsible for a particular product group and to the firm's local corporate headquarters in each country (the geographic dimension) – the latter aimed at presenting a single face to local customers.[13]

The reorganisation was hailed as a success. But a few years later (1998) Ericsson reorganised once more. While retaining the matrix structure, it abandoned the 1994 product dimension in favour of a focus on customer groups. Under this structure, unit managers would still report to heads of the various geographic areas in which Ericsson operated as well as to those of its executives responsible for a particular segment of its customers. These were divided into private customers, commercial enterprises and network operators.[14] ∎

Ford's global matrix

With the adoption of its 'Ford 2000' globalisation strategy, Ford needed a new organisation structure. To coordinate the development of new Ford products worldwide, Ford of Europe was merged with Ford's North American operations to form a single global structure for product development (see also Chapter 5). To implement its drive towards globalisation Ford adopted a global matrix structure, as shown in Figure 11.6.[15]

SELECTING COORDINATION MECHANISMS

In the final analysis, the firm's organisation structure is only one of the most obvious tools for achieving the required coordination. It is not the only means. Indeed, its impact is often exaggerated. Every company relies on a variety of coordinating mechanisms. Dependence on any single mechanism, such as organisation structure, is inadequate to the task and unlikely to bring about the desired result. Each company must choose the mix of coordination devices which best fits its strategy and internal situation. What works for one company may not work for another.

To illustrate, Figure 11.7 sets out two quite different coordination profiles, each comprising a different coordination mix. On the left-hand side, the mix of coordinating mechanisms and their character reflects a company which features a low degree of

Coordination mechanism	Low coordination profile	High coordination profile
Management career paths	Nationally limited	International rotation and career ladder
Headquarters role	Bankers role	Global role
Competence centres	None	Multiple
Information system	International information provided to national units only on a need-to-know basis	Information on firm's international activities and plans made available to national units as a matter of course
Planning system	Capital budgeting and national planning only	Integrated regional/global planning systems
Management recruitment and promotion	Nationally based	Provides for recruitment and promotion across national boundaries
Management reward system	Based on national company performance only	Based on international as well as national performance of firm
Communication system	Hub model (communication goes through parent company)	Electronic network linking all parts of the company
Purchasing	Decentralised	Selective global centralisation of purchasing
Company language	None designated	Common language for international communication
Management training	Develops national management skills	Develops international management skills
Use of cross-national teams	No	Yes
Composition of management	Nationals of home country	International
Board of Directors	Membership limited to nationals	International membership
Formal organisation structure	International division	Global/matrix

FIGURE 11.7 International coordination mechanisms

Source: Adapted from Leontiades, J. C. (1985), *Multinational Corporate Strategy*, Lexington Books.

cross-national coordination. The planning process in such a local player proceeds on a country-by-country basis. There is no global plan to integrate local activities with the firm's worldwide objectives. Policies vary from one country to another. Most management career paths are locally limited.

Within this same hypothetical company managers are rewarded according to the performance of their local business. No account is taken of the impact their decisions may have on the wider, regional or global, performance of the firm. Recruitment and training are geared to the needs of specific local operations. Recruitment for new staff is nationally limited. Information systems focus on financial information. Occasional visits by senior executives are used to maintain informal contact with the firm's operations in different parts of the world.

The profile on the right-hand side of Figure 11.7 represents a quite different type of company. The company has chosen a global type of organisation structure. It makes use of a planning process which links and integrates the firm's national and regional plans, aligning these with the firm's global objectives. It features multiple coordinating headquarters and teams which serve to decentralise coordinating authority and utilise skills and knowledge outside the parent company headquarters.

Global awareness and capability is also developed through personnel policies stressing global career paths, reward systems, worldwide job rotation and training. Other such mechanisms which can assist the global player in bringing about the desired degree and type of coordination are described in greater detail below.

Management recruitment

How and where the firm's managers are recruited will have an important bearing on the firm's general management culture and outlook. A widespread practice has been to draw top management from the firm's country of origin or home country. Because of this, it is still common to find, even in companies undergoing globalisation, that the upper levels of the corporate hierarchy are occupied almost entirely by managers with a common citizenship and ethnic background. Only managers from the firm's country of origin may advance to the upper reaches of the overall enterprise. Foreign nationals are limited to advancement within their own local affiliates. This has the effect of dividing the firm's management according to national background.

The more progressive companies, recognising the negative aspects of such a recruitment policy have implemented personnel systems designed to develop a pool of candidates from multiple national backgrounds for top management positions.

Reward systems

Reward systems linked to performance are widely used. For the global firm, it is essential that the performance criteria employed are not restricted only to local performance. Systems which link rewards only to local performance, how well the firm has performed in a particular country, inevitably reinforce a local mentality. Hence, many companies operating internationally now take a broader perspective, linking the compensation of locally based executives to company performance in other parts of the world. Some portion of the compensation is linked to regional and global performance. (See also Chapter 12.)

Training

Training is another mechanism used by companies to communicate certain corporate practices and policies which are considered essential to operating as a coherent worldwide enterprise. Many managers will have only a limited view of the company's worldwide operations. Some of them will have developed their skills largely within a particular cultural setting, reflecting nationally focused beliefs and loyalties. Training with colleagues from many other parts of the same company exposes them to a wider, more global perspective. It also offers an opportunity for the company to transfer 'best practice' from one part of the world to another. Alternatively, the trainers may themselves travel to various parts of the organisation.

Ikea, the furniture retailer, has announced plans to set up an international 'university' for training its employees in its methods. Some of the firm's most experienced managers will travel to the company's retail stores around the world to carry out such training. The lessons offered will not only reflect the firm's international experience, they will also be adapted to the particular conditions of the local markets in which the training takes place.[16]

Career paths

It has been the practice in many international companies to make each foreign operation (subsidiary) responsible for developing its own managers. By and large such managers were not mobile. Career paths were restricted locally. Transfers outside the local unit where managers had begun their career were rare. Managers associated with the home office corporate headquarters, sometimes referred to as home office personnel, followed their own, quite separate career ladders. For the global company, career paths designed to provide managers with the experience and skills required for communicating with and understanding different cultures and nationalities can prove a valuable unifying force.

Such career paths are in fact a necessity if the firm is to become a truly global organisation rather than an international company added on to a domestic core. Nothing hampers communication and coordination between the firm's international units more than a split between those with international experience and those without. Coordination within the global enterprise requires that the chief executive as well as a high proportion of all senior managers have had extensive international experience.

Overcoming the traditional distinction between domestic and international staff requires career ladders that include systematic cross-national job rotation. Every candidate for top management within a global company should have had first hand exposure to multiple 'foreign' job assignments. Breaking down internal barriers requires that positions in one part of the firm must be open to candidates from other parts, whatever their geographic location. Global career path planning should be applied uniformly throughout the enterprise, with career differences based on distinctions between international and domestic managers eliminated.

Information systems

To be a global player requires an information system that collects and distributes information on global competition, markets, customers and other features.

Such information is still largely collected on a national basis, often by the local affiliates of the firm in a particular country. In the past, many companies have experienced difficulty in extracting such information from their local units which had collected the data in the first place. These were not always eager to provide others with information that could be used to check and perhaps limit their own performance or simply to benefit another part of the company.

Putting together information from local units requires that it is not only collected but also processed. This means putting it into a form that is consistent from one country to another, distilling out the relevant portions, interpreting the data and distributing the results. Once this is achieved, such information acts as the basic building block for thinking and acting globally.

At one time the sort of information which portrayed a global overview of the firm's total international operations was only available to staff at international headquarters. Available means of communication made the dissemination of such information throughout the firm's global network difficult. This is no longer the case. It is now possible quickly and economically to collect and distribute data on global trends and events to business managers in remote parts of the world, keeping them informed of world events and providing a better basis for understanding why certain actions which affect them have been taken. Managers in the firm's various internationally dispersed business operations can cooperate far better as regards global undertakings with other parts of the organisation if they have access to the same data. Misunderstandings are reduced and cooperation facilitated. Moreover, dissemination of this data contributes to decentralising much of the firm's global decision making as well as the implementation of global reward systems. It is required for the establishment of multiple headquarters coordinating centres.

Communication systems

The firm's communications systems themselves are a major variable, influencing not only data collection and dissemination but the whole range of activities that are involved in global coordination. Communication systems with capabilities enabling all parts of the enterprise to communicate with each other are relatively recent. In an earlier era, the costs and delays of international communication and lack of compatibility, particularly between computer systems in one part of the company and those in another, were a major obstacle. Today, computer-to-computer links, e-mail, video conferencing, satellite phones, faxes and so on make possible communications which put all parts of the enterprise into almost instant touch with each other.

Technology has improved not only the speed but also the scope of inter-company communications. The hub model, which routed all international communications through a central headquarters, has now been abandoned in many companies in favour of a global network system. The various parts of the firm are able to communicate and interact directly with each other – seeking advice, feedback and comment irrespective of distance, much as in any domestic company.

Purchasing: one stop shopping

Global suppliers that can meet the needs of the company on a global basis can be a powerful aid in coordinating their operations. Take for example advertising. One option for the firm wishing to implement a global advertising campaign is to retain various advertising firms throughout the world and then to attempt to communicate with them individually in coordinating their efforts behind the campaign. Alternatively, working with a global advertising firm with its own worldwide network of branches can make this task much easier. An agreement is made between the company and the global advertising firm on the type of promotion required. The global supplier of advertising then undertakes the coordination of its own network of branches to implement the campaign worldwide.

Use of a single global supplier of banking services can help to coordinate the firm's financial strategy, ensuring that desired levels of liquidity and credit are available to all of its international affiliates.

One stop shopping through global suppliers has the obvious appeal of reducing transaction costs, substituting a single agreement with a global supplier for the multiple agreements with the many individual suppliers that might otherwise have to be retained.

Company policies

Company policies are in fact decision rules that can also help the global company to coordinate its worldwide activities. For example, a company policy might be to implement a particular standard of product quality, or to reach such and such a standard of safety, or to retire employees at the age of 65, etc. Such policies may vary from one country to another – differentiating the firm's global operations. Alternatively, global companies may use these as a powerful instrument of global coordination by promoting uniform standards of product quality, safety and personnel policies throughout its worldwide business activities. Once agreed, they serve to reduce active intervention from headquarters.

The McDonald's fast food chain has evolved an extensive set of policy guidelines with reference to worldwide standards of product quality, treatment of customers, promoting and projecting the company image and so on. Such policies are communicated to franchisees, partly through extensive training programmes. They represent ongoing rules of conduct requiring little repetition.

Company language

Global companies increasingly employ managers of many nationalities. Communications methods have made giant strides but these are to some degree neutralised if the firm's managers in different parts of the world cannot communicate because of language differences. Swedish and Swiss companies have been leaders in adopting a common company-wide language.

The chief executive of ABB Asea Brown Bovari has stipulated that every global manager in his company must be able to communicate in English.[17]

Overlapping boards of directors

One of the oldest, but still effective, coordinating mechanisms is the use of overlapping membership in the global firm's various boards of directors. Senior managers on the board of one company subsidiary may also serve as board members of others. This not only disseminates information on the activities of the various subsidiaries but also helps to coordinate their activities. Similarly, managers from the board of subsidiary A may serve on the board of the firm's regional or global headquarters and vice versa.

World boards

Some companies are establishing regional and world boards of directors. Their brief is to review the company's activities and advise on policies and strategies on a regional or global basis. A major American manufacturing company established a world board with a view to integrating its international and domestic operations. Managers from different functional areas, coming from both the international and domestic parts of the company, were represented on the same world board. They were given joint responsibility for developing global strategies in specific areas of the firm's global business.

The total mix

It is the totality and mix of the coordinating devices such as those shown in Figure 11.7 that is important. How the various means of coordination are combined and balanced will determine whether the company achieves the desired coordination and at what cost. In other words, if the company is organised to compete effectively as a global player.

THE INTERNET ORGANISATION

A central theme throughout this text has been the impact of information technology and the changes that have shaped international/global companies. The internet is one of the most important of these. It will undoubtedly have a major influence on globalisation and global companies. Its influence is already being felt.

The rise and development of on-line retailers, like Amazon.com, the North American bookseller, is indicative of future developments. This company does business around the world using the internet to overcome many of the traditional barriers. This new approach promises to revolutionise exporting and other forms of international commerce.

In the case of exporting, customers can now be contacted directly more cheaply through the internet, calling into question the entire apparatus of agents and distributors. Small transactions directed at small and large markets become more economical, introducing new possibilities for addressing customers and markets once considered uneconomical.

The impact on organisation structure, just beginning, will be enormous. As we saw in Box 5.1, some hint of the changes to come is evident in the new internet supply strategies of the major automobile producers. A group of these, including General Motors, Ford and DaimlerChrysler have agreed to set up a joint arrangement to secure supplies through web page based, electronic markets.[18]

Suppliers from all over the world will be able to use these web pages to offer to provide parts and components for these car firms, the potential buyers. Such global electronic markets will bring together buyers and sellers for a particular industry. By reducing transactions costs, thus greatly expanding global supply sources, it is estimated that this will lead to significant savings for the purchasers.

Many of the same automotive firms are experimenting, on the distribution side, with the use of the internet to reach their customers. Such direct producer to customer contact opens up new possibilities of customised automobiles, designed from the factory for individual customers, as is already the case with certain computer makers. Needless to say, the implications of this for existing distribution systems are dramatic.

These internet related initiatives will undoubtedly influence organisation structures. Global firms taking advantage of the ability of this recent innovation to conquer distance will be particularly affected. Figure 11.8 is indicative of the direction of such change. On the supply side, companies will be able to secure supplies (a much larger percentage of their intake than today) through the use of electronic markets which use the internet to bring together sellers from all over the world with company buyers. On the distribution side, the producing company will use the same sort of electronic market (now in the role of supplier) to contact global customers directly.

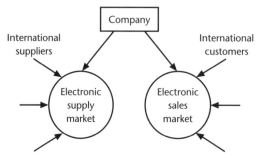

FIGURE 11.8 The global internet company

Major parts of the organisation will shift towards managing these electronic markets. Other parts of the company, company personnel dealing today directly with suppliers and distribution, for example, will find their jobs radically changed. If this method is successful, a number of production processes now carried out internally will disappear. Many administrative and clerical functions will be contracted out. Already some companies are using the internet to transfer certain administrative functions, such as data processing, programming and telephone services, to outside suppliers, many of them in the developing countries. Completed work is transmitted back to the purchasing company the next day.

The sharp lowering of transaction costs for functions carried on outside the firm means that companies will increasingly resort to external markets for their needs. The 'make or buy' decision will shift towards 'buy'. It is possible to envisage global coordinating companies, with little more than a small staff, managing the worldwide inflow of supplies and distribution of products through such means.

SUMMARY

- If it is true that structure follows strategy, then companies pursuing globalisation will have to change their structure. For export companies, the early organisation of their export activities is often simply an extension of the firm's domestic distribution system.
- The early American multinationals favoured the divisional type of organisation, grouping their international activities within an international division. Starting from smaller domestic markets, the European multinationals favoured the less elaborate mother–daughter form of organisation.
- Globalisation, with its emphasis on cross-border coordination, has caused firms to rethink their organisations. Improved communications technology has shifted the balance of advantage towards organisation structures that do not stop at national borders. These include global area, global product and global matrix structures.
- These global organisations shift the balance of power within companies away from the dominance by domestic parts of the enterprise, which characterises more traditional structures. They also reduce the significance of national borders within

the organisation. Change of this sort often comes incrementally, evolving over a series of transformations.

- Organisation structure is only one of many mechanisms which management can use to secure global coordination. Information systems, management career paths, communications systems and training are examples of other mechanisms important in bringing about the necessary coordination. Dependence on any single mechanism is inadequate. Each company must consider, select and develop a mix of such mechanisms to fit its requirements.
- A relatively new instrument already having a major impact on organisation structure is the use of the internet.

NOTES AND REFERENCES

1. Chandler, A. D. (1990), *Strategy and Structure: Chapters in the History of the American Industrial Enterprise*, MIT Press, pp. 44–9.
2. Bartlett, C. A. (1983), MNC's: Get off the reorganization merry-go-round, *Harvard Business Review*, March–April, pp. 138–46; also see Bartlett, C. A. (1981), Multinational structural change: evolution versus reorganization, in L. Otterbeck (Ed.), *The Management of Headquarters–Subsidiary Relationships in Multinational Corporations*, Aldershot: Gower.
3. Franko, L. G. (1976), *The European Multinationals*, London: Harper & Row.
4. Prahalad, C. K. and Doz, Y. L. (1987), *The Multinational Mission*, The Free Press.
5. Hedlund, G. (1986), The hypermodern MNC – a heterarchy?, *Human Resource Management*, Spring, vol. 25.
6. *Financial Times*, 14 March 1997, p. 1.
7. Sloan, A. P. Jr. (1990), *My Years With General Motors*, New York: Doubleday, p. 55.
8. Davidson, W. H. and Haspeslagh, P. (1982), Shaping a global product organization, *Harvard Business Review*, July–August, pp. 125–32.
9. *Financial Times*, 19/20 September 1998, p. 22.
10. *Business Week*, 26 September 1994, p. 18.
11. *The Wall Street Journal Europe*, 24/25 May 1996, p. 4.
12. I am grateful to the management of Cadbury Schweppes for their cooperation in this research.
13. *Business Week*, 12 December 1994, p. 52.
14. *Financial Times*, 29 September 1998, p. 21.
15. *Financial Times*, 23/24 April 1994, p. 11.
16. *Financial Times*, 24 September 1998, p. 20.
17. Taylor, W. (1991), The logic of global business, *Harvard Business Review*, March–April.
18. *The Wall Street Journal Europe*, 28 February 2000, p. 1.

12 Developing a global scorecard

In sporting games, the procedures for calculating the scores of the various contestants are usually fairly clear. But in business there is more than one method of keeping score. Moreover, the procedures used by business firms may change depending on circumstances and data availability. Today, companies embarked on globalisation are undergoing major changes which will require them to reassess their system of scorekeeping. If the game has become global, then scorekeeping will have to reflect this.

THE BALANCED SCORECARD

Recently there has been a general upsurge of interest in performance scoring systems. Questions have been raised concerning the methods companies have been using to measure their performance. In particular, there have been doubts about the usefulness of relying on accounting/financial measures as the main indicators of company performance. The gist of the argument is that conventional financial measures, such as the company's balance sheet, profit and loss statements, return on investment, etc. are too narrow. Exclusive reliance on these does not provide all of the information management needs today to assess company performance.

A number of experts have pointed out that the emphasis on financial measures excludes crucial information of which managers should be aware. This reflects a growing feeling that no single set of measures can capture the various changes that need to be monitored, hence the interest in developing a 'balanced scorecard' which looks at the company and its performance from a number of different perspectives. Measures that consider the company's performance in areas such as customer satisfaction, company innovation and learning, it is suggested, are likely to give management a more balanced view of the firm's performance.[1]

Information relevant to the firm's strategic direction is often lacking in the more conventional measures. It is not enough for performance indicators to identify the company's historic financial performance, where it has been. This is useful and necessary, but also needed are indicators which give some insight as to where it is heading. Igor Ansoff identified this issue some years ago in his pioneering book on corporate strategy.[2] Ansoff points out that although the overall objective of the firm is profitability, this measure can only be reliably estimated looking ahead over a relatively short period of time. For interpreting the firm's longer term future, Ansoff forwarded a number of 'proxy measures', such as sales growth, market share, new products. These did not measure profitability directly, but were indicative of where the firm was heading, that is, its likely profitability over the longer term. Ansoff's proxy measures did not simply reflect current performance, they were diagnostic in that they helped management to assess the factors underlying profitability. Some writers today refer to such measures as indicators of 'strategic health'.[3] Equipped with such performance measures, management is better able to anticipate future profitability and to act accordingly.

Recent discussions on this issue echo Ansoff's view of the need for performance measures that point towards the future rather than simply record what has happened in the past. There is also considerable agreement in the current debate on the fact that company performance measures may change over time, as company priorities and situations change.[4] To be relevant, performance scoring has to be updated in the light of changing circumstances.

Considering the magnitude of the changes introduced by globalisation, it is remarkable that there has been so little discussion in the current debate regarding scoring methods for global companies. In approaching this subject it will be useful first to distinguish between two quite different types of performance measurement.

PERSPECTIVES ON SCORING

Whatever the nature of the firm, whether it is local, international or global, there are two distinct perspectives shaping scoring systems. One perspective relies on 'autonomous' measures which focus on the performance of the firm without reference to its competitors. Here we also find most of the traditional financial measures of company performance, including for example, the value of company sales, profitability, total costs, unit costs and similar, financial measurements. Autonomous performance may also include non-financial measures such as growth in unit sales, product quality, productivity, new product development, customer satisfaction and so on. The focus of these measures is essentially internal.

Based on such measures, whether the firm is winning or losing is judged according to its own performance independent of the performance of other companies. For example, 'This year we earned a 25% return on invested capital' or 'Our sales increased by 20% this year compared to the previous year' or 'We met our objective of reducing pollution by 20%'.

This type of performance measurement has the added advantage of using data which is available internally and fairly precise. Often it originates in the accounting department, drawing on the services of a trained staff using approved methods and educated in what must surely be the second oldest business profession. It has been suggested that after receiving accounting reports, managers are either happy or sad, but never wiser.

A quite different perspective looks at the firm's performance relative to that of other firms and particularly its rivals. Rivalry performance scores are relative measures. The score achieved depends not only on the actions of the subject firm but also those of its rivals. A 'gain' is registered only if the firm outperforms one or more of its rivals. A loss is registered if it performs less well than its rivals. The best known of these rivalry measures is market share, measuring the percentage of total sales attributable to the firm compared to its competitors. Rankings against rivals also fall into this category. For example, 'Our product ranked first in reliability' or 'We reduced our costs by 10% more than our nearest competitor'.

Rivalry measures are more recent. They are necessary to tell management how it is doing in the competitive contest. Whether it is gaining or losing financially may be irrelevant in the long run if the firm cannot compete. In giving management a view of the firm's competitive performance, rivalry measures also help to pinpoint its strategic capabilities, its strengths and weaknesses. It is difficult to define the firm's core competence and/or competitive advantage without such information.

Of course, autonomous measures may be converted into rivalry measures simply by using the former as a basis for comparison with competitors. For example, comparing the firm's sales or profits or productivity against those of its rivals. 'Our sales have grown 20% faster than those of our major competitor'. This is a rivalry type performance measure and quite different from a presentation of the firm's sales on their own.

Characteristics of the two scoring perspectives

The two scoring perspectives have different characteristics. Rivalry itself is essentially a zero sum game. One firm's gain finds its immediate and equal reflection in the losses of others. A gain in competitive position of one firm, be it measured in market share or relative product quality or other such comparative measures, necessarily reflects a loss of competitive position by one or more rivals.

The same does not apply to autonomous measures. All firms may improve their own (autonomous) performance simultaneously. A rising tide 'raises all boats' and in a rapidly growing market it is possible for all firms to improve their sales and profitability or to surpass their objectives. It is not possible for all competitors to improve their rivalry scores, just as it is not possible for all firms to improve their market share.

Autonomous measures are not only different in nature but often give different signals. It is not surprising therefore that these two measures may occasionally yield scores which point in opposite directions. Figures on company sales, profits and so on, may signal to management that there is an improvement in performance, the firm is winning, while rivalry measures show just the opposite, the firm is falling behind its rivals. A firm with a 20% or 100% increase in profits may still be losing market share. Increases in profits and other inward looking measures may continue for some time alongside decreases in rivalry performance.

By the same token, rivalry measures may show an improvement while autonomous indicators register a drop.

Hewlett Packard reduced its prices for personal computers in the second quarter of 1998 to increase its market share. The move succeeded in dramatically increasing that company's market share but overall profitability declined.[5] Of course, this divergence cannot continue indefinitely. Beyond a certain point a decline (or improvement) in rivalry performance will eventually impact on financial criteria. It will be reflected in sales and profitability. This is hardly a novel discovery. Consistent failure against rivals, e.g. a market share approaching zero, will inevitably diminish financial performance. This has not kept companies from ignoring the obvious.

The British motorcycle industry, when it was the world's leading producer, experienced improved sales and profits, even while its market share deteriorated. It was losing the game while its finances improved. Eventually, the inward looking financial score followed the same direction as the rivalry measures. The latter, rivalry measures, will often lead inward looking measures.

Performance balance

Certain decisions will require information on the firm's autonomous performance score, such as company sales, income and costs. Other decisions will require measures which provide the essential signals on its performance relative to competitors.

Both types of performance measurements are required. This is not only to tell management how it is doing in each particular category, but also to achieve a balance between the two types of performance. Management cannot, for example, continually reduce prices to increase market share ('buy market share') without a consideration as to the impact of this on its autonomous profit performance. Striking a balance, making the trade-off, between these two types of performance criteria is a strategic decision. To make the decision requires information on both.

Companies operating internationally

The sorts of changes in scoring performance required by firms embarking on globalisation may best be illustrated by reference to practice within the early multinational companies. We have already noted the difficulties of communication over distance that characterised the early multinationals. Communication between the parent company and its subsidiaries was necessarily kept to a minimum. This required that the parent company allow its subsidiaries considerable independence. Once established in a foreign country the latter developed their own methods and strategies almost as individual businesses. It is not surprising that in this context the parent company adopted a banker role. Scorekeeping concentrated on monitoring the local financial performance of the multinational's individual national subsidiaries.

The main measurement tool was the budget. Once the budget was agreed, variations from budget became the key performance criteria. Local units reported their results periodically to the parent company, usually quarterly or even annually. Costs, sales and profits were calculated for each local unit in considerable detail and projected over the following year. Companies and managers that exceeded their budgeted sales/income/profits were considered to be winning. Those falling behind these targets were underperforming. Performance measurement relied heavily on autonomous financial measures.

Management at the corporate centre was responsible for reviewing the performance of the various local units, comparing their results against budget targets. It was also responsible for monitoring the firm's worldwide performance. In these early multinationals this was typically arrived at by summing up the financial results in its various local operations expressed in conventional accounting terms. Given the communication realities of that era, global strategies were vestigial or non-existent.

SCOREKEEPING GLOBALLY

The above approach measures the firm's performance internationally, country by country, rather than globally. It is entirely inadequate for scoring the performance of global companies. The fact that such companies have developed the capability to see and to act globally in a coordinated manner has opened up new possibilities. Global players are able to implement global strategies and to develop global competencies not available to more locally oriented firms. Implementing these, however, entails certain costs. New communications systems are required as well as staff trained to use them, also personnel trained in interpreting global markets, competitors, social trends and economies. Is it worth it? Are the results claimed for the new approach being delivered? If not, what signals can management depend on to help it anticipate events and implement corrective action? To answer such questions will require major changes in performance measurement. As indicated in Figure 12.1, global firms will continue to use both autonomous performance measures and rivalry measures. To meet the needs of the global firm, however, these measures will have to be made locally as well as globally. The four dimensions of performance measurement in the global firm are indicated in the figure.

Local performance in global companies

In global companies, monitoring of local performance is still vital. 'What has been our performance in a particular country or region?' will remain a key question, first,

FIGURE 12.1   Dimensions for performance measurement in the global firm

for assessing local management performance and determining local management incentives, including financial reward systems and promotions.

It is also necessary for diagnostic reasons. Management within the global firm needs to understand the reasons behind geographic variations in the firm's performance. Differences between countries and regions are bound to influence its performance. Does the drop in company sales in a particular country reflect underperforming local management or does it reflect a downturn in the local economy? Higher unit costs locally may reflect local inefficiency or perhaps the fact that wage rates in country A are different from those in country B. Similarly, local differences in competitors, markets, tariffs, infrastructure, institutions and a host of other local conditions will influence local performance. Lumping different national locations together, measuring the firm's performance there as if they were a single environmental unit, masks underlying differences which may be responsible for local performance variations. Keeping score of each local unit's performance within its own local environment helps (but only helps) to isolate the effect of local conditions on performance.

Local performance assessment is also necessary for identifying best practice. Within the global enterprise, there will be significant variations in productivity, quality and reliability between various local operations. Once these are known, those local units with the best practice can be encouraged to transfer their methods to other company units which may also benefit from them.

There is also the need to assess one local business against another, perhaps in another part of the world, for investment purposes. In allocating capital to its various local operations management needs to have some notion of expected return. This is not the only or even the decisive consideration behind such decisions. Investment may be made for strategic reasons which are immediately concerned with securing the highest return (see Chapter 3). That is not to say that such decisions are made without reference to their likely return. Estimates of expected return, based to some degree on past performance, are a necessary part of the overall decision.

There are also considerations of balancing the firm's total worldwide portfolio of investments. Some writers have indicated that such portfolio balancing has no place in a global company. With its much closer coordination across boundaries, a business in one location cannot simply be dropped from the firm's portfolio without affecting, perhaps disastrously, the global firm's operations elsewhere.[6]

There is certainly some validity in this. Compared to the multi-domestic type of enterprise, there is less scope for dropping and adding entire units. Nevertheless there is still considerable flexibility, even within a closely coordinated global enterprise to shift investment away from some operations and to increase investment in others. With suitable planning, such portfolio decisions can be, and are, made without jeopardising the smooth operations of the overall company (see also Chapter 13).

SCORING GLOBAL PERFORMANCE

The main changes in performance measurement in companies going global will be the greater emphasis on scoring performance at the global level and particularly the firm's worldwide performance against its rivals. As indicated in Figure 12.1, global companies will still need to develop autonomous performance measures of global performance. They will need to assess their firm's global performance in terms of worldwide profitability, costs, output, capacity utilisation and similar such measures. For companies that are already operating internationally, most of the information required for this type of performance measurement will be familiar and readily available from internal sources.

The same is not the case with respect to global rivalry measures. This type of information will typically not be readily available to the firm embarking on globalisation, but it is essential. Global firms are playing in two different competitive contests. They are engaged in rivalry within particular national and regional territories pitting themselves against companies there competing for the same local markets. They are also engaged in a global competitive contest, an altogether different thing. Rivalry performance in any particular local territory may differ widely from that at the global level. The global firm may be very successful against rivals in a particular local market but may be struggling globally.

Simply adding up the scores submitted by the firm's various local operations will not provide the necessary information on its global rivalry performance. For example, summing local measures of market share in the various national markets where it competes is not likely to yield information on the company's global market share position. This would leave out countries and competitors where the firm does not operate. Any attempt to measure global market share must take into account all the countries that market the products or services the company deals in, even those in which the firm does not have a presence. The same is true of other measures of rivalry performance.

Global firms that do not already have this type of information must seek to obtain it. Its usefulness extends beyond performance measurement. Management needs this type of information to think global. This is difficult if the data on which it bases its judgements comprises individual sets of national performance measures.

The strategic dimension

Without measures that compare the firm's performance to its competitors globally, management lacks the information required to answer the 'Where are we?' type of questions. It is not able to say, without performance indicators such as global market share, comparative sales growth, unit costs, product quality and so on, whether it is winning or losing the global competitive contest. It is unable to identify its current positioning within the global competitive league. Is it a major global player or a niche player? Lacking global rivalry performance measures it also lacks vital information on why and where it is winning or losing the global competitive contest. Against which competitors are we gaining sales? Is it a matter of comparative productivity, customer loyalty, product quality, etc? In which part of the world are we growing faster (or slower) than the competition?

It is in raising such questions and providing answers to them that global level management can begin to address the second set of questions that management in the global company must answer, the 'Where are we going?' type of questions. Performance assessment against global rivals is required if the firm is to identify its points of strength and weakness against global competition as a basis for developing a global competitive strategy. Information of this sort on a world scale provides the signals vital to both diagnosis and strategic thinking for global firms.

A shift in emphasis

More important than any single measurement is the shift of performance priorities. Unlike the early multinationals, the emphasis in the global enterprise is on maximising global performance. Local performance is considered an interim measure, a means to an end. The bottom line is global performance. This is the main objective to strive for, even at the expense of sacrificing the performance of some of the firm's local operations. Management in a particular local unit may be asked to forego certain opportunities or incur additional costs in order to benefit other parts of the global enterprise. A promising manager or product developed by the firm's business operations in Germany may be transferred out to one of the firm's other local operations if it is considered that the manager or product would contribute more from there to the firm's overall global results. A new innovation produced in France may be transferred to another part of the company in another location if this contributes to better world-wide performance. New operations may be established which are in themselves not profitable if they contribute to global profitability. (For a fuller discussion of this point see Chapter 3). This priority on global level performance affects the way such firms score performance at the local level.

IDENTIFYING LOCAL PERFORMANCE IN GLOBAL COMPANIES

The closer cooperation and integration between the global firm's various international business operations makes the contribution of each local unit less easily identifiable.

In the early days of Ford's European operations, the cars produced by the company and the associated costs incurred were clearly attributable to one or other of the firm's largely independent national production facilities. The conversion in 1967 of Ford's various European businesses into a unified regional organisation, integrated its various automobile plants into a single European production system.

Cross-national integration of Ford production systems meant that its different national businesses began to work together much more closely. An automotive component produced in Belgium could be shipped to England or Germany for further work. The same component would then be grouped with other automotive parts produced by Ford facilities in many other countries to produce the final product. This sharing of production and other activities across national borders made it more complicated and difficult to assess just what each operation contributed towards bottom line performance. Transfer pricing reflecting different national tax requirements may add to the difficulties.

The added complexity of measuring local performance is part of the cost of becoming a global enterprise. Such firms will have to devote added time and effort to devising accounting systems which estimate cross-border contributions from one part of the global enterprise to another. Scorekeeping at the local level will have to take into account local efforts whose ultimate payoff is in another part of the world. This means that there will be greater reliance on accounting mechanisms such as transfer pricing to measure local performance where there is a transfer of resources from one part of the global enterprise to another. Cost centres will also find increasing use, particularly where the entire output of a particular production unit is transferred to another part of the company, rather than marketed locally.

Managers of the firm's local operations will increasingly be assessed and rewarded on their contribution to the firm's global performance. This is already happening. It is not unusual for bonuses in companies undergoing globalisation to be based not only on what is achieved locally but also on the contribution to the firm's overall global performance.

Integrating local and global plans

The procedure for setting performance targets will also change. Global coordination, a hallmark of the global enterprise, will affect local budgets and therefore local performance objectives. This can and has led to disputes. Are local budget objectives realistic? Do they take account of local interests? Of global objectives? Minimising the possibility for friction and disagreement requires an interactive type of planning, quite different from the quasi-autonomous budget process characteristic of the multinational company. Within the global enterprise, managers in charge of local operations will have to take greater account of global company objectives, coordinating local plans with the firm's wider aspirations.

As outlined in Chapter 10, the planning process within the global firm may be initiated by managers from global headquarters who begin by communicating the broad outline of the firm's worldwide objectives and plans. These serve as a basis for discussion. Local managers are asked to respond, indicating how their local units might contribute, or be unable to contribute, to such plans. Interaction between the two levels continues until agreement is reached on planning objectives and budgets which reflect both local and global thinking and take into account cross-local contributions, from one local planning unit to another.

Integrating local and global performance

Global players need to measure their performance both locally and globally. A narrow preoccupation with local performance can obscure the wider global perspective. The company may be gaining locally but not doing at all well globally. Focusing on global aggregate performance scores, e.g. the global market share of the company as a whole, can obscure the contribution and relationship of the various parts. It can hide vital local situations influencing overall performance. In the final analysis, the two are closely related and must at some point be considered together. Local and global performance cannot remain separate. An appreciation of the global firm's overall performance requires that they be integrated, the signals and implications of one set of measures related closely to those of the other. For the most part, this integration takes place in the mind. However, displaying the entire portfolio or network of the firm's local operations against those of its global rivals provides a broader local/global perspective which may aid this process.

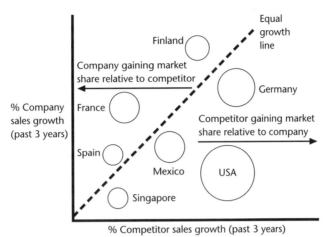

FIGURE 12.2 International comparison of changes in relative market share
Source: Adapted from Leontiades, J. C. (1985), *Multinational Corporate Strategy*, Lexington Books.
Note: Circles are proportional to latest total industry sales in territory.

Figure 12.2 depicts the local market share performance of a particular global player, in all of its different national markets against a global competitor in the same local markets. This global/local perspective offers additional information and a view of performance which is quite different from that obtained either by viewing each local situation individually or by considering the aggregate market share of the company. Management is able to see at a glance where (in which local situations) the firm is gaining and losing against its rivals. It is able to evaluate the various parts in relation to the whole.

Certain performance features specific to companies operating internationally are particularly difficult to interpret as global aggregates. Political risk is an example. Risk is a key element of performance. A high rate of return associated with a high risk is quite different from a high rate of return associated with a low risk. In terms of political risk, the nation state (a local score) remains the natural unit of analysis. Arriving at the firm's overall global risk by simply totalling up its political risk exposure in its different national operations around the world, including high risk countries in the same calculation as those with minimal risk, hides at least as much as it reveals. This implies that the global firm should assess political risk in each country individually. But for global companies, that still leaves the problem of arriving at some estimate of their total political risk exposure.

The firm's global performance in this respect can best be interpreted as a portfolio of national risk/return situations indicating both the political risk and the associated return for all of the countries in which it operates, as illustrated in Figure 12.3.

DEVELOPING A GLOBAL SCORECARD

We may now summarise some of the above discussion relative to the development of a global scorecard.

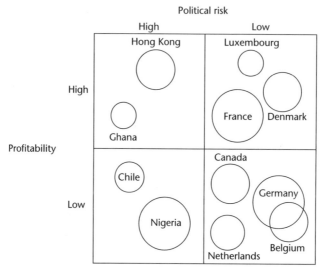

FIGURE 12.3   Political risk vs. profitability

Note: Circles are proportional to company sales.

All firms gather a wide number of measures to assess their performance. Even where the emphasis at the top of the corporate hierarchy has been primarily on financial indicators, a more detailed inspection will reveal other performance measures being used in various parts of the organisation, such as employee turnover, productivity per employee, customer complaints, product rejects and so on. The interest in a balanced scorecard gives more weight to certain non-financial measures, viewing them alongside traditional financial indicators to arrive at a more balanced view of the firm's overall performance.

The firm embarked on globalisation is probably already engaged in international business activities. It will almost certainly have made extensive use of autonomous performance measures such as sales and profitability to assess performance. Some information of this type will also have been used to measure the firm's worldwide performance across all of its international and domestic operations. Measures assessing the firm's position in particular countries and regions relative to its local rivals will also very likely have been developed. Global rivalry measures are a different thing. These are likely to be lacking. Global rivalry measures will be required, not only to assess the firm's performance globally but also to provide vital information required in developing a global competitive strategy, an area that differentiates the global firm from its international predecessors.

Once again it is a matter of the right balance. The combination of local/global measures that constitutes the best balance varies from one company and industry to another. Much will depend on company priorities and strategy. Another factor is the degree of globalisation. Aircraft companies such as Boeing and Airbus may be expected to place greater emphasis on global rather than local measures. Automotive producers may place equal emphasis on local and global performance. The local/global mix of performance indicators may also be expected to shift over time. As an industry or

- Autonomous and rivalry performance measures used to assess company performance locally and globlly

  > *To implement*: will probably require development of new global rivalry measures.

- Global performance becomes the top priority

  > *To implement*: local performance becomes an interim objective which management may purposely choose to sub-optimise if it improves global performance.

- Coordination between local and global objectives to establish local budgets and performance targets

  > *To implement*: requires the development of interactive planning procedures between local and global levels of management.

- Increased need to measure local contribution to other parts of the enterprise

  > *To implement*: requires development and application of mechanisms such as transfer of pricing to identify local contribution.

- Integration of local and global performance measures to arrive at overview of company performance, locally and globally

  > *To implement*: development of measuring techniques that aid development of a local/global perspective of performance.

FIGURE 12.4 Characteristics of global performance measurement

company becomes more global, there will inevitably be a tendency for greater emphasis on global performance measures.

Figure 12.4 summarises some of the characteristics of global performance measurement and the steps required by companies moving towards globalisation (particularly multinational companies) to implement them.

SUMMARY

- Companies which are going global undergo changes which make it advisable for them to review their systems for measuring performance. There are also more general reasons for such a review. Traditional financial measures tend to be too narrow and backward looking – showing where the firm has been. Also needed are diagnostic performance indicators which contribute to strategic analysis and provide some insight as to the company's future direction.
- Scoring methods fall into two distinct categories. One type consists of autonomous performance measures. These take an internal perspective, focusing on the firm's performance without reference to competition. The other type, rivalry measures, assess the performance of the firm relative to other companies and particularly its rivals.
- The two types of measure have different characteristics. Rivalry measures are purely relative, a gain by one firm (e.g. in market share) reflects a loss by another. Autonomous measures do not share this characteristic, all firms may improve their sales. Both types are useful, a balance is required between the two.

- The earlier multinationals measured performance country by country. This is unsuitable for global companies. Global companies need to measure performance globally as well as locally. This means they have to measure their rivalry and autonomous performance locally as well as globally.

- The main change in performance measurement for companies undergoing globalisation will be the greater emphasis on performance at the global level and particularly against rivals. Simply adding up the performance of the multinational firm's local operations will not provide global rivalry measures.

- The greater integration of the global firm's operations makes local performance measurement more difficult. Accounting systems will have to be adjusted to take account of the greater cross-border activity and cross-contributions between one part of the global company and another. Local budgets will be affected as will the setting of local performance targets.

- Local and global performance cannot remain separate. An appreciation of the global firm's total performance requires that management has an integrated view of local as well as global performance. Displaying the performance of the firm's various local operations as part of a global portfolio can aid this process.

NOTES AND REFERENCES

1. Kaplan, R. S. and Norton, D. P. (1992), The balanced scorecard – measures that drive performance, *Harvard Business Review*, January–February, pp. 71–9.
2. Ansoff, I. (1968), *Corporate Strategy*, Penguin Books, pp. 52–5.
3. Markides, C. C. (2000), *All the Right Moves*, Boston: Harvard Business School Press, p. 101.
4. Clark, P. J. (1997), *The Balanced Scorecard* (working paper A/T No. 97–14: Centre for Accounting and Taxation Research, Department of Accountancy, University College Dublin), May, pp. 1–24.
5. *Financial Times*, 15 May 1998, p. 16.
6. Porter, M. E. (Ed.) (1986), *Competition in Global Industries*, Harvard Business School Press, p. 19. Also see Porter, M. E. (1985), *Competitive Advantage: Creating and Sustaining Superior Performance*, The Free Press, p. 381; Gluck, F. W. (1980), Strategic choice and resource allocation, *McKinsey Quarterly*, Winter, p. 21.

13 Geographic positioning

A key aspect of any global strategy concerns the geographic positioning of the firm's plants and facilities. To an extent greater than is sometimes realised, the globalisation of business has progressed through the ability of companies to establish subsidiaries and operating facilities in various international locations. Its presence in multiple locations in different parts of the world has provided the international company with access to customers and resources it could not otherwise have reached. Considered in their totality and in relation to markets, supplies and competitors, these locations represent the firm's geographic positioning.

Decisions on where to locate the firm's international facilities have often been made on a piecemeal basis. Multinational firms have generally established their foreign bases in response to perceived needs and opportunities as they arose. The global firm, however, is not so much interested in individual site locations as in the global distribution of its worldwide system of plants, offices and other facilities. Its geographic positioning depends on its overall international network of site locations. Management in such companies is concerned with questions such as the following: Does the company's network of sites provide access to major world markets? If the company is aiming for a major share of the world market for its products, is it presently operating in locations which make this possible? How do its locations position the firm relative to the competition? Is it competing on a me-too basis, following rivals into the same locations? How do its locations differ from those of rivals and for what reasons? Is the firm's worldwide system of facilities consistent with its strategy?

Questions along these lines have received surprisingly little attention in the literature. In particular, there has been a lack of practical guidance regarding locational decisions faced by managers of firms pursuing a global strategy. Most treatments of the subject have assumed the perspective of the traditional multinational company. The key question for this type of company has been: Which country offers the best location for our next investment?

TRADITIONAL LOCATIONAL ANALYSIS

Conceptually the solution to the above question is simple. The company's new facility (whether it is a plant, office or research centre) should be located in that part of the world which maximises its overall contribution to the firm. Since most global companies will already have existing plants and operations in other parts of the world, the location of the new plant should be the one which maximises the contribution of the new facility to the firm's existing international network.

Putting this prescription into effect raises some practical problems. Since the criteria as stated here are essentially financial, financial analysis has been a basic tool used to evaluate such site possibilities. But as already noted (in Chapter 3) strategic considerations, such as the blocking of a rival, may dictate investment in certain sites that entail little or no identifiable financial return. In such cases, the strategic benefits to the entire system may be so far in the future or so difficult to pin down that they cannot be calculated.

In addition, financial analysis while useful in evaluating individual sites does little to help management identify the various strategic options regarding location possibilities, or to relate these to its existing network of sites. The sheer expense of carrying out detailed investigations, particularly those covering the level of detail required in a financial evaluation, greatly limits the number of options that can be considered. In his research on the foreign investment decision process in major multinationals, Yair Aharoni found that 'even the most cursory investigation of each of more than 150 countries in the world is practically impossible'.[1]

The great number of possibilities for new sites has meant that many firms arrive at location decisions with little or no systematic search. Perhaps the most effective and widely used method is 'try it and see'. We know that companies most often expand abroad first through exporting.[2] The great merit of this approach is that it provides, at minimal risk, direct contact and practical business experience with a particular location, exposing its many peculiarities and possibilities. It also often involves low risk in terms of company resources and, perhaps because of this, is frequently characterised by minimal systematic search and evaluation. After the firm has gained a certain amount of knowledge and experience about a foreign market through exporting, it is in a much better position to judge the advisability of further commitment to the location in question.

However, in a fast changing economic climate this try it and see approach leaves much to be desired. A failed exporting test of a particular market may not have cost the firm much in the way of investment, but the time required and the extensive delay this may cause in the investigation of alternative sites become less and less acceptable. Furthermore, there will be occasions when a new facility will so change the firm's prospects in a particular location that past experience based on exporting is of little relevance.

SCREENING NATIONAL MARKETS

For these reasons companies engaged in international markets have developed a number of techniques to help them evaluate possible new locations. In the following sections we begin with the simplest of these, moving on to more sophisticated approaches aimed at evaluating the firm's overall global geographic positioning.

Country screening is one of the earliest such aids. Given the large number of global location possibilities, many firms have felt the need to engage in some form of screening to sift through the various national options. The aim of screening is quickly and cheaply to eliminate as many undesirable locations as possible, leaving only a relatively few promising possibilities for more thorough subsequent examination. The more promising site locations can then be subjected to a much more detailed investigation, usually involving on-site inspection, the development of a strategy suited to that site, and finally a financial projection of likely returns.

Screening criteria

Techniques for screening new national market possibilities range from the informal, largely intuitive evaluations of potential sites to the more quantitative, computer based techniques.[3] They are essentially similar in that they evaluate possible locations against selected screening criteria such as size of market, consumer income, legal requirements, institutional features, consumer buying habits and other variables considered relevant to establishing a facility in a new location.

Some experts have recommended a two-stage screening process. An initial screen identifies attractive national locations on the basis of national market characteristics. A further screen using characteristics more specific to the firm and its customers is used to narrow these down to a manageable number of possible locations.[4]

The more sophisticated investors apply such criteria in the form of rating scales (Figure 13.1 provides an abbreviated example).[5] These apply a system of weights to the various criteria, according to their importance. The general procedure for developing such a rating scale is as follows.

1. Screening criteria are chosen which are considered to be indicative of (correlated with) the potential of a country as a national location. 'Potential' may refer to consumer income, total (product) sales, sales growth, political risk, etc., depending on the firm's own priorities and objectives.
2. Each country is rated according to its performance on each of these criteria, usually on a numerical scale from one to 10, e.g., if high per capita gross national product is considered favourable, countries with a high per capita gross national product would be rated towards the top of the scale.
3. A numerical weight is applied against each criterion rating, to reflect its overall importance.
4. The weighted ratings are calculated for each country. Those with the highest score are selected for more intensive examination, usually involving on the spot investigation and a projection of risk and financial returns.

Screening criteria	National rating (1–10)	×	Weight (1–10)	=	Combined score
Political stability	_____		_____		_____
Government attitude to foreign companies	_____		_____		_____
Repatriation of capital	_____		_____		_____
Repatriation of earnings	_____		_____		_____
Investment incentives	_____		_____		_____
Tariff protection	_____		_____		_____
Restrictions on foreign managers	_____		_____		_____
Taxation	_____		_____		_____
Exchange rate stability	_____		_____		_____
Per capita income	_____		_____		_____
Gross national product	_____		_____		_____
Prospect for economic growth	_____		_____		_____
Rate of inflation	_____		_____		_____
Size of market	_____		_____		_____
Market growth rate	_____		_____		_____
Industry capacity utilisation	_____		_____		_____
Industry legislation	_____		_____		_____
Support facilities	_____		_____		_____
Distribution access	_____		_____		_____
Competitor concentration	_____		_____		_____
Industrial relations	_____		_____		_____
Availability of supplies	_____		_____		_____
Industrial standards	_____		_____		_____
Wage rates	_____		_____		_____
Raw material costs	_____		_____		_____
TOTAL COMBINED SCORE					_____

FIGURE 13.1   Rating scale for screening national environments
Source: From Leontiades, J. C. (1985), *Multinational Corporate Strategy*, Lexington Books.

The general concept of screening is to reduce the many possible candidates to a smaller number which can economically be examined more closely. It is a method which finds wide application. Medical screening employs the same principle to identify persons at risk from a variety of medical conditions. New product ideas are screened to select the most promising possibilities, and so on.

However, applying the rating scale approach to screening international site locations entails a number of possible pitfalls. The following are particularly relevant for global companies.

Neglect of regional/global, political and other linkages

Since each country is rated and assessed individually, there is no provision for identifying important linkages and relationships between countries. For example, it may be optimal to locate a plant in one of the countries of the European Union even though individually it receives a low rating scale score if, from there, the product can be shipped tariff free to other European countries with superior market opportunities. Hence the proliferation of plants in Ireland.

Assessed on its own, the country might receive a relatively low rating by some firms. The Irish market is relatively small, but companies located there are able to ship their products tariff free to France, the United Kingdom, Germany, and other members of the European Community. This has attracted much foreign investment to Ireland by companies not so much interested in the intrinsic characteristics of that country as in its links to other members of the European Union. Other cross-national links in industrial standards, safety and environmental legislation, etc., are increasingly to be found and may have an important bearing on location decisions.

Failure to take sufficient account of firm's ability to compete

Traditional screening methods are frequently biased towards interpreting market potential in terms of national market 'attractiveness'. This in turn means a heavy emphasis on criteria indicative of market demand, such as economic growth, size of product/market, market prices and similar criteria which bias the result towards the selection of the larger, faster growing national markets considered attractive in terms of overall demand.

Yet it is observable that many firms do quite well in smaller, less prosperous national markets while some companies who actually establish operations in the larger more prosperous countries have been known to fail. No matter how attractive and generally favourable the economic and political environment offered by a particular country, it is of little avail if the company in question is not able to compete there success-fully. Traditional screening methods, relying as they do on a single rating scale, tend to confuse two quite separate and distinct sets of national characteristics: those that refer to the general attractiveness of a particular national market and those that refer to the ability of a new foreign company to compete there successfully.

Weakness in identifying regional/global strategic possibilities

Applying a screening process to each country considered individually may overlook regional and global strategic considerations in the distribution of the firm's overall network of facilities. In an increasing number of global industries, particularly those in the high technology areas, long term growth and even survival requires that the firm is able to compete directly in certain key national market locations, even though these may not be considered optimal when considered strictly on their own merits. A screening method which permits the analyst an overview of global demand and locational possibilities is required in such cases.

PORTFOLIO SCREENING

A more recent approach, portfolio screening differs from the above method in that it does not attempt to assess country locations individually, nor does it attempt to filter out the 'best' countries. Rather, it presents an overview of many potential sites, view-ing location possibilities as a portfolio of investment sites. This broader approach, simultaneously taking into account multiple site options, aids the identification of different possible regional/global locational options and strategies. Moreover, it is able to take into account the firm's ability to compete in particular locations.

The portfolio method is based on a matrix (Figure 13.2) of possible site locations. This classifies possible locations along two dimensions. Two rating scales are used to assess both the attractiveness of a particular location as well as the firm's ability to

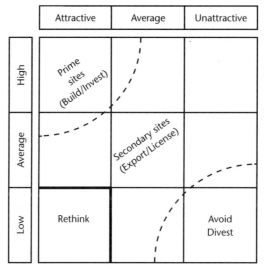

FIGURE 13.2 National market attractiveness

Source: From Robinson, S. J. Q. and Wade, D. P. (1978), The directional policy matrix – Tool for strategic planning, *Long Range Planning*, 11, (June).

compete there. The national attractiveness rating of each national location is based on the more traditional screening criteria indicative of the political and economic climate, including such variables as total size of the product market (or markets), gross national product, national economic growth as well as market growth rates, per capita income levels, political stability, exchange rate volatility and analogous variables, the precise selection depending on the strategy, objectives and situation of the firm carrying out the screening.

What constitutes attractiveness with reference to national location may therefore vary from one company to another. However, there is considerable agreement that both economic as well as political/institutional criteria are important.[6]

Assessing ability to compete

Since traditional screening methods for national locations stress attractiveness, the criteria associated with this dimension will appear familiar. The following measures aimed at assessing national markets from the standpoint of the firm's ability to compete there are either omitted altogether from traditional screening methods or lumped together (and hence not separately identifiable) with the attractiveness criteria. Outlined below are four general categories which each company will want to consider in developing a rating scale which rates national locations along the 'ability to compete' dimension.

Government attitude to new foreign entrants

A country may have a generally favourable political climate in terms of government stability, industry legislation, and regulations governing the repatriation of capital and income and still be unwelcoming or even hostile to new foreign companies and/or particular companies entering specific industries, e.g. telecommunications and defence industries.

Each company will have its own priorities and interests which will dictate the specific measures most appropriate for its situation, but examples of those which can be used to indicate the government's attitude to new foreign entrants include:

- industry regulations and standards which favour domestic companies;
- measures of foreign direct investment flows, both incoming and outgoing;
- legislation which restricts the transfer of foreign managers, technicians, technology or components.

Fortunately, information of a political nature that once would have been extremely difficult to gather on an international scale is now becoming widely available through the development of government agencies and private sources, and in particular specialised news services and private publication services such as Business International.

Likely competitor response to foreign entry

How likely are competitors to respond adversely against a new foreign company? The rate of capacity utilisation in the industry within the country in question provides a useful indicator. If the firms competing in the territory are already operating at near full capacity they will have limited resources (and motivation) to divert against a new competitor. Particularly if the market in question is also growing rapidly, they will feel less threatened, when operating at high levels of capacity utilisation, than in a situation where plant is underutilised and customers hard to find.

The degree of industry concentration is another possible screening criterion within this overall category. In highly fragmented industries the cohesiveness and industrial organisation required to mount a concerted response against new competition is generally less than in highly concentrated industries dominated by a few large firms. Estimates of buyer concentration can similarly prove useful, particularly if there is an oligopsony/oligopoly situation in the country, linking a few buyers closely to a small number of sellers.

Competitive strength of firms already in the market

It is important to assess not only the probability of competitor reaction against new market entry but also the likely effectiveness of such a response. Clearly, the technological capability of firms already competing within the territory in question will be important in those industries where technology is a major competitive variable, particularly if the new entrant is in possession of a technology not presently to be found there.

'Market power' refers to the ability of competitors to influence other firms or agencies in a way which may adversely affect the new entrant's possibilities of success. Such power cannot be directly measured but can often be ascertained from external evidence, such as ownership of managerial links. Cross-membership on boards of directors can also be indicative of this.

Availability of supplies and infrastructure

Ability to compete is also likely to depend on the availability of certain supplies and infrastructure, for example, the availability of distribution systems.[7] In certain cases even local suppliers are unable to secure entry due to blocking measures by competitors regarding distribution systems. For example, in Britain local breweries operate a system of loans and financial incentives for pubs which are thereby effectively tied to the local brewery, presenting a formidable entry barrier to outsiders.

Plotting the position of each country on a matrix such as that in Figure 13.2, according to the results of both sets of screening criteria, enables management to interpret the distribution of national site possibilities in terms of both the attractiveness of the market as well as the firm's ability to compete there. Those locations which rate high in terms of both (upper left-hand corner of Figure 13.2), represent the prime sites and clear candidates for closer consideration. However, it should be noted that certain of the secondary sites may represent a better fit with reference to the firm's overall strategy and the geopolitical considerations mentioned above.

Of particular importance will be those countries classified in the lower left-hand corner of the matrix, countries representing attractive markets but where the firm is for one reason or another poorly placed to compete. Can anything be done to improve competitiveness in these areas? Should the firm consider divestment or reduction of its commitment in certain countries, i.e., the right-hand side of the figure and particularly the lower right-hand corner?

MAPPING THE NETWORK

The portfolio method can be further developed to indicate the geographic positioning of competitors. Having classified the various national sites into the various boxes on the matrix, it is a simple matter to indicate which countries already provide sites for the international facilities of its competitor or competitors.

Any attempt to assess the firm's locational positioning relative to competitors must also consider that national boundaries do not necessarily define the competitive arena. Increasingly, the significance traditionally accorded to national boundaries is breaking down. In particular, countries that belong to regional trade groups with preferential trade agreements may enable a company located in one national site to compete freely in other member countries.

This is a crucial aspect of the emerging global competitive environment. The portfolio presentation of location possibilities can be readily coded to indicate which national locations represent countries which are members of regional trade groups. This is of special significance in the light of rapidly emerging trade groups which allow member countries preferential access to each other's markets. The appearance and growth of such country groupings has undermined the significance of traditional country-by-country analysis.

For example, in Figure 13.3, Brazil, China, Australia and Germany represent the prime sites which emerge from the screening process as possible new national locations (though the firm will also want to consider the possibility of further expansion in existing

National market attractiveness

		Attractive	Average	Unattractive
Our ability to compete	High	UK* (EU) Brazil (MER) China† Australia Germany† (EU)	Canada (NAFTA) Argentina† (MER) Ireland* (EU) New Zealand Hong Kong Finland (EU)	Malaysia* (AS) Norway (EF) Turkey* Morocco Denmark (EU)
	Average	France*† (EU) Venezuela† (MER) Japan Spain (EU)	Italy*† (EU) Sweden* (EU) Belgium (EU) Holland (EU) Saudi Arabia Switzerland (EF)	Peru (MER) Nigeria* Greece* (EU) Tunisia Portugal (EU)
	Low	USA† (NAFTA) Mexico (NAFTA)	Thailand (AS) Philippines* (AS) S. Korea	India* Paraguay* (MER) Chile (MA) Peru (AN)

Notes:
* Country where firm already has existing facilities
† Country where firm's major competitor has facilities
Membership in major regional trade groups indicated within parentheses:
AS = Association of South East Asian Nations
EU = European Community
EF = European Free Trade Area
MER = Mercosur
MA = Mercosur Associate
AN = Andean Community

FIGURE 13.3 Classification of potential and existing plant sites
Source: Adapted from Leontiades, J. C. (1988), Global location strategy, *Journal of Global Marketing*, 1 (4), Summer.

locations). However, before jumping to conclusions about these locations, the firm making the evaluation must take into account that it already has facilities established in Paraguay, a member of the same trade group (Mercosur) as Brazil, giving it preferential access to that country.

It should also consider that its existing plants in the United Kingdom, France, Ireland, Sweden, Italy and Greece already provide tariff free access to Germany. In addition, it should be noted that treaties between the European Union and the European Free Trade Area indicate that the company may have preferential access to members of the latter (Switzerland in Figure 13.3).

The most important attributes of a particular company site may not lie within the country of its location. If the country in question is a member of a trade group, the major attribute of the location may be the access it provides to other member countries. Many companies locate in Ireland and Belgium not so much because of their internal characteristics but because of the ready access they provide to other members of the European Union.

The regional groupings to be thus plotted are not necessarily confined to trade groups. In an increasing number of cases various regional legal and product standards associated with particular industries are a vital element of competitive strategy and location decisions. At one time, the strategy of the television producers turned about the division of the world's markets into three regions using technical television standards, PAL, SECAM and NTSC. These were probably more important than any national or regional barriers in their impact on location strategy.

Portfolio interdependence

A possible difficulty in applying the portfolio method has to do with the interdependence of the firm's various facilities. The portfolio concept as used in the corporate strategy literature finds its clearest application in firms comprising separate, independent businesses. In such cases the composition of the firm's portfolio of business may be altered without bringing the whole enterprise to a halt. Hence the portfolio concept may be applied to the more traditional multi-domestic type of company operating its foreign business units as largely independent businesses.

A number of authors have cast doubt on the applicability of the portfolio concept to firms pursuing a global strategy.[8] They point out that truly global firms are run with a high degree of interdependence and not as a portfolio of independent businesses which can be dropped and added without damage to the overall enterprise.

It is certainly true that global companies feature a higher degree of coordination and hence interdependence between their international sites. Business activities in one part of the world are functionally dependent on those in another, e.g. business unit A supplies unit B which supplies unit C, so that the firm's freedom to drop and add business units to its portfolio is severely curtailed.

But one must be careful to distinguish the type of portfolio at issue. As applied here, portfolio analysis is used to refer to geographic locations, not the business activities themselves. New activities may be initiated in new locations and old ones shifted from existing locations without necessarily disrupting the interrelated functioning of the enterprise.

IBM at one time closed down operations in India, then opened up a new plant in Mexico. It is demonstrably true that even the most highly integrated global competitors have some freedom, often considerable, in shifting the location of their facilities, i.e., they are able to alter their geographic portfolio.

GEOGRAPHIC POSITIONING AS A TOOL FOR INTERPRETING STRATEGY

Devising a global strategy implies an attempt to understand competitor behaviour and strategy on a world scale. Since the particular countries and regions where firms have chosen to locate their facilities represent major decisions and are an integral part of corporate strategy, the global distribution and pattern of such facilities can yield valuable clues and indications as to competitor strategy, objectives and positioning. The type of geographic data shown in Figure 13.3 permits network-to-network comparisons, the firm's network of global locations compared with that of a competitor. The figure shows at a glance that the firm's major competitor has a network which features facilities in a larger number of the world's more attractive world markets. Such information is essential for devising the firm's own positioning strategy.

A global overview of competitor site locations can also yield valuable information on competitor strategy and areas of vulnerability and competence, as indicated in the following sections.

Changes in global strategy

Traced over time, the changes in the geographic distribution of a competitor's facilities provide strong indications as to changes in its global strategy. The fact that facilities generally require a long lead time before they are completed means that early notice of new investments can often give advance warning on competitor strategy.

BOX 13.1

Signalling a change of strategy

Cable and Wireless (C&W), the British telecommunications firm, made a major commitment to the Pacific region when it purchased the Hong Kong telephone company. The same year saw the firm expand rapidly into the North American arena. C&W formed a joint venture with the Missouri–Kansas–Texas railroad subsidiary of Katy Industries, laying optical fibre cable link to commercial centres in the American South West. About the same time, C&W was active in optical fibre telecommunications links between Washington and New York. This gave C&W a unique geographic positioning relative to its competitors, while most of the major communications firms, with the exception of Sweden's Ericsson, had their major facilities and operations clustered near their home markets and closely adjacent territories. It is evident that C&W was busy developing operations that linked major commercial centres in the Pacific, North America and Europe. Its distinctive geographic spread clearly anticipated its global strategy. This was described a few years later by C&W as a plan to build a 'digital highway' linking the world's major financial centres.

Like most strategies, this was the subject of evolutionary change. The point is that the general direction of such change was signalled by changes in the location of C&W facilities, long before the new digital highway strategy was announced. ■

Areas of vulnerability

Foreign investments expose companies to risks, such as those associated with exchange rates and political and economic circumstances, which may provide opportunities for firms familiar with a competitor's global network to identify particular areas of vulnerability and opportunity brought about by such risks.

A case in point is provided by Midland Bank, now HSBC, one of Britain's largest banking institutions. Its acquisition of the American bank Crocket turned out disastrously and Midland had to subsequently divest itself with substantial losses on property and development loans. Later, it was announced that Midland had to set aside reserves of nearly 1.5 billion dollars as bad debt provisions in connection with loans to Third World countries. Both of these losses were highly publicised and provided an opportunity which the National Bank of Australia (NBA) was quick to capitalise on. For several years NBA had been seeking acquisitions in Europe to expand its retail banking network outside the Pacific region. With demand for banking facilities increasing rapidly, acquisition opportunities proved very scarce. But Midland's overseas difficulties signalled just such an opportunity. NBA spotted it and took advantage of Midland's circumstances to acquire one-fifth of its retail network.

Competence

Geographic location can also help to identify areas of competitor competence, since the type of expertise a company needs to succeed is subject to change from one part of the world to another. At one time, the Swedish telecommunications company Ericsson focused many of its activities in developing countries. This necessarily required the development of expertise and competence in producing products suitable for their telecommunications needs, such as small, modularised telephone exchanges and the managerial skills needed to deal with the particular needs and aspirations of governments in developing countries. But Ericsson's major presence today in telecommunications in the more advanced industrial countries signals the development by that company of a different product mix, different managerial skills and competencies.

Marketing and the specific type of marketing competence required to succeed will also vary with geography. A different marketing approach and different techniques are required to succeed in China and the Eastern bloc countries as opposed to free market economies.

Finally, global location analysis can provide useful insights regarding competitor strategy and vulnerability by addressing the following questions:

1. What is the global pattern and emphasis (particularly with reference to new locations) of the competitor's global network of site locations? Are these consistent with past strategy or do they signal a major change of direction?
2. What is the positioning of the firm's own network of facilities with respect to major competitors and markets?
3. What particular high risk areas of the world is the firm committed to and what are the possible adverse consequences of such risks for competitors?
4. What does the positioning of competitor facilities tell us about competitor competencies in technology, political relations, marketing, etc.?

SUMMARY

- A key aspect of a global company's strategy concerns the geographic positioning of its facilities. This refers to the location of its worldwide network of facilities in relation to global markets, competitors and supplies.

- In selecting national locations, companies find that the large number of possible sites in different parts of the world, makes a detailed, on the ground analysis of all possible locations impractical. Multinational companies have therefore developed a number of techniques to evaluate potential locations for foreign based plants and other facilities which economise on their time and resources.

- These techniques all rely on some form of screening to select the most likely national sites. The (small) group of countries which result from the screening is then subject to much more detailed analysis.

- Most often, screening techniques depend on rating scales. These list the criteria which the company considers most important in selecting a new site, rating each national site according to its performance on each criterion. These may be further refined by weighting the score of each criterion according to its importance.

- Such rating scales have a number of weaknesses, including their relative inability to take account of relationships between countries. They also have a tendency to underweight the importance of competition and a general inability to depict an overview which highlights regional and global strategic opportunities.

- Portfolio screening is a more recent method which presents an overview of many national sites. Two rating scales are used to rate and to map national sites along two dimensions. Possible sites are rated according to their attractiveness as markets and also according to the firm's ability to compete there. This method can be further developed to take account of the location of competitors' sites and to indicate trade group membership.

- A global mapping of such locations is useful in highlighting the positioning of the firm's overall network of facilities relative to global markets and competitors. It can also be useful in providing insights regarding a competitor's global strategy and areas of vulnerability.

NOTES AND REFERENCES

1. Aharoni, Y. (1966), *The Foreign Investment Decision Process*, Boston: Division of Research, Harvard Business School, p. 79.

2. Johanson, J. T. and Vahlne, J. E. (1977), The internationalization process of the firm – a model of knowledge development and increasing foreign market commitments, *Journal of International Business Studies*, Spring–Summer, pp. 23–32.

3. Goodnow, J. D. (1985), Developments in international mode of entry analysis, *International Marketing Review*, Autumn, pp. 17–30.

4. Wind, Y. and Douglas, S. P. (1972), International market segmentation, *European Journal of Marketing*, 6 (1), pp. 17–25.

5. Stobough, R. B. (1969), Where in the world should we put that plant, *Harvard Business Review*, January–February, pp. 129–30.

6. Goodnow, J. D. (1985).

7. Farmer, D. (1981), Source decision making in the multinational company environment, *International Journal of Physical Distribution and Materials Management*, II, (2/3) pp. 5–15.

8. Porter, M. E. (Ed.) (1986), *Competition in Global Industries*, Harvard Business School Press, p. 19. Also see Hout, T., Porter, M. and Rudden, E. (1982), How global companies win out, *Harvard Business Review*, September–October, pp. 98–108; Gluck, F. W. (1980), Strategic choice and resource allocation, *McKinsey Quarterly*, Winter, p. 21.

14 Interpreting the global competitive environment

All companies operate within an environmental context which influences their performance. It is generally accepted that thinking strategically requires an understanding of the firm's competitive environment.

Global players function in an environment quite different from that of local companies, operating over many countries and regions with widely different environmental conditions. Managers in such companies are increasingly faced with the task of making sense of this diversity. Which countries and regions offer the best opportunities? Which of our competitors are benefiting from them? These and similar questions present managers of companies operating globally with the need to evaluate a wide number of environmental conditions covering many countries.

Interpreting the environment

The advice to managers to 'interpret the firm's environment' suffers from the fact that literally everything outside the firm itself qualifies as 'environment'. Philosophers tell us that, for someone standing on a beach, understanding the environment implies knowledge of every grain of sand. Obviously this is not a practical prescription. Particularly in the case of the global company, the term 'environment' interpreted in this fashion includes a formidable number of countries, and an almost infinite number of items to be considered. Any practical analysis of the global company's environment will necessarily have to be focused in a way which brings it within the information processing capabilities of management. In short, some means must be found to narrow the scope of what is meant by environment.

Following the work of researchers in the field of industrial organisation, the approach throughout this text (see Chapter 2) has been to narrow the scope of our analysis by focusing on industry sectors. But even limiting environment by industry still leaves a large number of factors to be considered.

A further method used to simplify the analysis is to concentrate only on those factors (within the industry) which affect player performance. These are after all the crucial variables of interest to managers. The method outlined in this chapter follows this procedure.

PROCEDURE FOR GLOBAL INDUSTRY ANALYSIS

Today, there is an increasing amount of information readily available on the performance of companies. Brokerage firms and a wide number of financial institutions issue regular reports on the performance of most companies which qualify as global. The aim here is to use such information on player performance to identify those key features in the global industry environment which have influenced it.

Identifying the global players

The first step is to identify the players. The global players in a particular industry are those firms which meet the following criteria:

- First, they must meet the traditional criteria of industry members. That is, they are firms producing similar products or services.
- Secondly, they must each be engaged in global rivalry. Rivalry on a global scale requires a world view, a global vision, of markets and competitors and coordination of the firm's worldwide operations accordingly.

  Firms which qualify under both of the above criteria comprise the global players of a particular industry sector. Excluded from this definition are multi-domestic companies and exporters which conduct their rivalry on a country-by-country basis.

Interpreting the global competitive environment also requires that we know the major characteristics of the global rivals within the industry, such as the following:

1. **Nationality**. What is the nationality, the home country, of the various players? Firms begin their operations in a particular national location. In doing so they acquire a nationality which is important and continues to influence even the most global players. There are special links between the global firm and its 'home country' in terms of laws, cultural ties and even emotional affinity which make nationality an important element.

   A few firms have broken this link, moving to new countries. This is a practice which may well grow in the future. But even in such cases, it is important to know the player's new 'home' country.
2. **Geographic deployment**. How have the various players deployed their operations globally? What geographic regions and markets have they concentrated on? Where are their major markets and supply facilities? Inevitably, there will be major differences in the geographic distribution of the various players' assets and the intensity of their commitment to different countries and regions. It is important

to identify these locational differences. They serve to differentiate the various players and their relationship to the global industry environment.

3. **Geographic constraints on the players.** Are there certain constraints on the various players which limit their geographic mobility or that of certain of their proprietary assets? For example, not all players are allowed to operate in Cuba or China. Also, certain patents, marketing rights and contractual agreements may be valid in some parts of the world and not others. It is quite common to find that purchased proprietary rights are valid for some countries but not others.

4. **Global player alliances.** What links have these players formed with other firms that help them to compete? Are these alliances limited to particular locations or global in scope?

5. **Degree of global player domination of the industry.** It is important to assess the degree to which the industry as a whole is globalised. Is the industry dominated by the global players, as in the case of aircraft engines, or are they a relatively small minority in an industry dominated largely by local players, as in the case of the brewery industry?

Identifying global player performance

The next step in the analysis is to evaluate the performance of the global players in the industry. Understanding the global industry environment requires a knowledge of how the member firms have performed. Who are the lead companies in the industry? Which companies are lagging?

Whatever the industry, some firms will be doing better than others. These are the industry leaders. Others will be surviving, that is keeping pace with the global industry average while still others are performing below average. Fortunately, the availability of financial and sales information has developed to the point where much of this data is now readily available.

Figure 14.1 illustrates a method of grouping the various global players according to their performance as indicated by their profitability and sales growth (measured in a common currency). Profitability refers to the level of profits over the past few (3–5) years expressed as a percentage of the firm's capital. Sales growth refers to growth in global company sales over the same time interval. The winning companies are those with the best relative performance in profitability and sales growth.

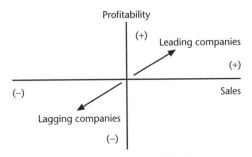

FIGURE 14.1 Assessing relative global performance of industry players

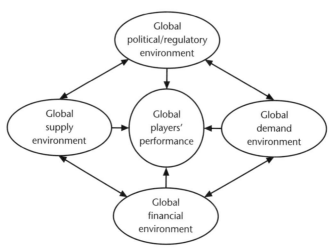

FIGURE 14.2 Interpreting the global industry environment

As far as possible, the performance of the players should also be identified according to location. Which countries and regions exert the most significant influence on overall sales and profitability? Which players are benefitting from favourable environmental conditions in particular countries and regions? Which locations have adverse environmental conditions, setting back player performance?

The global industry environment

In any large company, management's view of the overall external environment is brought together from various piecemeal observations. Those responsible for purchasing have their own view of what constitutes the firm's environment which is quite separate from the perception of marketing managers or those concerned with accounting and finance. It is part of the task of top management to pull these various perspectives together to form an overview of the firm's overall global external environment.

Analogously, the global industry environment is viewed here as made up of four interrelated sub-environments, as shown in Figure 14.2. Understanding how these sub-environments have contributed to the success (or failure) of the various players will help us to understand the environmental features influencing global player performance. But first we need to examine each sub-environment individually, as outlined below.

The global demand environment

The demand for the products of the industry derives from various national and regional markets where buyers purchase the product or service produced by this industry. Any analysis of the global industry demand environment requires that we identify the various local markets which comprise the world market for this industry and how they have contributed to total global demand. Which are the core markets for this industry, those few national/regional markets which are the main battleground for industry leadership? Which markets have been the growth leaders, which areas of weak demand? In some parts of the world growth in demand may have been negative. In short, how have the various national/regional markets performed?

To answer these questions we may first look to a number of primary indicators. These are features, often in numerical form, which are representative of the global demand environment.

Primary indicators

Global industry sales. We need first to arrive at some idea of total global industry demand. What is the size of the total world market for this industry (total industry sales) and what has been its growth? Such demand estimates should preferably be measured in both value terms, e.g. what is the value of total global sales over the relevant period and, where possible, the number of units sold. Is there evidence of overcapacity or demand which cannot be met?

The sales performance of the industry as a whole provides a useful benchmark for interpreting the performance of the individual players. Which players have experienced sales growth faster or slower than the industry as a whole?

Geographic distribution of industry demand. In each industry there are certain key world markets, sometimes no more than two or three, which determine global industry leadership. Which countries/regions represent these key markets? Which countries and regions are enjoying highest (and lowest) level of demand? Which players are most committed to such markets?

Secondary indicators

There are also secondary indicators that are useful in gaining a deeper understanding of the demand situation in those countries and regions identified as especially significant for the global demand situation. These secondary indicators help to explain underlying conditions bringing about change in the primary indicators.

The business cycle. Over any given time interval, the various markets of the world will be experiencing different phases of the business cycle.

These cyclical movements can have a major impact on market demand and player performance. Those players in markets in the upswing phase of the cycle will be experiencing a favourable increase in demand on this account. But this may not accurately reflect the long term trend.

For example, Japan experienced a downward phase of its economic activity during most of the 1990s while during the same period the United States was enjoying an exceptionally high rate of economic growth. Getting at the underlying trend of demand in these countries requires that the different national cycles and their temporary nature is taken into account.

Stage of market development. Industries experience different stages of development which will vary from one country to another. For example, the automobile industry is in a mature stage in its development in most Western countries. Demand is characterised by a high level of per capita car ownership and relatively slow growth, largely for replacement purposes.

In China and many developing countries the same industry is just emerging. It is in its early developmental stages, characterised by low levels of car ownership and a high growth rate. Countries in different stages of development will have a quite different influence on the overall demand environment as well as the various global players.

Fashions in demand. To what degree do the observed changes in demand reflect temporary fashions or fads? Various products such as clothing, food, entertainment services and so on experience fashions in demand which may vary from one country to another.

Exchange rates. Despite the pace of globalisation in many aspects of industry, exchange rates remain a peculiarly national phenomenon. Each country has its own currency with its associated rate of exchange relative to other currencies.

Variations in exchange rates can affect market demand, particularly for imported products. As with the business cycle, such influence may be temporary. In assessing the demand situation in any particular country, a review of recent exchange rate changes (and the prospect of future such changes) can shed additional light on the overall demand picture there.

Prices. Information on prices and particularly price changes make an important contribution to the picture of overall global demand. Have there been major price changes? If so, how are they distributed – which countries?

Political initiatives. Governments influence industry demand through their direct purchases, for example the purchase of defence goods. Included also under this heading are the political initiatives relating to the establishment of regional trade groups, such as the EU, Mercosur, etc. Such regional groupings may impose changes in tariffs and other national border restrictions which influence demand.

Relating global players and industry demand

As far as possible we should associate the various global players with the countries and regions identified above as having a major influence on global industry demand. Which players have been associated with the markets where demand is increasing and are having a positive influence on industry sales? Which have been associated with those having a negative influence?

Even where two players are represented in the same market, there will be a difference in terms of their commitment. One will have a relatively greater stake than the other, hence the impact will not be the same.

The global supply environment

Global players draw supplies from different parts of the world. Many of them rely to a great degree on their country of origin as their major supply source. Increasingly, however, there is a move to capitalise on the capability of such firms to develop international supply sources from countries offering lower costs, superior quality and other potential for competitive advantage. These various supply sources and their characteristics are important elements of the global supply environment.

Analysis of the global supply environment requires that we identify the major sources of supplies for the global players. Which countries or regions offer supply advantage in terms of cost, quality and availability of supplies to the industry? Are there conditions within the industry's present supply sources which point towards future changes in the global supply environment?

Primary indicators

Supply availability.   Have any global players experienced supply shortages during this period? If so, which particular players and countries were involved?

Supply prices.   Have the prices of supplies used by the industry remained stable or have there been major changes in price over the period under review?

Secondary indicators

There are also secondary indicators which help to explain the supply situation in particular countries or regions. For example, wages are an important element in determining supply costs. Players producing labour intensive products and drawing their supplies from countries with lower costs will have a cost advantage over those not so favourably situated. Here again the aim is to understand the supply situation, identifying the most significant locations and the factors relevant to the supply situation for the global players. Such secondary factors to consider include the following.

Labour costs.   Labour costs will influence the supply purchases of global firms and particularly their unit costs. Which players are making use of low cost labour to reduce the cost of their supplies? Wages vary widely not only from one country to another but also within the same country over time. Which countries and regions are the major providers of such low cost supplies? What changes are taking place in labour costs today which will influence supply sources tomorrow? The low cost source of today may be seen as expensive tomorrow. Countries such as Singapore, South Korea and Taiwan are no longer seen by many firms as low wage countries.

Natural resources.   Supplies may well be affected by changes in the price and availability of certain natural resources. Changes in the global supply environment due to depletion and discovery can bring about sharp changes in the prices of these products as supplied to global companies. Seasonal supply variations, as in numerous agricultural products, are another source of change in supply prices and availability which can influence player performance.

Technical change.   Are technological developments changing the supply situation of the industry? For example, new machinery may reduce the labour content of certain components to the point where it is not worthwhile to produce them in low wage countries.

New supply sources. What changes have there been during this period in the geographic distribution of industry supply sources? Are there new sources of raw material which have altered the supply situation of some or all of the global players?

Exchange rates. How have changes in exchange rates affected the global supply situations? Global players purchasing supplies from 'abroad' pay two prices: the local currency price of the product purchased, and the local price converted through the exchange rate into the currency of payment. Both of these affect the overall price of the product to the global player.

Political initiatives. Have government changes in political orientation, trade barriers and other legislation influenced the global supply environment? With the thawing of the East–West Cold War, there is now greater access to Russian supplies in the form of cobalt, natural gas, timber, finished metal and many other materials which are purchased by some global players. Government initiatives may also affect the global supply environment through agreements relating to tariff rates (through the World Trade Organization) and the formation of regional trade blocs.

Reviewing the global supply environment

In reviewing the global supply environment special note should be made of events altering supply prices in specific locations, such as changes in wage rates, productivity, tariffs and raw materials costs. Have there been major changes during this period in the geographic location of the industry's supply sources? The security of supply? What are the major changes in supply prices? Which global players have had their performance affected?

The global industry political/regulatory environment

Global players operate within a political and regulatory environment which provides the 'rules of the game'. As indicated earlier, government decisions may affect the various players indirectly, as through their impact on markets and supplies. Government decisions may also influence global players directly.

Some instances of this direct influence are obvious. For example, expropriation of company assets has affected a number of players and industries in the past. Less drastic measures may take the form of government subsidies to various players or investment restrictions. The French government received the permission of the European Union to grant major financial support to Crédit Lyonnais, one of the world's largest banks. Governments exercise more particular vigilance and influence in some industries than in others. Such industries include those associated with public broadcasting, high technology, airlines or medicine. Governments also employ a number of methods to restrict or encourage players from certain locations, as in the case of the US government's restrictions on doing business with Cuba.

Closely related to purely political decisions are the laws and regulations, often specific to particular industries, including those relating to matters of safety, food and drug standards, tariffs and border controls, pollution regulation, industrial standards and special industry taxes.

Unlike most competitive contests, the rules set by the various governments can and do vary markedly from one location to another. Here again, the task of the industry analyst is to first acquire an overview of the global environment, going on from there to identify those countries and regions where political decisions and regulations have had the greatest influence (positive or negative) on the performance of global players.

Primary indicators

Government ownership. Are some of the global players owned or partially owned by government? Many governments have an ownership interest in global players. In some industries (e.g. telecommunications, automobiles, aircraft, petroleum) major global players are owned or partially owned by government, with government representatives taking an active role in decision making.

Government promotion of company products. Are any global players being actively supported by government visits and the exercise of government influence aimed at promoting the sale of their products? Governments are increasingly taking an active role in boosting the sales of their own companies. The president of the United States has actively promoted the products of certain global companies as has the prime minister of the United Kingdom.

Government policies. The performance of global players is often influenced by policies of the various governments under whose jursidiction they operate. An example is the impact on Boeing of the decision by several European governments to support the construction of large scale passenger aircraft.

Government rules and regulations. These are more specific than policies, spelling out rules of company behaviour. Of particular interest is the introduction of new rules and regulations. Included here are industry standards and regulations regarding work practices, product safety and pollution. Also tariffs, work permits, enforcement of proprietary rights, etc.

Government financial incentives and penalties. Which governments have been particularly active in awarding financial incentives (or penalties) and which players have benefited? In implementing their political and economic objectives, governments may award financial incentives to certain players (e.g. as an incentive to invest, to export or to provide employment). In some cases they may impose financial penalties, the extreme case being expropriation of the firm's assets.

Political risk. Which countries and regions are characterised by exceptional political risk for global players operating there? Government risk refers to unexpected change outside the established political system. Government coups and revolutions are obvious examples. These can influence player performance and the overall economic climate even if they do not actually take place.

Secondary indicators

Having located the countries/regions where such developments have proved important for the industry, a more fundamental analysis requires that we try to assess the underlying conditions behind these events. In particular, changes in the following government and government related situations should be noted.

Social trends. Social trends may bring pressure on governments to enact legislation affecting industry. Recent examples are to be found in public attitudes relating to pollution, health and safety, working conditions and animal experiments. Which industries and players have been affected by such legislation? Are there identifiable trends and distinctions in this respect between different countries? For example, certain restrictive legislative measures regarding cigarette advertisements do not apply in China or most African countries.

Domestic economic conditions. Have domestic economic conditions affected the political/regulatory environment in certain countries? National economic conditions, such as unemployment or an unacceptably low rate of economic growth may pressure governments to enact legislation that affects global players. A number of the developing countries dissatisfied with their economic performance have passed legislation providing financial incentives for foreign direct investment. Within the industrial countries, unemployment has brought about active opposition from some labour unions to the international sourcing of supplies.

Shifts in political orientation.   Changes in fundamental government objectives and attitude, even though not directly related to the industry may introduce changes which affect industry players. The changes in the former Soviet Union and its fragmentation ushered in a quite different political and regulatory environment which affected the competitive behaviour of many companies operating there.

Balance of trade. An adverse trade balance may motivate government legislation affecting global players. This may take the form of changes in trade barriers. Virtually all treaties governing tariffs and other trade barriers have escape clauses which permit major changes in such trade barriers under certain adverse conditions, usually as a last resort.

Government trade policy. Many governments are adopting trade policies aimed at specific national objectives. So-called 'strategic trade' objectives may include the support (defence) of certain industries, irrespective of the dictates of free trade.

Another expression of trade policy is the decision of the governments of the United States, Mexico and Canada to participate in a North American Free Trade Association.

International agency policies and rules of trade. A number of international agencies, such as the World Trade Organization, the OECD, the United Nations, the G7 countries or regional trade groups such as the European Union enact legislation which affects trade barriers, rules governing foreign direct investment and other measures influencing global players.

Overall

What have been the major high points during the period under review in the overall global political/regulatory environment? In which particular countries and regions have such policies had the most significant impact on the global industry? Which global players have been affected?

The global industry financial environment

All companies doing business across national boundaries operate in the context of an international financial environment which can exert a major influence on their performance. Exchange rates are a major concern for global players. As indicated earlier, they can change global player performance through their effect on market demand and supply. An increase in the value of the yen versus the US dollar raises the price of Japanese products exported to the United States. At the same time it increases the cost of US products in Japan.

Exchange rate changes also affect the money value of player earnings, sales and assets. Global players are necessarily dealing with foreign currencies whose value (the value of one currency in terms of another) is subject to change. For example, companies holding cash in a depreciating currency will experience a loss relative to other currencies.

Over any given interval of a few years, it is to be expected that various players will experience many such changes in exchange rates. Indeed many of these will cancel each other out, losses in one currency being matched by gains in another. But within any given time period, the financial environment will have an important influence on global player performance. Some will gain, others will lose. Exchange rate fluctuations merit special attention in arriving at any interpretation of the global industry environment.

Primary indicators

Changes in currency exchange rates.   What has been the exchange rate situation during the period examined? Have changes in exchange rates affected the demand for the products/services of the various global players? Even with the development of sophisticated hedging techniques, global players may remain exposed to changes in exchange rates which may alter the value of their assets, costs, sales and earnings.

Cost of capital.   Despite the internationalisation of capital markets there are still significant variations in cost and availability of capital from one part of the world to another. An important competitive advantage of Japanese global companies during the 1970s and 1980s was their ability to raise capital cheaply. The cost of capital may be measured by the prevailing interest rate and/or the price/earnings ratio of equity shares. Are certain players gaining a competitive advantage through access to cheaper capital? If so, from which countries?

Secondary indicators

Factors which may help to explain current or future changes affecting the financial environment in specific countries include the following.

Trade balance. The balance of a country's trade, whether it has a surplus or deficit in its exports and imports of goods and services, is often indicative of changes in exchange rates. The persistent trade deficit of the United States has resulted in a long term decline of the dollar, particularly with reference to the Deutschmark and the yen.

Foreign investment. Foreign investment contributes to capital inflows and a strengthening of the currency of the country receiving the capital inflow together with a weakening of the currency of the country losing the capital.

General economy. Economic conditions affecting the entire economy, such as the business cycle, may lead to measures influencing the financial environment. For example, government initiated changes in the rate of interest to stimulate or depress economic activity.

Changes in forward rates of exchange. Currency weakness or strengthening will usually be reflected in published 'forward rates'. These quote the rates of exchange today between currencies which will be exchanged at some future date.

Currency speculation. Major movements of currency due to speculative activity on the international currency and capital markets may be instrumental in exchange rate variations. Which national currencies have been subject to such speculative activity? With electronic transfer of financial assets, such capital movements are increasingly volatile and may adversely influence currency stability.

Restrictions on capital repatriation. Despite the recent trend towards liberalisation of capital, governments still occasionally attempt to restrict the free movement of currencies and capital. Such attempts may affect global players directly, e.g. restricting the repatriation of capital. They may also serve as an indicator of financial difficulty, signalling a possible future devaluation of the national currency.

Overview of the global financial environment

Analysis of the global financial environment should identify which currencies and capital markets have had a major influence on which global players during the period under review. Where is the cost of capital cheapest and which players are benefiting? What are the prospects for the future? Which players are benefiting from their present commitment to certain currencies? Which are being negatively influenced by adverse developments in the currencies they are associated with?

KEY ENVIRONMENTAL FEATURES

For global players, the most important features of the global industry environment are those able to influence their performance. The above analysis attempts to identify these key environmental features by noting which of them are associated with changes in player performance.

The last step in the environmental review is to bring together the most significant primary and secondary indicators of environmental conditions which have been identified as having the greatest impact on player performance. This includes those indicators which appear to have had the most influence on the performance of the losing players as well as those which help to explain the performance of the winners.

The environmental conditions which have influenced player performance will not have been distributed evenly across the globe. Market demand will have been stronger in some parts of the world than in others, exchange rate fluctuations will have influenced companies with certain national locations more than others, and so on. As far as possible, the countries or regions where these conditions have had the strongest impact on player performance should also be identified.

PROFILE OF THE GLOBAL INDUSTRY COMPETITIVE ENVIRONMENT

Finally, the information developed from the above procedures should be assembled into a profile of the global industry competitive environment. This industry profile should cover:

1. The performance of the overall industry. This should include information on total market demand for the industry's products or services as well as the growth in industry sales over the selected period.
2. The global players. Who are they and what are their characteristics in terms of nationality, geographic concentration, alliances and other notable features?
3. The performance of the individual global players, particularly the winners and losers. What has been the performance of the global players in terms of their sales, growth and profitability?
4. Which environmental features (primary and secondary indicators) have been identified as having a significant influence on the performance of the industry players? Changes in these indicators during the period under review are of particular significance.
5. What were the major locations (countries and regions) where these environmental features exerted their greatest influence on the performance of global players? For example: which countries or regions have most influenced the demand for the products/services of certain players? Which have offered a supply advantage (or disadvantage)? Which are associated with major political/regulatory impacts on global players? Which countries or regions have been associated with major changes in their financial environment?
6. How were the various players in the industry positioned relative to the countries and regions identified in step 5 above? For example, which players had operations in countries which exposed them to major changes in markets during this period? Which players were located in countries where they were able to benefit from (or were adversely affected by) changes in markets or the supply situation? Which were located in countries which exposed their performance to the impact of government initiatives and changes in financial markets?

SUMMARY

- Managers of global companies, like those elsewhere, are faced with the task of interpreting their business environment. To narrow the number of variables, the procedure outlined here takes an industry based approach. It focuses on identifying the environmental features within a given global industry which influence global player performance.

- The first step is to identify the global players. They must be firms producing similar products or services (in the same industry) and engaged in global rivalry.

- We should also know the major characteristics of these global rivals, such as their nationality, alliances, deployment, geographic constraints and the degree of industry globalisation.

- Understanding the global industry environment also requires a knowledge of how the global players within it have performed. Who are the leaders and laggers in the global industry?

- For purposes of analysis, the global industry environment itself is subdivided into four interrelated sets of environmental conditions, or sub-environments. Understanding how these sub-environments have contributed to the success (or failure) of the various players will help us to understand the environmental features influencing player performance.

- Global industry demand is one such sub-environment. The main features to examine are a number of primary indicators: factors directly related to demand. A number of secondary indicators can also be useful in understanding the behaviour of the primary indicators.

- Analysis of the global supply environment requires that we identify the major sources of supplies for the global players. Primary indicators include supply availability and supply prices.

- The global political/regulatory sub-environment is rich in factors which can influence player performance. Primary indicators include government ownership of some of the global players themselves, government subsidies and industry regulations as well as industrial policies.

- Global companies are also influenced by international financial conditions. Primary indicators of such environmental influences are changes in exchange rates and the cost of capital. Secondary indicators include national trade balances, foreign investment, currency movements and capital repatriation.

- The next step in the environmental review is to identify the most significant primary and secondary factors which have had the greatest impact on player performance.

- The information developed from the above procedures should be assembled into a profile of the global industry competitive environment. This should include data on the overall industry and the market for its products, the identity of the global industry players and their performance. It should also include a summary of the main primary and secondary environmental conditions influencing player performance and their location, as well as an indication of how the various players were positioned relative to these.

Index

Note: **Bold** page numbers indicate chapters.